SOLUTIONS FOR NETWORKED DATABASES

SOLUTIONS FOR NETWORKED DATABASES

How to Move from Heterogeneous
Structures to Federated Concepts

Dimitris N. Chorafas
Saint-Laurent d'Eze
Alpes Maritimes, France

Heinrich Steinmann
Union Bank of Switzerland
Zurich, Switzerland

ACADEMIC PRESS, INC.
Harcourt Brace & Company
San Diego   New York   Boston   London   Sydney   Tokyo   Toronto

Copyright © 1993 by ACADEMIC PRESS, INC.

All Rights Reserved.
No part of this publication may be reproduced or transmitted in any form or by any means, electronic or mechanical, including photocopy, recording, or any information storage and retrieval system, without permission in writing from the publisher.

Academic Press, Inc.
1250 Sixth Avenue, San Diego, California 92101-4311

United Kingdom Edition published by
Academic Press Limited
24–28 Oval Road, London NW1 7DX

Library of Congress Cataloging-in-Publication Data

Solutions for networked databases: How to move from heterogeneous
structures to federated concepts   / Dimitris N. Chorafas and Heinrich Steinmann.
        p.   cm.
      ISBN 0-12-174060-9
      1. Distributed databases.   2. Computer networks   I. Steinmann,
Heinrich, 1931-   II. Title.
QA76.9.D3C4758   1993
005.75'8–dc20   92-36765
                                                                              CIP

PRINTED IN THE UNITED STATES OF AMERICA

93 94 95 96 97   QW   9 8 7 6 5 4 3 2 1

CONTENTS

PREFACE

The approach and purpose of this book are different from those of many other publications on databases. It is not intended primarily to describe theoretical aspects, though the basic theories are discussed. Rather, it explains the most up-to-date developments in standards and ad hoc solutions aimed at providing cross-database connectivity for networked databases.

The tension between the need for innovation and the requirement for practical solutions—not to mention standards capable of commercialization—has always made the job of managing high technology a challenge. Yet without high technology we can have neither innovation nor valid solutions in database management.

"Interoperability is the No. 1 item on customers' agendas today," said the marketing vice president of a major American computer manufacturer. The solution to cross-database connectivity is not just technical. It is primarily managerial and it depends on: "Whether or not we have the intellectual vitality to face the new era of information technology."

Along such frontier spirit, this book intends to go beyond informing the reader on principles and breakthroughs concerning heterogeneous databases. It aims to stipulate consideration of different and better ways to solve problems connected to networked databases—demonstrating solutions which have been able to overcome some of the thorniest problems we have faced so far in this domain.

This book is written for specialists in computers and communications. As graduate engineers with management experience, we fully reject the dichotomy often made between an *engineering-oriented* and a *management-oriented* text. It is a fake division.

This sort of ill-conceived dichotomy from college onward to professional life is responsible for the huge computer-management gap created over 35 years of practice and is still around, to the detriment of everybody. The gap has to be closed—the organization and contents of this book constitute our contribution.

The book is divided into three parts. Part I addresses itself to the advent of the *multidatabase*, which has at its roots the concept of a corporate database. This is treated in Chapter 1 in a way which brings together database and knowledgebank concepts, reliability and availability characteristics, as well as the synergy necessary to create and sustain *federated databases*.

Chapter 2 examines the alternatives of centralized and distributed databases, showing when, how, and why we have been led from the former to the latter. But distributed databases must be managed as Chapter 3 explains, and there are different ways for doing so, ranging from a common denominator to added value.

Networked databases must be treated as a corporate resource. Chapter 4 documents this issue by emphasizing the evolving goals in a dynamic organization. It is up to computer professionals to face the networked database challenges, as Chapter 5 suggests, and this calls for a cultural change in database management.

Part II rests on three pillars: schemata, data dictionaries, and protocols. Schemata and metaphors with distributed databases are the theme of Chapter 6, which establishes, on the basis of how schemata are handled, the difference between loosely and tightly coupled approaches to networked databases.

"Can we solve cross-database problems through the able manipulation of schemata?" asks Chapter 7. It answers this query by demonstrating that efforts toward a global schema have not given commendable results. By contrast, the able usage of the semantics of schema integration can lead toward efficient solutions.

Two chapters concentrate on the increasingly sophisticated data dictionary. Chapter 8 highlights guiding lines and results from the generic Japanese efforts in designing and developing an electronic data dictionary. The Information Resource Dictionary System (IRDS) in the United States is the theme of Chapter 9.

Networked databases need first-class protocols to sustain their impact. Chapter 10 tells the story of ANSI SQL, the productization efforts of the SQL Access Group and what IBM has to offer. Chapter 11 elaborates on the concepts and standards behind application programming interface (API), formats and protocols (FAP), and remote data access (RDA).

Part III is dedicated to real-life cross-database application, particularly some of the most successful implementations which can presently be found in the domain of networked databases. As the reader will appreciate, there exist both ad hoc and commodity software solutions. The Distributed Relational Data Architecture (DRDA) introduced by IBM in 1990 is the subject of Chapter 12. Chapter 13 focuses on the DataLens concept and its productization as one of the most agile commercially available solutions.

The excellent effort by the General Telephone and Electronics Laboratory in developing the intelligent database assistant (IDA) is discussed in Chapter 14. This presentation also includes the implementation of IDA, which has been done by GTE in its operations in California (CALIDA).

Solutions to the problems presented by heterogeneous networked databases can only be given through basic studies which address the underlying problems, not through cosmetics and the revamping of old, impotent approaches. A project which addresses the issues of effective data sharing and modeling is the Data Access Integrated Services (DAIS) that is presented in Chapter 15.

One of the most generic developments available today for software portability and cross-database access is the Multivendor Integration Architecture (MIA). The last three chapters of this book (16, 17, and 18) elaborate on this very important project which has been initiated by Nippon Telegraph and Telephone (NTT) and in which DEC, IBM, Hitachi, Fujitsu, and NEC participate.

As the largest investor in computers and software in Japan—a role similar to that of the Department of Defense in the United States—NTT has made the MIA specifications the pivot point of its procurement services. In the United States, both Project Carnot of MCC and Digital Equipment rest their strategy on MIA.

The power underpinning the MIA, DAIS, IDA, and DataLens is the able exploitation of know-how. Unlike capital, *knowledge has no fixed limits.* It is not a finite substance to be diminished by division and neither does it multiply through arithmetic manipulation. On the contrary, the more knowledge other people enjoy, the more each person will have individually.

This is a fundamental premise in the implementation of networked databases and in one paragraph crystallizes what we have learned during the intensive research which led to this book. This research took place during 1991 and 1992 in North America, Japan, and Western Europe: 85 organizations and 196 executives participated in it.

The names of senior executives, specialists in computers and communications, as well as faculty members who contributed to these research projects are found in the Acknowledgments. To all of them we wish to express our appreciation for their advice and assistance.

Let us close by presenting our thanks to everyone else who also contributed to making this book successful: to our colleagues for their advice, to some of the organizations being visited for reviewing selected parts of the text, and to Eva-Maria Binder for the artwork, the typing of the manuscript, and the index.

Dimitris N. Chorafas
Heinrich Steinmann

ACKNOWLEDGMENTS

The following is a list of organizations and their senior executives, specialists in computers and communications, and faculty members who contributed to the research projects on which this book is based. The list is subdivided by country and the organizations are arranged alphabetically within these subdivisions.

United States

American Airlines

> Jeffrey A. HARTIGAN, Managing Director, Advanced Technology and Enduser Technology
> Mary ALEXION, Managing Director, Corporate Data Management
>
> *4200 Amon Carter Blvd., CP2 Mail Drop 2517, Ft. Worth, TX 76155*
>
> Susan L. DUNLAP, SABRE Computer Services
> Todd FITZGERALD, Manager, Database Administration
> Warren ELLIOTT, Manager, Data Models
> Brenda MORYAN, Manager, Data Planning
> Sam ANTURI, Technical Planning
> Phil HARTLEY, Advanced Technology, Object-Oriented Applications
>
> *P.O. Box 619616, Dallas/Fort Worth Airport, TX 75261-9616*

Andersen Consulting

> Bruce B. JOHNSON, Director of Research
> Michael DE BELLIS, Center for Strategic Technology
>
> *100 S. Waker Drive, Chicago, IL 60606*
>
> Stanton J. TAYLOR
>
> *69 West Washington Street, Chicago, Illinois 60602*
>
> Charles W. McDONOUGH
>
> *400 Renaissance Center, Detroit, Michigan 48243*

Associative Design Technology

John C. EDWARDS, President

Two Westborough Business Park, Westborough, MA 01581-3199

Bankers Trust

Dr. Carmine VONA, Executive Vice President

One Bankers Trust Plaza, New York, NY 10015

Beatrice/Hunt-Wesson

John L. ESTES, Director, Information Systems and Services
Elaine M. GIDCOMBE, Manager, Systems Development

1645 West Valencia Drive, Fullerton, CA 92633-3899

BBN Communications Corporation

Jeff MAYERSOHN, Senior Vice President
Dr. Gilbert FALK, Director, Telecommunications Consulting
A. LYMAN CHAPIN, Chief Network Architect

150 Cambridge Park Drive, Cambridge, MA 02140

BBN Systems and Technologies Corporation

Steve JEFFREYS, Staff Scientist, Laboratories Division

10 Moulton Street, Cambridge, MA 02238

Chemical Bank

Frank A. KORAHAIS, Vice President, Information & Technology
    Management Division

96 Wall Street, New York, NY 10005

John E. CANTELLA, Vice President, Systems Development Department

55 Water Street, New York, NY 10041

Chicago Board of Trade

Glen W. BELDEN, Vice President, Information Systems
James D. WHITE, Vice President, Computer Systems and Operations
Richard N. LEE, Manager, Administrative Information Systems
Frank CHERECK, Manager, Network Computing
Veronica MURPHY, Database Administrator
Mark JESSKI, Supervisor, Administrative Systems

LaSalle at Jackson, Chicago, IL 60604

Citibank

Colin CROOK, Chairman, Corporate Technology Committee

399 Park Avenue, New York, NY 10043

Daniel SCHUTZER, Vice President
Sholon ROSEN, Vice President
Dr. Alexander J. PASIK, Assistant Vice President

909 Third Avenue, New York, NY 10022

John DAVIES, Vice President
Robert HSU, Vice President

1 Huntington Quadrangle, 4th Floor, Melville, NY 11747

Harvard Software (HSC)

Thomas GUTCHIGIAN, Vice President, Software
Jim DUDMAN, Product Manager

1661 Lincoln Blvd., Suite 101, Santa Monica, CA 90404

Hewlett-Packard

Dr. Ming-Chien SHAN, Manager, Cooperative Information Management,
    Hewlett-Packard Laboratories
Prof. Witold LITTWIN, University of Paris (currently at Hewlett-Packard)
Abbas RAFII, Manager, Database Technology
Philippe DE SMEDT, Database Technology
Weimin DU, Database Technology
Dr. Rafi AHMED, Database Technology

1501 Page Mill Road, 3U-4, Palo Alto, CA 94304-1126

Douglas DEDO, Product Line Manager, Commercial Systems Division

Hewlett-Packard Company, 19111 Pruneridge Avenue,
    Cupertino, CA 95014

Hughes Aircraft

Bhadra K. PATEL, Senior Scientist, Systems Technology Laboratory
Mae MA, Project Leader, Database Integration

Command and Control Systems Division, Bldg. 618, MS P325,
    P.O. Box 3310, Fullerton, CA 92634-3310

Hughes Research Laboratories

Son DAO, Senior Staff, Knowledge Based Systems, Artificial Intelligence
    Center

M/S RL 96, 3011 Malibu Canyon Road, Malibu, CA 90265

Inference Corporation

> Dr. Alexander JACOBSON, President
> Dr. Philip KLAHR, Vice President, Professional Services
>
> *550 N. Continental Blvd., El Segundo, CA 90245*

Kendall Square Research (KSR)

> Alex DONNINI, Director of Marketing
> Dr. David S. REINER, Director of Commercial Software Development
> Robert H. DORIN, Manager of Technical Support Commercial Products
>   Group
>
> *170 Tracer Lane, Waltham, MA 02154-1379*

LAC-USC Medical Center

> Dr. Bharat N. NATHWANI, Professor of Pathology, President Intelligraph
>
> *1200 N. State Street, Los Angeles, CA 90033*

Lotus Development Corporation

> Peter HARRIS, Systems Architect
>
> *55 Cambridge Parkway, Cambridge, MA 02142*
>
> Steven L. SNEDDON, Chief Technologist
>
> *One Rogers Street, Cambridge, MA 02142*

Microelectronics and Computer Development Corporation (MCC)

> Dr. P.E. CANNATA, Manager, Carnot Project
>
> *3500 West Balcones Center Drive, Austin, TX 78759-6509*

National Association of Securities Dealers (NASD)

> Robert N. RIESS, Senior Vice President, Technology & Development
>
> *1735 K Street, N.W., Washington, D.C. 20006*

Santa Clara University

> Dr. Mohammad A. KETABCHI, Director of Engineering Design Center
> *Santa Clara, CA 95053*

Security Pacific Automation Company

> Dale P. TERRELL, Executive Vice President
> *Security Pacific Plaza, 333 S. Hope Street, Los Angeles, CA 90071*

Terryhill Associates

> Meir BARTUR, Partner
> Marc D. GUREN, Partner
>
> *1900 Sepulveda Boulevard, Los Angeles, CA 90025-5620*

Thinking Machines Corporation

> Dr. Craig W. STANFILL, Senior Scientist
>
> *245 First Street, Cambridge, MA 02142-1214*

TRW Systems Engineering

> Dr. Anthony T. MATERNA, Manager, Data Integration Systems
>
> *Software & Systems Laboratory, DH6/2753, P.O. Box 6213, Carson, CA 90746*

UBS Securities, New York

> Dr. KRAENZLIN, Manager of Information Technology
>
> *299 Park Avenue, New York, NY 10171-0026*

University of Southern California, School of Business Administration

> Dr. Jack R. BORSTING, Dean
> Prof. Dr. Alan ROWE, Professor of Management
> Dr. Dennis McLEOD, Professor of Computer Science
>
> *Los Angeles, CA 90089-0871*

University of Virginia

> Prof. John ROSENBLUM, Dean
> Prof. Brandt R. ALLEN, Director, The Executive Program
> Prof. William W. SIHLER, Executive Director, Center for International Studies
> Prof. Robert J. SACK, Chairman, Information and Technology Committee
> Frank MORGAN, Manager, Executive Education
>
> *Darden Graduate School of Business Administration, P.O. Box 6550, Charlottesville, VA 22906-6650*
>
> Dr. Anita K. JONES, Professor and Department Head, Computer Science
> Dr. John L. PFALTZ, Professor and Director, Institute for Parallel Computation
>
> *Thornton Hall, Charlottesville, VA 22903*
>
> Philip M. NOWLEN, Dean, Division of Continuing Education
>
> *P.O. Box 3697, Charlottesville, VA 22903*

World Bank

Karl G. JAHR, Director, Information, Technology & Facilities Department
Emmitt S. SUMMERS, Jr., Chief, Services and Systems Support Division,
Cash Management Department
Pilarisetty MADHUSUDAN, Manager, Systems Programming

The World Bank, 1818 H Street, N.W., Washington, D.C. 20433

Xerox Corporation

Mark C. MALETZ, Manager, KBS Competency Center

780 Salt Road (Building 845-20C), Webster, NY 14580

Japan

Bank of Japan, Institute of Monetary and Economic Studies

Yoshiharu ORITANI, Chief Manager
Masahi NAKAJIMA, Assistant Manager
Nobuko KUWATA, Researcher

2-1-1 Hongoku-Cho, Nihonbashi, Chuo-ku, Tokyo 103

Center for Financial Industry Information Systems

Shigehisa HATTORI, Executive Director and Member of the Board
Masao TAKAYANAGI, Director, Electronic Banking Research
Fumitaka HAYASAKA, Deputy Director, General Administration and
Planning

*16th Floor, Arc Mori Building, 12-32, 1-Chome, Akasaka, Minato-ku,
Tokyo 107*

Dai-Ichi Kangyo Bank

Shunsuke NAKASUJI, Assistant General Manager and Director, Informa-
tion Technology Division
Kiyomo AKAHANE, Database Administrator
Misako YOSHIDA, Systems and Operations Planning

1-5 Uchisaiwai-cho, 1-Chome, Chiyoda-ku, Tokyo 100

DEC Japan

Dr. T. KOBAYASHI, Director of Research and Development
Yoji OGINO, System Engineer, Integration Services
Yasuko MORI, Database Specialist
Kikuzo ABE, District Sales Manager
Takao NODA, Financial Sales Division

134 Goudo-cho, Hodagaya-ku, Yokohama 240

EOS Software

Takeharu KOBAYASHI, President
Sumio ISHIZAKI, Professor at Sanno College and Consultant to the
  President
1-12 Sumiyoshicyo, Shinjuku-ku, Tokyo 162

Fuji Bank

Yasuo FUNAMI, Deputy General Manager; Chief, Systems Planning
  Division
Otemachi, Chiyoda-ku, Tokyo

Fujitsu and Fujitsu Research Institute

Masuteru SEKIGUCHI, Member of the Board, Fujitsu Research Institute
Tatsuji IGARASHI, Manager, Research and Planning Division, Fujitsu
Kazuaki WATANABE, Manager, Technical Support Center, Fujitsu
Takashi KIMOTO, Manager, Systems Laboratory
Kiyoshi ASAKAW, Chief Researcher, Neural Networks
1015 Kamikodanaka, Nakahara-ku, Kawasaki 211

Hitachi

Dr. Fumihiko MORI, Manager, System Development Laboratory
Haruyoshi YAMANOUCHI, Manager, Banking Systems
Kazuo MASAI, Senior Engineer, Database Department
5030 Totsuka-cho, Totsuka-ku, Yokohama-shi 244

Institute of Space and Aeronautical Science

Prof. Dr. Kozo FUJII
Yoshinodai 3-1-1, Sagamihara, Kanagawa 229

Japan Electronic Directory Research Institute (EDR)

Dr. Toshio YOKOI, General Manager
Mita-Kokusai-Building Annex, 4-28 Mita, 1-Chome, Minato-ku, Tokyo 108

Japan Research Institute, Subsidiary of the Sumitomo Bank

Koji SANO, Manager, Software Development Division
Akihito SAKAI, Vice-Chief, Software Development
3-1-31 Minamiaoyma, Minato-ku, Tokyo 107

Laboratory for International Fuzzy Engineering

> Prof. Dr. Toshiro TERANO, Executive Director
> Dr. Tomohiro TAKAGI, Deputy Executive Director
> Itsuko FUJIMORI, General Manager, Research Administration
>
> *Siber Hegner Building, 3rd Floor, 89-1 Yamashita-cho, Naka-ku, Yokohama-Shi 231*

Mitsui Taiyo Kobe Research Institute and Mitsui Taiyo Kobe Bank

> Teruhisa TAKASHIMA, General Manager, System Consulting
> Yoshiaki IWAMARU, Deputy GM, Financial Systems
>
> *16-6 Shinjuku, 2-Chome, Shinjuku-ku, Tokyo 160*
>
> Masato FURUKAWA, Senior Vice President, Systems Development Division, Mitsui Taiyo Kobe Bank
>
> *4-1-4 Kami-Osaki, Shinagawa-ku, Tokyo 141*

NEC and NEC Management Systems Research Institute

> Kotaro NAMBA, Senior Researcher, NEC MSRI
> Isao KAMOI, Engineering Manager, Database Development
> Takeshi YOSHIMURA, Manager, Basic Technologies Research Lab
> Yutaka KIMURA, Researcher on Object-Oriented Databases
>
> *5-29-11 Shiba Minato-ku, Tokyo 108*

Nippon Telegraph and Telephone

> Dr. Fukuya ISHINO, Executive Manager NTT, Director of the Communications and Information Processing Labs
>
> *1-2356 Take Yokusuka-Shi, Kanagawa 238-03*
>
> Masao KIMURA, Division Manager, Building Design and Construction
>
> *No. 21 Mori Building, 4-33 Roppongi-Chome, Minato-ku, Tokyo 106*

Sanwa Bank

> Shoji SAKAMOTO, Deputy General Manager
> Toshio HORIKAWA, Assistant General Manager—Databases
> Akira FUJIWANA, Database Expert
>
> *1-1 Otemachi, 1-Chome, Chiyoda-ku, Tokyo 100*

Sumitomo Bank

> Akimoto TANAKA, Director, Operations Administration Department
> Shigeo MORIWAKI, Assistant General Manager, Domestic Banking Planning
>
> *3-2 Marunouchi 1-Chome, Chiyoda-ku, Tokyo*

Acknowledgments **xxiii**

Tokyo International University

Prof. Dr. Yoshiro KURATANI

FI Bldg., 6F, 1-26-5 Takadanonaba, Shinjuku-ku, Tokyo 169

Tomin Bank

Kuwiki MASAI, General Manager, Systems Development Division
(Tomin Bank)
Hideo KOISHIAWA, General Manager, TCS Systems Development
Company (Subsidiary of Tomin Bank)

3-11 Roppongi, 2-Chome, Minato-Ku, Tokyo 0106

Toshiba

Tadahiro OHASHI, Manager, Computer Applications Department
Kazuo KAWAMURA, Manager, Financial Sector Systems
Willie SHA, Stock Trading System Analyst
Miss SATO, Bond Trading System Analyst

1, Toshiba-Cho, Fuchu-Shi, Tokyo 183

Toyo Information Systems (TIS), Subsidiary of the Sanwa Bank

Yukio URATA, General Manager, Business Systems Division
Katsutoshi YAMASHITA, Deputy GM, Business Systems Division
Hiroshi SHUNOHARA, Assistant GM, Systems Consulting Division
Kumiko TOTSUKA, Manager, Systems Integration

4-6-1 Ginza Chuo-ku, Tokyo 104

UBS Tokyo Area Office

Peter BRUTSCHE, Executive Vice President and Chief Manager
Helmut LASKA, Director of Regional Logistics
Graham MELLOR, New Director of Regional Logistics
Dr. Peter BERWERT, Manager, Regional Information Systems
Masaki UTSUNOMIYA, Manager of IT, UBS Investment Banking
Dan CERRI, IT UBS Trust Bank
Tom KOZLOSK, IT UBS Trust Bank

Fukoku Seimei Building 5F, 2-2-2 Uchisaiwaicho, Chiyoda-ku, Tokyo 100

Yamaichi Securities

Morihiro MATSUMOTO, Deputy General Manager, Strategic Planning
and Product Development
Toshihiro HATTA, Manager, Financial Strategy
Masaaki HASHIMOTO, Deputy Manager, Systems Planning
Norio KOMAKO, Assistant Manager, Systems Planning

Fukuoka Bldg., 4F, 8-7 Yaesu 2-Chome, Chuo-ku, Tokyo

United Kingdom

Abbey National

> Mac MILLINGTON, Manager, Group Systems
> Nick GOODMAN, Project Leader, Finance & Banking System
>
> *Management Services Division, Chalkwell Drive, Shenley Wood, Milton Keynes MK5 6LA*

Andersen Consulting

> Hugh MORRIS, Partner
> Dr. Gilles LAFUE, Director, European Research Division
>
> *2 Arundel Street, London WC2R 3LT*

Associative Design Technology

> Mathew TOMAS
>
> *23 Forthbridge Road, London SW11 5NX*

Bank of Scotland U.K. Banking (East)

> Colin S. McGILL, Divisional General Manager
>
> *P.O. Box No. 12, Uberior House, 61 Grassmarket, Edinburgh EH1 2JF*

Barclays Bank

> Peter GOLDEN, Information Technology Director, Markets Division
> Brandon DAVIES, Head of Financial Engineering Global Treasury Services
> Graeme M. SKELLY, Manager, Financial Engineering, Global Treasury Services
>
> *Murray House, 1 Royal Mint Court, London EC3N 4HH*
>
> George BIGBY, Chief Data Architect, Group Information Systems, Technology Organization
>
> *Radbroke Hall, Knutsford, Cheshire WA16 9EU*

Barclays de Zoete Wedd

> Neil G.A. EVERINGHAM, Director
>
> *Ebbgate House, 2 Swan Lane, London EC4R 3TS*

Chemical Banking

> Graham BLAND
>
> *180 The Strand, London WC2R 1EX*

Coopers Lybrand Deloitte

   Ian L. BRIGGS, Manager, Knowledge Engineering Applications
   Samit KHOSLA, Manager, Object-Oriented Systems

   Plumtree Court, London EC4A 4HT

County Natwest

   Sam GIBB, Director of Technology
   Cyril KILBRIDGE, Business Systems Analyst
   Chris BAKER, Business Systems

   135 Bishopsgate, London EC2M 3UR

County Natwest Investment Management

   David MAGUIRE, Manager, Information Technology

   43/44 Crutched Friars, London EC3N 2NX

County Natwest Securities

   Don F. SIMPSON, Manager, Information Technology

   135 Bishopsgate, London EC2M 3UR

London Stock Exchange

   John D. SCANNELL, Head of Network Operations/SEAQ
   Diane IMTHRUN, Network Operations/SEAQ

   London Stock Exchange, London EC2N 1HP

National Westminster Bank

   Andy F. MILLER, Senior Manager, IT Planning, IT Strategy & Policy
      Department

   10/11 Old Broad Street, London EC2 1BB

Noesis Ltd.

   G.J. MASKELL, Director

   10 Cobden Road, Brighton, East Sussex BN2 2TL

UBS Phillips and Drew

   Hansruedi WOLFENSBERGER, Vice Chairman
   Dr. Peter JACKSON, Area Director of Information Technology
   Urs BRYNER, Former Area Director of Information Technology

   100 Liverpool Street, London

Sweden

Irdem HB

> Gian MEDRI
>
> 19, Flintlasvagen, S-19154 Sollentuna

Nordbanken

> John LUNDGREN, Project Manager, Business Systems
>
> 24, Smalandsgatan, S-10571 Stockholm

Skandinaviska Enskilda Banken

> Mats ANDERSON, Manager of Systems Architecture and Technology
>
> 2, Sergels Torg, S-10640 Stockholm

Svenska Handelsbanken

> Lars O. GROENSTEDT, Senior Vice President
> Peter ININBERGS, Systems Analyst
>
> 11, Arsenalgatan, S-10670 Stockholm

Swedish Bankers Association

> Bo GUNNARSSON, Technical Director and Coordinator of Bank
> Automation
>
> Box 7603, S-10394 Stockholm

Other Countries

AVT/Eurosept

> José MOREJON, Director of AVT
>
> 13, rue Gilbieri, 69002 Lyon, France

Bank of Norway

> Lars Erik RUSTAD, Data Security Chief
>
> Bankplassen 2, Postboks 1179 Sentrum, 0107 Oslo 1, Norway

Banque Scandinave en Suisse

> François JEANNET, Director
>
> Cours de Rive 11, P.O. Box 901, 1211 Geneva 3, Switzerland

Ciba-Geigy, AgroDivision

Pamela Ann BATHE, Director of Logistics
Stefan JANOVJAK, Information Manager
Meike BUEGLER, Information Architect

Schwarzwald Allee, 4002 Basel, Switzerland

Bim Systems

Olivier DECLERFRAYT, General Manager
Didier HECK, Technical Director

30, rue de Lisbonne, 75008 Paris

Fellesdata AS

Forde IHLEN, Chief Consultant

Nedre Skoyenvei 26, P.O. Box 248, Skoyen, 0212 Oslo 2, Norway

Union Bank of Switzerland

Ulrich RIMENSBERGER, Director of Telecommunications
Kurt WOLF, Director of IT Technology in Investment Banking/Area
    Europe
Hans WALTHER, UBILAB (Union Bank of Switzerland Research
    Laboratories)

45 Bahnhofstrasse, Zurich, Switzerland

University of Ottawa

Dr. John Scott COWAN, Vice Rector, Resources and Planning

550 Cumberland, Ottawa, Ontario, Canada K1N 6N5

PART I

Advent of
the Multidatabase

CHAPTER 1

Developing a Corporate Database Concept

1.1 Introduction

The problems posed by the exponential growth of information handling to practically all industries in the decade of the 1990s are becoming increasingly pressing. Database resources are that much more valuable when we can provide seamless access to the people who need them. For this reason, able solutions to the management of networked databases are at a premium.

One of the most urgent tasks facing financial institutions and industrial organizations is to identify opportunities for improving the design and use of their corporate databases. To do so, it is necessary to:

- Assess the current state of the art
- Evaluate whether the needs of endusers are being met
- Identify the pressing problems in database interoperability
- Outline opportunities for improvement

The configuration of a corporate database can be expressed in terms of primitives and a properly designed conceptual integration schema. This should permit flexible and efficient cross-database query processing as well as transaction handling.

The relative importance of technical and managerial issues associated with data organization and management is, to a substantial measure, determined by:

- The distributed and/or centralized approaches which prevail
- Existing data types, schemata, and semantic descriptions
- Special characteristics of state-of-the-art implementation(s)
- *Database management systems* (DBMS) and their heterogeneity or compatibility

- Current and anticipated daily operational requirements
- Longer term perspectives and the way we approach them

Every environment has its needs. Scientific data usage, for example, is characterized by large volume, low update frequency, and almost indefinite retention. Other priorities characterize the business environment.

In the past, it has been generally safe to assume that scientific data resulting from experimental observations was never thrown away. But the future volume of collected *information elements* (IE) will be staggering. The *Magellan* planetary probe, for instance, will generate a trillion bytes of data over its five year life—including more image IE than all previous planetary probes combined.

Business database applications are often input/output (I/O) intensive. Solutions have to keep up with I/O requests from multiple distributed computer units. One way to eliminate the I/O bottleneck is to maximize the I/O bandwidth, but this poses other problems.

Both with business and with scientific databases, most challenging is the fact that they rest on an array of incompatible supports. The computer industry has been careless in this regard and user organizations today are hampered by a diversity that verges on anarchy. Incompatibilities pose a substantial barrier to data access by those who need it. They also create challenges which are technical, logistical, and organizational.

Both in scientific and in business environments, analytical approaches using multiple data sets from different incompatible databases are becoming an increasingly important and powerful tool for managers and professionals. Hence, organizational, logistical, and technical solutions have to be found.

1.2 Fundamental Notions for the 1990s

Both centralized and distributed database implementation rests on a number of basic concepts which have been found to be fundamental in understanding the whole system. The work which we do in this domain can be assisted by the semantics and descriptive power of the methodology which we use—but which is the better methodology?

Because of the growing need for *networked databases*, a significant problem facing the information scientist today is the bewildering array of commercially available database management systems. Another is the nearly total incompatibility of custom-made:

- Database interfaces
- Data structures
- Computer operating systems
- Network protocols

All of these issues need to be mastered in order to examine potentially relevant data. Experience teaches that the best way to face the associated challenges is to start with the fundamentals.

One of the fundamental notions is the rapidly increasing amount of *multimedia*[1] information stored and retrieved by computers. Another basic notion is a growing demand for solutions able to support *convenient access* to databases distributed across networks.

A logical integration of these databases is needed in order to provide seamless access to information elements spread across multiple preexisting systems. But to perform such logical integration, we need to overcome many obstacles arising because of technical as well as organizational reasons.

Organizational and logistical reasons see to it that databases are not only spread geographically and/or by functional area, but also that they belong to different business units. These databases retain their independence in terms of authority and responsibility, yet they need to work in unison on certain projects through networking.

These prevailing conditions are not new. What is new is that the organizational not the technical issues hold the upper ground, and organizational problems cannot be effectively solved by brute force. Precisely because of conflicting organizational and logistical interests, the better model is that of a loosely coupled system, like that of the Swiss Confederation. In this system each Canton has plenty of local authority and the central government respects it. But the central government also controls it to make sure centrifugal forces do not tear the system apart.

In a technical, computer-enriched sense, this is the model of *federated databases*. They are networked but operate peer-to-peer, as shown in the right side of Figure 1.1. This contrasts to the left side, which represents the centralized repository system like the one Napoleon instituted in France with Paris as the pivot point.

In a concept dominated by centralization, the resources may be physically distributed, but logically they are centralized (and at times over-centralized). In a peer-to-peer system characterized by federated databases, every player has a certain amount of independence.

---

[1]Text, image, graphics, icons, data, and voice.

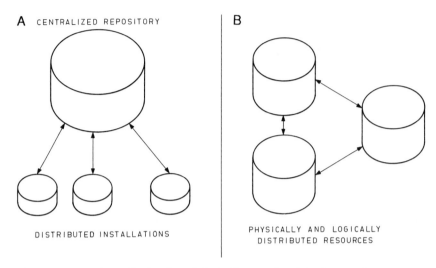

Figure 1.1 (A) Physically distributed, logically centralized database, and (B) federated databases operating peer-to-peer.

We will be looking into the technical details of federated databases in Chapter 6 when we talk of schemata and metaphors. However, what is important to underline at this point is that even with fully centralized solutions there is a great deal of *diversity* with which any technically valid approach has to cope. Such diversity is largely due to:

• Different data models for each of the DBMS in the network
• Different design decisions made in connection to each database
• Possibly conflicting values for related IE stored in different
   databases—which may even be located in the same room

We will be stating the obvious by underlining that able solutions cannot be attained through the now traditional languages and the database concepts of the 1970s or 1980s. But can we define an effective model which will permit us to face current and coming challenges in an able manner?

The answer lies in a three-dimensional (3-D) approach to database design, implementation, and maintenance. The facilities supported by database management, as a whole, must expand to offer services across the 3-D spectrum as shown in Figure 1.2. The axes of reference are distributed information elements, object management, and knowledge engineering.

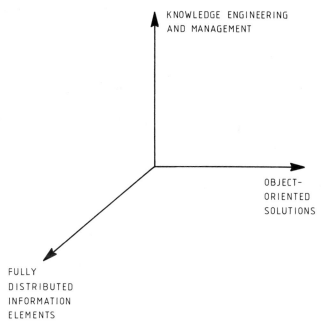

KNOWLEDGE ENGINEERING
AND MANAGEMENT

OBJECT-
ORIENTED
SOLUTIONS

FULLY
DISTRIBUTED
INFORMATION
ELEMENTS

Figure 1.2   Most real-life database management problems in
the 1990s and beyond will be three-dimensional.

Distributed information elements will reside in networked databases
which are to a significant extent local and autonomous, yet part of a
networked solution.

The services required in the domain of object management must be
able to efficiently store, retrieve, and manipulate nontraditional data
types such as images, icons, text, graphics, and documents—in short
multimedia. Object-oriented types of problems abound in computer
aided design, office automation, treasury/forex operations, portfolio
management, and other applications.

The contribution of knowledge engineering rests on the ability to
store and use a collection of rules that are part of the semantics of the
application. These rules describe a course of action as well as integrity
constraints. They can also allow the derivation of information elements
that are not directly stored in the database.

1.3 What Is the Sense of Database Operations?

Most real-life database management problems that will arise in the
1990s and beyond are inherently 3-D, as shown in Figure 1.2. Ideally,

the distributed database being described through this coordinate system is a single integrated entity on which both logical and physical operations take place.

To fulfill the objective of interoperability among networked databases, object and rule management capabilities must be added at the *tactical level*. These have to be more powerful than the DBMS services we have known so far. But there is as well a conceptual, *strategic level* of reference even more important than the tactical. This strategic level calls for a clearer definition of what a corporate database *is*, and *is not*.

A *database* is an organized collection of information elements set up to fulfill a certain purpose. Such purpose might have been enunciated at the design phase or developed through usage—the second alternative being much more likely than the first.

During the research which led to this book, the majority of organizations interviewed said that their databases grew, more or less, like wild cacti. The purpose of their existence and the perceived benefits came *after* the databases' growth—hence the drive currently under way to put sense and organization into database structures.

New departures in database design, implementation, and management are more important as networked corporate databases are increasingly accessed on-line by:

- Endusers with *ad hoc* dynamic requirements approaching the database through a query language
- Teleprocessing routines for transaction chores which become more and more complex as well as polyvalent

Both address information elements in the networked database, that is, encapsulated callable entities. An IE can be a bit, byte, field, record, file, major chunk of a database, or the whole database itself—and it has to be handled in a dependable way, as we will see in the last sections of this chapter.

The enduser wants to have not only dependability but also agile, friendly approaches to stored information. This is a different viewpoint from that of the database designer who looked at the database in a different sense, as:

- The repository of corporate IE structured according to a data model
- These IE being multimedia or single media, depending on the implementation

For both the enduser and the specialist, however, the concept of a corporate database and its management is becoming increasingly important. As we work with huge amounts of computer-stored IE, we need to be able to organize and access them efficiently, facing in an able manner the challenge of databases communicating over *global networks*.

Since databases are built to be used, we are evidently interested in the performance which we get from them. Database performance can be measured in terms of *response time* and *transaction throughput*, two issues which do not need to be synonymous though they are often taken as such.

One reason why we are interested in database performance is that the database resources of large firms are worth billions, even if they do not appear on a balance sheet. At American Airlines, for example, jetliners show up as assets, but the information system that runs SABRE, the reservation service, is not on the balance sheet.

Yet Wall Street securities analysts figure that as a profit center SABRE makes more money for American Airlines than the planes do. Traditionally, information technology has been taken almost entirely as an intangible asset, that is why it is nowhere to be seen on the balance sheet. But in the 1990s, this is changing.

The change is triggered by the fact that database operations start being seen as *asset-generating activities*. Poor organization and management of the networked corporate database leads to poor profit and loss (P&L) results. Good organization and management requires not only the manipulation of information but also of knowledge—and learned users understand the difference between the two.

1.4 The Concept of Corporate Databases and Knowledgebanks

The corporate database is increasingly becoming a storehouse of multimedia information which should be addressed in a seamless way by the three main levels in an organization for which computer applications are written. Top to bottom:

1. Top management decisions requiring complex, analytical queries
2. Allocation and optimization problems addressed by professionals
3. Transactions and settlements, many of which are of a clerical nature

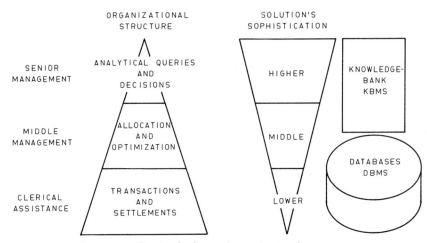

Figure 1.3   Solution specification by layer of organizational structure.

Figure 1.3 presents these three layers of reference and also suggests that increasingly sophisticated software is necessary to meet each layer's needs for capturing and managing complex, corporate-wide information and knowledge.

The aim of any systems solution being projected today should be to build applications using both information and knowledge in the database. This cannot be provided economically with nonintegrated database structures and with obsolete third-generation-type languages.

American and Japanese studies document that more than 75% of important management functions have no support whatsoever from computers, in spite of large sums of money which have been thrown at the problem. The same studies indicate that in order to address analytical queries as well as allocation and optimization decisions, we need *knowledgebank management systems* (KBMS).[2]

The issue of databases and knowledgebanks boils down to this: To retain their competitive edge in a rapidly changing, global marketplace, companies must be able to utilize in an efficient manner their information resources and the knowledge which they acquire:

• Raw data, events, and values are stored in the database
• Knowledge assets are handled through the knowledgebank

[2]See also D. N. Chorafas *Knowledge Engineering*, Van Nostrand Reinhold, New York, 1990.

The knowledgebank includes the rules necessary to exploit in an *intentional* manner the contents of the database. At the same time, knowledge assets in *corporate memory* represent the experience and wisdom which managers, professionals, and other employees have acquired.

We typically use both data and experience in forming judgments, making choices, elaborating policies and procedures, and handling complex organizational and market relationships. This permits us to reason about past as well as present business success and failures and to project about things to come—positioning ourselves against the market forces.[3]

The safekeeping and able utilization of corporate knowledge is most critical for business success. But while the storage of information elements has more or less been mastered, it is quite difficult to capture, store, and distribute knowledge throughout an organization in any automated way.

Both knowledgebanks and databases should be handled by means of a systematic methodology. Over the longer run, we should aim at the standardization, integration, and access to knowledge resources. Such resources help provide a dynamic model of a system (physical or logical) containing information elements which must be efficient, updatable, and secure.

Since it is the dynamic model of an active system in operation, the corporate database must be designed, implemented, and maintained in a way able to provide:

- A concise, understandable representation of structures, functions, and operating states characterizing the organization
- Efficient access to facts and values describing the actual status of the corporate system
- Simple access procedures for a consistent update as functions, states, and values change within our operating environment
- Real-time response to analytical *ad hoc* queries made by users—whether persons, programs, or machines

Questions regarding the nature of comprehensive information contained in the database have not yet been fully resolved. We know, however, that effective solutions must reflect not only the context of applications but also the ways users interact with stored information.

Bearing such requirements in mind, the systems and procedures we develop must reflect both knowledge and information requirements and be able to cover:

[3]See also D. N. Chorafas *Risk Management in Financial Institutions*, Butterworths, London and Boston, 1990.

- Acquisition of information and knowledge
- Quality assurance and error control
- Real-time storage and retrieval
- Operations in a distributed topology
- Processing as well as presentation
- A visualization solution very friendly to endusers

The dissemination of information and knowledge is critical because of the inherently complex and changing nature of problems which companies are facing today. The goal is to develop and maintain flexible approaches that enable us to successfully capture, store, and use corporate knowledge and information to solve critical enterprise-wide problems, develop competitive products and services, and sustain a steady market advantage.

Such approach is part and parcel of a strategic effort which starts with a search for a valid answer to the query: "What kind of computers and communications facilities do our products and markets require and what will they require in the future?"

1.5 Information Solutions in a Knowledge Society

The able use of concepts and processes of scientific analysis can enrich us with immense powers. Francis Bacon (1561–1626) phrased this in one short sentence: "Knowledge is power"—which like any other form of power has to be exercised.

A *knowledge society* revolves around the creation, transfer, storage, and usage of both know-how and information. In an era where the knowledge society is rapidly becoming a reality, database resources are as important as natural, human, financial, and social resources. It is important to appreciate that in the current post-industrial era, our products, services, processes, and structures are becoming knowledge- and information-intensive, increasingly oriented toward their handling by means of heuristics, algorithms, networks, and databases.

New types of software underpin computer processing, leading to the industrialization of knowledge and information. The acceleration of the deployment of networked databases helps in strengthening the service industry. The ternary sector of the economy has been largely supported by advanced information systems.[4]

[4]See also D. N. Chorafas and H. Steinmann, *Expert Systems in Banking*, Macmillan, London; New York University Press, New York, 1991.

Through software, solutions must be developed which can capture dynamic information processes and human expertise. The domestication of knowledge enables us to solve complex tasks more quickly and accurately than otherwise would be possible, but also underlines:

• The need to build solutions on a virtually homogeneous database platform, in spite of physical and logical incompatibilities
• The wisdom of using intelligent broadband networks interlinking workstations and databases
• The growing requirement for supercomputing to perform process simulation, information filtering, and complex transaction processing chores

The challenge of the 1990s and beyond is to extend and integrate knowledge engineering and data management technology to the point where problems can be solved successfully by having on-line access to information and knowledge resources.

Knowledge engineering underpins the *new type of software* which is available to those who know how to take advantage of it. Software is the logical layer in solutions involving computers and communications—but its nature is changing. The same is true of physical supports. Presently, the physical layer of the information industry, which is supporting the "informatization" of society, is *electronics*. Tomorrow it will be *photonics*: Optical cables for communications, optical disks for databases, and optical switching for computing.

Since the 1980s, microprocessors have been used in every field of industry and society. Semiconductor products are so widespread and so fundamental that in Japan they are called *the rice industry*. But in the 1990s, we have begun to see knowledge engineering chips becoming the "staple food" of our culture.[5]

An orderly transition to a knowledge society includes the need to be conscious of the details of all the mechanisms involved, logical as well as physical. We must observe the dynamics of the technologies of the future in order to obtain the added value they make possible in information processing and knowledge handling.

The informatization of society is taking place in multiple dimensions: geographical, demographic, and sociostructural. But it can be handled in an able manner only when we are able to understand the functions of real-world objects and use computers to execute these functions effectively.

---

[5]For instance the fuzzy engineering and neural network chips developed by the Laboratory for International Fuzzy Engineering (LIFE) in Yokohama.

Able performance requires a blending of concepts from a number of disciplines: knowledge engineering, database design, communications, and man–machine interfaces. We need agile enduser interfaces to deal with issues such as:

- Images and vector graphics
- Voice and other sound recordings
- A variety of text forms
- The more classical data
- Compound electronic documents

At the bottom line, this is a database problem compounded by the need for agile human windows with enduser selectable lists, menus, pop-up forms, color, and graphics.

To sustain interactivity and improve it, database access must be seamless and uniform, but the user interface should be customized to meet the needs of every individual. This has to be done in a knowledge-enriched manner.

The more sophisticated people to whom future systems will be addressed (and where the highest return on investment can be found) are very demanding. Many companies fail to understand the fact that information solutions in a knowledge society are primarily directed to these more sophisticated people. These are the companies which are spending money for nothing.

1.6 The Reliability of Large Databases

One of the basic requirements in sustaining the momentum of a knowledge society is the development, utilization, and maintenance of *large databases*[6]—both private and public. Large databases are not little databases which have grown up; complex databases pose novel and taxing requirements in terms of:

- Conceptual design
- Development perspectives
- Implementation
- Exploitation
- Steady upkeep

---

[6]There is no precise yardstick to say what is a large database, but this label can apply to structures beyond 500 gigabytes. For over 2 or 3 terabytes we talk of very large databases.

The able utilization of large and very large databases requires a high degree of parallelism and involves a large number of components. As in any system, one or more of the component units can fail, affecting performance and availability. Hence the need for fault tolerant solutions.

Quantitative analysis is necessary to compare the relative effect of different parameter values on system-wide availability. Since fault tolerance is obtained at the cost of additional resources, the designer's task is to:

- Minimize such cost for a given level of *reliability*[7]
- Make trade-offs by choosing an appropriate *system architecture*

With networks, we are after the so-called *"four 9s"* —99.99% reliability. At least a *"three 9s"* (99.9% reliability) figure should characterize networked databases.

Though 99.99 and 99.9% reliability is a difficult goal to obtain, many companies do not even make an effort in this direction. It is therefore not surprising that, as a result, their databases feature a reliability of 90% or less, two or three orders of magnitude less than what is required.

The major components of a large distributed database structure are processors, central memory modules, magnetic disks, and optical disks.[8] These resources are dedicated to storage and parallel-processing chores needed to exploit stored information. Because of the size of a distributed database, the amount of replication has to be carefully controlled. With regard to operations, an update transaction will change many information elements; hence the need to know the location of the master copy. After a failure, reintegration of failed components has to be followed by system recovery.

In a reliability sense, three issues are crucial to the operation of the components, subsystems, and the networked database system as a whole: fault, error, and failure.

A *fault* is a defect in a component or subsystem. Faults result in errors which lead to invalid component states and to *failures*, i.e., loss of service. Within a networked environment, database locality, hence a *federated* solution, enhances system reliability, whereas centralization concepts diminish reliability, often to a significant degree.

---

[7]Reliability is not an ability. It is the probability that a system will operate without failure over a specified period of time under established conditions.

[8]Magnetic tapes, too, but these should be weeded out of the system.

Database *errors* may be transient, intermittent, or permanent. Permanent errors are *hard errors* while transient and intermittent errors are often viewed as *soft errors*. Soft errors, however, are very difficult to locate and account for the large majority (up to 90%) of all unwanted events.

A fault tolerance approach to database reliability should protect against both soft and hard errors. Error detection and correction techniques are vital, as is knowledge engineering-enriched software which sees to it that after failure the database takes a corrective action through recovery.

This can involve reconfiguring to isolate a failed component, as well as restructuring. If a single failed component affects no other during recovery, we are faced with a single failure. If a failed component tears down other parts of the system, then the faults are propagated and the networked databases drift. Simultaneous failure of more than one component is a multiple failure. If after a single failure effective operation continues, then the database system is *gracefully degrading*.

Reliability is improved through redundancy. *Physical redundancy* can be obtained by having extra devices in the database network, or by extra time for diagnosis and recovery. The latter is known as *temporal redundancy*.

One form of physical redundancy is the use of backups able to mask faults and permit reconfiguring of the database to get around faulty components. Temporal redundancy assists in retrying operations to recover from transient soft errors.

There is *also logical redundancy*, which is typically software supported and has to do with how information elements are distributed. Knowledge engineering provides logical support to database reliability and can be used with several classes of redundancy service.

1.7 Networked Databases and Reliability Measures

Knowledge engineering constructs can be used for pretesting components, subsystems, and systems of the networked databases. They are also used for instituting and exploiting a *quality database*, which should be created to assist in terms of *reliability* and *dependability*, the latter in a data integrity sense.

One of the principal threats to *data integrity* in many systems arises from data duplication. Large databases have plenty of it. Maintaining consistency among several copies of the same information element is difficult and is a major factor in the development of inconsistencies in a database.

This reference is valid whether we talk of centralized or of distributed databases. The exact topology and fine or coarse degree of distribution should be an issue transparent to the enduser—who is, however, dearly interested in data integrity.

The point of this last reference is that it is not enough to interconnect databases and other computer resources in order to obtain a reliable system on which users can depend for their operations. Effectively networked databases demand much more than that, including the appropriate reliability measures.

The way we appreciate the reliability of networked databases changes quite radically when we stop looking at them as arrays of hard disks supplied wholesale by a vendor and we start examining them as a vital corporate resource. When the asset-generating issue (of which we spoke in Section 1.3) is brought under perspective, quality programs are initiated and real improvements can be made.

This change in course and outlook is true of all database structures, whether centralized or distributed, but it is more valid with the latter than with the former. That is why prior to discussing distributed versus centralized alternatives, partitioned databases, schemata, metaphors, and protocols through which IE can be accessed, it is proper to face the intricate aspects of the reliability challenge.

The general schema of the system to which reliability measures will be addressed is shown in Figure 1.4. Distributed corporate resources communicate among themselves, with a central repository, with other computers, and with a myriad of workstations through a network. The goal is availability of database resources, and this greatly depends on how information elements are distributed and duplicated. Data fault tolerance is attained by proper placement of information elements within this networked environment.

For instance, one method is to have two or more copies of each IE in different places of the database network. People who are long on enthusiasm but short on judgment will duplicate practically everything—but this is the wrong approach.

The right way of improving the reliability of a networked database requires simulation studies and appropriate metrics. Two statistics are commonly used to evaluate system reliability at runtime:

• *Mean time between system interrupts* (MTBSI)—which particularly addresses hard failures

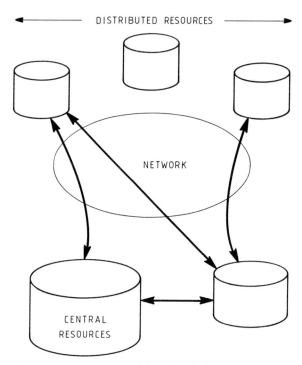

Figure 1.4 Networks and distributed databases for real-time management.

- *Mean time of system interrupt* (MTOSI)—reflecting repair, restart, and recovery[9]

To improve both statistics, physical redundancy techniques are used only after appropriate experimentation. To help increase the availability of each component through duplication or triplication, we must know our goals, our operating environment, and the resources at our disposal.

Duplication strategies for processors are called *processor pairing* and for disks, *disk mirroring* (duplexing). These are mainly techniques to be used at the single device level, but stimulation and optimization, hence experimentation, permits extending them to the system level.

[9]See also D. N. Chorafas *The Handbook of Data Communications and Computer Networks*, McGraw-Hill/TAB Books, New York, 1991.

Processor pairing allows masking of soft failures and increases tolerances of hard failures. Disk mirroring is used to increase MTBSI in a logical, data-oriented sense, provided the network operating system is able to maintain a consistent image of all elements at any time.

1.8 Fault Tolerance Means Availability

Our attitude, we said, changes when we look at networked databases as corporate resources rather than platforms on which we park our bits and bytes. Many companies have been slow to grasp the change taking place or have been hobbled by inertia, but those who understand what they do are keen to apply the appropriate metrics.

While MTBSI and MTOSI are important at system level, they are influenced by the component-by-component reliability measures concerning the attached units. For each component, reliability measures are expressed through the statistics:

* *Mean time between failures* (MTBF)
* *Mean time to repair* (MTTR)

One of the problems in terms of practical implementation of these statistics is the lack of fundamental, theoretical studies beyond the hardware level. Yet, we need to implement both soft failure and hard failure algorithms.

This is true about all networked resources: processors, main memory, and disks, as well as power supplies, connecting busses, gateways, and other linkage devices.

Apart from processor pairing, at the *processor level* soft failures have to be addressed through transaction recovery and software reinitialization. Hard failures require system reconfiguration.

At the *memory level*, software failures are approached through parity and error correction codes, transaction recovery, and software reinitialization. Hard failures call for memory reorganization, mirroring, and reconfiguration.

Storage disks too have soft failures which call for error correction codes and techniques such as the aforementioned disk mirroring. Here again hard failures are approached through system reconfiguration.

Failures of busses and gateways are treated by means of protocol retries and error detection/correction codes and also by way of redundancy in linkages and switches along the data paths being used.

With reliability statistics available, based on the measurement of performance, the favored parameter-characterized fault tolerance is *availability*. At the device level, with MTBF and MTTR, the availability of a component is given by:

$$\text{Component Availability} = \frac{\text{MTBF}}{\text{MTBF} + \text{MTTR}}$$

Estimates of the MTBF and MTTR of each component should be known before availability can be estimated. This is just as valid for system availability:

$$\text{System Availability} = \frac{\text{MTBSI}}{\text{MTBSI} + \text{MTOSI}}$$

Availability of a fault tolerant database system can be defined by assuming that the entire networked database should be available at any time, from any place, for access by authorized users.

$$\text{Availability} = \frac{\text{Time the entire database is available}}{\text{Total time}} \times 100$$

It is relatively easy to quantify and therefore to justify that the specified fault tolerant techniques meet established availability goals. This is true when we are able to calculate the availability of subsystems consisting of multiple components.

The management of overall reliability of networked databases requires the development of a *quality database* focused on availability, managed through knowledge engineering, and enriched by accessing as well as updating appropriate transaction tables. A valid methodology is a "must," for instance specifying that:

- Aborted transactions are restarted when the distributed database leaves the pause state.
- The system remains in passive state until the reconfiguration is completed.
- Newly arriving transactions are queued behind the transactions to be restarted.

The accesses of the coordinator must be global. The network control center (NCC) must have the ability to find IE stored on the failed device(s). Subsequently, the reintegration process requires that the contents of the repaired components are updated with respect to all transactions or other operations which have taken place during MTTR.

Transaction handling, query processing, and optimization techniques are very intimately related to component and system fault tolerance. This statement is valid from the initial design and onward since efficient solutions to data storage depend on the type and frequency of transactions made and queries asked.

In conclusion, to design a real-time database system, the developers have to understand the application and devise a network scheme that is acceptable from the transaction and query processing viewpoints as well as in terms of fault tolerance. Both the required response time and reliability are to a significant extent application dependent, contrary to what is written in most books.

CHAPTER 2

Distributed versus Centralized Database Solutions

2.1 Introduction

One or more computers accessed by multiple users through nonintelligent terminals or personal computers emulating dumb terminals (for instance through 3270 protocol) constitutes a *centralized* system. All database services and applications are provided in a monolithic way. As a result, growth over time:

- Leads to bottlenecks
- Reduces the level of service ability
- Ends in disruptions with users feeling frustrated

An important characteristic of centralized systems used to be the single-site database shared by multiple users (people, terminals, programs) with different requirements. Unfortunately, for many companies, due to bad advice or resistance to change this poor centralization habit has been extended to multiple sites which act as one block.

Inflexibility, high cost, and low return on investment are the inescapable results of solutions which are bought from the vendor wholesale without proper questioning. Centralization imposes constraints and limitations upon the utilization of information resources, particularly when the users are many and fairly dispersed in topology.

By contrast, in a *distributed* environment, databases and applications reside on computers interconnected by means of a network. By off-loading functionality, a distributed solution can dramatically improve efficiency and productivity as well as cost-effectiveness and performance.

A distributed approach delivers better and more flexible services to users, enables faster solutions to local problems, improves accountability, and reduces communications costs. It also minimizes the risk of total system failure, but presents constraints as well. One of the more important of these is *heterogeneity*—which is not alien to centralized solutions as well.

Significant advantages are presented by the use of distributed approaches, which explains why user organizations are increasingly looking toward integrative solutions. But we must be able to confront in an able manner the handling of operations in such a landscape which consists of a large number of databases.

In a distributed interactive environment, users do not have complete knowledge about all *database schemas*. Among the challenges faced by database specialists are to:

- Define the location and type of networked databases
- Educate themselves about the expanding information space and its organization
- Provide the means for seamless accessing to the stored information elements (IE)
- Give the user the tools to efficiently manipulate IE in the targeted database

System integration[1] is the key to an effective solution. An integrative project can be divided into two phases: First, finding the IE location after the application space has been defined. Second, providing the user with the ability to efficiently access networked databases and training the user on their use.

2.2 The Increasing Complexity of Database Applications

The difference between successful and unsuccessful efforts in the management of networked databases is that those which are successful look to the user as being the king in any solution. The user must be able to navigate to solve query or transaction requirements in a distributed database, even if the networked resources are heterogeneous and hence incompatible.

[1]See also D. N. Chorafas *System Architecture and System Design*, McGraw-Hill, New York, 1990.

This means that the user must have the ability to effectively handle transaction processing and query resolution with full knowledge of local databases and database management systems. Another prerequisite is sharing of information in large distributed structures by building *views* of applications and hence providing linguistic support by which the user can dynamically investigate information elements.

- Solutions must always account for the fact that *ad hoc* database access is very important.
- Authorized endusers must have the freedom to access, query, or modify contents.
- Most importantly, any solution must be open to evolutionary requirements.

These references are just as valid for distributed and for centralized database approaches. But networked databases bring in an added dimension in terms of problem complexity, while they provide greater flexibility and a faster, better user service.

The concept of networked databases did not come out of the blue sky. It has been promoted by the increasing complexity of business and industrial applications and the heterogeneity of system environments. Both reasons have made centralized databases inappropriate.

As leading-edge organizations have found out through experience, advanced applications are best developed by means of distributed cooperative resources. However, these too present new challenges in terms of:

- An exploding demand for on-line database storage and retrieval
- Representations of information elements in a network-wide sense
- Complex interactions among the tasks required to achieve processing objectives

Based on a sample of statistics and projections from leading companies, Figure 2.1 shows the exponential growth in database requirements. From 100 or so gigabytes of storage in the early 1980s, corporate databases will feature 10 terabytes or more by the end of the 1990s—an increase of two orders of magnitude in less than 20 years.

Even at the level of 100 gigabytes, centralization of database resources was tedious and inefficient. But it is totally absurd today and it will be absolutely impossible by the mid-1990s. Only networked databases can confront the growing applications complexity.

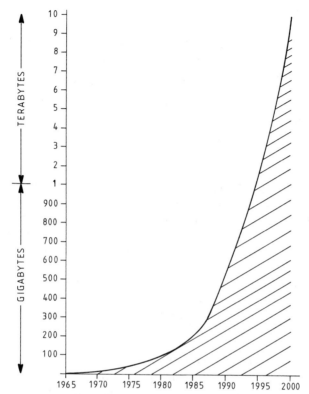

Figure 2.1   Throughout business and industry demand for
storage is increasing dramatically.

A long transactions environment is the case in point. We have briefly
talked about long transactions in Chapter 1. The following three examples explain what they mean in terms of technological solutions and
database accesses[2]:

• Skandinaviska Enskilda Banken is one of the first European
  financial institutions to bring alive a long transactions
  environment. The application focuses on portfolio management,
  giving the client buy/sell and other investment advice.

Run under IBM's hierarchical database management system, IMS
(which is a severe mistake), this application requires 1000 database

---

[2]See also the discussion in Section 3.3, Chapter 3.

accesses per transaction—versus 8 to 10 accesses which a classical transaction needs. The difference is 10,000%.

Interestingly enough, this figure of 1000 database accesses per long transaction would not have been that much better under IBM's relational database system, DB2. American banks said so, and so did COVIA.

- Owned by United Airlines, British Airways, and other carriers, the COVIA information system must handle 100,000 transactions per second. Some of them are long transactions, and their number is growing.

COVIA started by running its long transactions under the MVS operating system and DB2, on an IBM 3090/600. They executed at the rate of less than 20 per second. To bring this example to the point of absurdity, if all of the 100,000 transactions per second were long transactions, COVIA would have needed 5,000 IBM 3090/600 mainframes at about $5 million apiece.

As a result, COVIA benchmarked a full application with all inputs/ outputs on a new supercomputer (by Kendall Square Research). Compared to the large IBM mainframe, the cost-effectiveness ratio was 2000%.

- In London, Barclays Bank and BZW made the same reference in regard to their financial engineering applications. Under its new management, Barclays got going and is well launched in financial engineering to regain its competitiveness.

Said the manager of Financial Engineering at Barclays: "To handle the models we are doing at subsecond, we would have to dedicate a large IBM mainframe per trader. We simply cannot invest £3.5 million ($5.8 million) per trader. Hence we use high technology."

2.3 Is Cultural Change a Prerequisite?

These real-life references are brought into perspective because long transactions, simulators, optimizers, and expert systems are the competitive tools of the 1990s. But even the best and most sophisticated mathematical models cannot function alone. They need steady access to reliable networked databases.

Let's make no mistake about it, long transactions are on a steady increase and the earlier an organization prepares for handling them the better off it is. Companies often resist change because they are pursuing two contradictory aims:

1. Save the status quo
2. Keep up competitiveness at the same time

Only clear-eyed managers and technologists can see that it is unlikely that both aims can be met. Crucial choices are necessary and a cultural change is a prerequisite in moving from aim 1 to aim 2.

The main problem is not to lose control over events. Pull and push by the market is the moving gear behind the new environment and nobody can really resist the competitive market forces for long.

Skandinaviska Enskilda, for example, forsees plenty of long transactions in the years to come as the merger wave under way in Sweden leads to a great number of analytical requirements. Enskilda Banken projects that the coming environment in the financial industry will split between two major classes:

- The more traditional reservation type
- The newer and more demanding competitive type

Reservation type applications are both simpler and better known. In terms of database requirements, they represent the aforementioned classical 8 to 10 database accesses. By contrast, competitive type transactions are much more demanding and have many unknowns. They cannot be handled through the patched-up, stereotypical approaches of the past.

But a new technology strategy like that of fully distributed, networked databases can make sense *if* and *only if* a number of steps are decided by top management and religiously observed by everybody. These include:

- The proverbial long hard look
- Cultural change necessary to make it possible
- Proper design of the distributed databases network
- Valid projection of competitive type applications
- Rapid software development timetables
- A well-studied transition plan toward competitive type
  applications

A networked databases strategy will of course entail much more detail, but the foregoing points help in bringing to the foreground the fact that the enlarging business horizons have important technology aftermaths.

We must learn from the leaders in this field in order to be able to implement worthwhile applications.

Developing appropriate software paradigms to support communicating databases and cooperative work is one of the major challenges facing not only the computing and communication industry but also the user community. Solutions must point in an effective manner to the direction of distributed service implementation.

Such solutions necessarily have to deal with heterogeneous database systems and long transaction models. They have to define new correctness criteria for control of interactions among cooperative tasks, some of which will necessarily be long-running applications. Since experience in this domain is still thin, this can only be achieved via an iterative trial and error process.

2.4 Distributing the Information Elements

Many issues are impacting the distribution of information elements in today's environment of networked databases. Therefore, there is need for a methodology to help in the analysis of user requirements and business functions and to provide a technical basis for efficient distribution of information elements.

It is evident that technological subjects raised and presented by distributive activities have to be explored in depth, concentrating on the areas of efficiency in solutions, greatest potential risk, and data integrity. Database architecture and database administration must also be viewed in the context of a distributed processing environment, logically integrating the database but physically partitioning it. Partitioning can be vertical or horizontal.

The *vertical partitioning* of a database is useful when the database is too large or volatile to be serviced by a single engine. Vertical partitioning also provides a limited form of fault tolerance in the sense that the loss of a single database computer does not necessarily halt all transaction processing.

If we partition the database on the basis of a number of attributes corresponding to main accounts or client entities, this will be vertical partitioning. By contrast, if the partitioning job is done along the lines of functional subsets, this will be characterized as *horizontal partitioning*.

The possibility of both vertical and horizontal partitioning has to be carefully studied. Future trends as well as standards for distributed database technology must be explored. Among the most significant tools are:

- Distributed data dictionaries
- A thorough analysis of design strategies
- Object-oriented technologies
- Performance issues proper to the specific implementation on hand

Performance issues have many aspects. In Chapter 1 we have spoken of response time, but the cost function too must always be kept in perspective.

Figure 2.2 presents in a nutshell the trend curves of three different projects which evaluated distributed database structures against the alternative of centralization. The exponential growth curve reflects a fast growing data load.

The two trend curves show order of magnitude variation. Quite evidently, detailed studies are necessary within every specific transaction control system which addresses itself to cooperative tasks interacting with each other by sharing objects stored in databases. A *distributed* cooperative model allows more local:

- Autonomy
- Flexibility
- Reliability

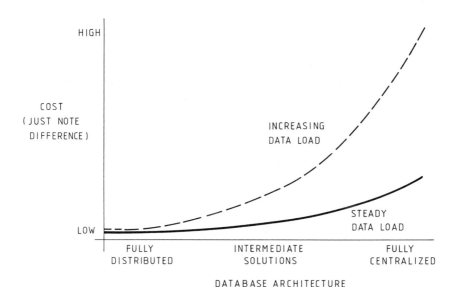

Figure 2.2   Costs increase exponentially with growing data load under centralized conditions.

This is done with greater efficiency than is the case with a *centralized* scheme. In a distributed cooperative model, applications are controlled by a set of tasks properly defined through a sequence of interactions which have to be studied in advance and properly dimensioned.

An effective distributed cooperative model, however, requires that several technical issues are addressed, including the way to observe and control the progress of an application that supports long-running activities. This is particularly important since the dynamic interactions among users can be complex precisely because they require iterative and cooperative processes.

Any authorized on-line user (person, terminal, or program) may change the cooperative objectives just as this user affects the inputs and the outputs. This raises a number of queries:

- How can the shared resources be reliably manipulated?
- How do we define and determine when a cooperative objective is attained?
- What is the criterion for controlling interactions among multiple iterative tasks?

Able answers to these queries must be given within the *technological* perspectives of the 1990s—not of the 1980s or 1970s—as well as the current and projected *operational* requirements.

Solutions advanced by foremost organizations involve visualization at enduser level, knowledge engineering, object orientation, and prototyping. Complex programming models are being developed on high performance computers; intelligent networks are designed to handle broadband communications; and enduser requirements are answered through interactive multimedia applications.

2.5 Standards for Data Management

The user community should be encouraged to develop methods to foster the distribution of databases and to reward those which are properly managed. There should be a standard for database organization and the storage of relevant information elements in appropriate database structures, as well as the *regular pruning* and secure handling of databases.

Over time, the problem of the increasing volume of stored IE will force some hard decisions with respect to their retention. At some point it will become necessary to decide:

- Whether to discard some of the information elements in storage
- Which criteria should be used for pruning purposes

Studies along this line of reference will lead to major policy decisions which cannot be made by database specialists only but will necessarily involve senior management as well.

Therefore, through business and industry, management will be well-advised to start promoting and funding workshops to investigate and recommend policies relative to the organization of distributed databases and pruning of stored information elements.

Account must be taken of the many nontechnical barriers to the successful solution of database management problems. These include peoples' unwillingness to release data in a timely fashion (as well as to get rid of those becoming obsolete) and the shortage of individuals trained to analyze information.

Today, in a growing number of observed cases, people access databases and massage the information without *really knowing* what data they access—or its semantics. It is therefore important to resolve the computer literacy problems hindering the development of a sound information management and usage policy.

On the more technical side, a crucial issue in data management perspectives concerns the *quality of information elements*. The quality of the networked databases depends on:

- The quality and dependability of the data sources from which they are fed
- The soundness of design of each local database both in absolute terms and in relation to the demands of the applications
- The criteria established for the various types of data being handled within a given environment

Due to its polyvalence and the dynamic requirements to which it must conform, such a database cannot be constructed without active participation from the user community to which it is addressed. In a way, it is immaterial whether the database is centralized or distributed, as in either case it has to be:

- Designed by a database architect
- Run and maintained by the database administrator
- Accessed by a myriad of users

Therefore, the database must benefit from the advice of the user community to which it addresses itself in the first place. Just the same, the users have to be equipped with state-of-the-art interactive workstations able to reach the networked databases in a seamless manner.

Standards must be devised to assure the compatibility of information elements for verification, among other reasons. Quality targets must also be defined to guaranty that data (whether collected internally or purchased from external sources) is consistently reliable.

Such controls should relate primarily to the accuracy and comprehensiveness of the information elements being supplied. Whether or not it is decided to buy data from public databases, the work of harmonizing and quality-controlling all information in a company's private databases must still be carried out. Assuring the quality of information elements is a steady job, not a one-time proposition. A dynamic database will be steadily confronted with new information elements which by adding themselves to the existing lot may alter its structure.

Even if a neat solution is found during the architectural design, (for instance along the reference shown in Figure 2.3), the time will come when the new inflow will upset the existing balances.

Particularly crucial in terms of a steadily updated design is the placement of reference data. Placement problems become more difficult

<table>
<tr><td></td><td colspan="2">BUSINESS LINE</td></tr>
<tr><td></td><td>CROSS-BUSINESS</td><td>SPECIFIC TO
THE LINE</td></tr>
<tr><td>GEOGRAPHY-
WIDE</td><td>GLOBAL
DATABASE
PERSPECTIVES</td><td>DISTRIBUTED
ELEMENTS
BY
BUSINESS LINE</td></tr>
<tr><td>TOPOLOGY

OF
LOCAL
IMPORTANCE</td><td>DISTRIBUTED
ELEMENTS
OF GENERAL
IMPORTANCE</td><td>LOCAL ELEMENTS
BY
BUSINESS LINE
(REALLY LOCAL)</td></tr>
</table>

Figure 2.3 Classification of information elements by business line and topology.

where IE specific to more than one of the quarter spaces shown in Figure 2.3 are compounded by product types or customer types. An example is transnational, country-specific, and client-specific IE.

In these cases, the database architect must be able to distinguish scope of usage at the individual placement level in order to know which copy of an IE is the master. This requires indicating country, client, or product priorities to which the organizational and marketing functions are associated.

The reason for placing so much importance on the master copy is that, as we should know in advance, it is unavoidable that discrepancies will eventually develop between some of the copies of the same IE distributed through the networked database. It is therefore imperative to preestablish:

- Which copy of the information element in reference the database administrator will regard as the master
- Which procedures should be followed so that all other IE are calibrated against that master copy

The proper definition of standards and their integration into workable solutions can become a foundation from which business and industry serve themselves with a valid, easy-to-use, cross-database approach. But networked solutions have prerequisites and the reliable handling of master copies is one of the center points.

2.6 Adopting an Open Architecture

Standards do not emerge in an orderly, well-defined manner. It is either a market leader or the users and the marketplace that creates them. That is how *de facto* standards are set. If successful, they are normalized by national and international standards organizations such as the American National Standards Institute (ANSI) and the International Standards Organization (ISO).

De facto standards are formalized through national and international standards organizations because major users keep on driving for *open systems*. Contrary to what some vendors say about their parochial protocols or other wares, a truly open system implements *all* of its protocols and interfaces according to standards which have been established by neutral organizations and institutes.

One objective of the observance of standards in protocols and interfaces, IEEE underlines, is to enable properly engineered applications software to:

- Be ported across a wide range of systems with minimal changes
- Interoperate with other applications on local and remote systems
- Interact with users in a style which facilitates portability

As a matter of general principle, open systems are not proprietary. Generically, they operate along very different lines than closed systems do.

The first major difference with open systems is that no vendor really has a lock on them, though vendors do try to create supposedly better versions—or dialects—which are incompatible with the normalized standard. Every time one hears "my version is better . . . ," what is essentially being said is that it is incompatible to the open system standard in reference.

There is, however, much more than a normalization process characterizing open systems. Their underlying strength is conceptual. Using a metaphor from thermodynamics:

- Open systems do not absorb and hoard entropy, hence they don't wear and tear like closed systems.
- Closed, proprietary systems are thought to be self-contained, providing little or no flow of ideas, matter, and energy between themselves and the outside world.

According to the second law of thermodynamics, *entropy* is a measure of the amount of energy *unavailable* for useful work in a system undergoing change. Entropy is also the degree of disorder in a system or a substance.

Organization aims to decrease the amount of entropy. It is a matter of common experience that disorder will tend to increase if things are left by themselves. In computers and communications and in heuristics, entropy is a measure of the information content of a message evaluated as to its uncertainty.

If the level of requirements increases in a systems sense, as it often does, open solutions can always deal with it. In contrast to closed, proprietary approaches, open systems are *self-organizing* and therefore *they evolve.*

Once a closed system reaches its limits or breaks down, there is little hope of it being put back together again. But the open system is subject to steady change by absorbing input and adapting itself to the environment stimuli.

As a process, the drive toward open systems is fueled by the economic necessity of the user community to leverage existing computers and communications investments: software, hardware, protocols, gateways, operating systems, DBMS, and applications programs.

Ideally operating systems (OS) and DBMS must run in an open software environment embodying standard data models, data description, and data manipulation languages the way the Multivendor Integration Architecture (MIA) aims to do.

This is a new awareness, as database management systems and programming languages have historically defined their own esoteric and proprietary "standards." But, as investments in applications software mounted, user organizations found out the hard way that this is a bad policy which negates the possibility of reusable software.

What the leading-edge user organizations today are particularly after is the ability to assure *seamless communication* among networked databases and the interconnected world of terminals, workstations, and computational resources. Under the banner of the Open Systems Interconnection (OSI)[3], the standards bodies and user organizations talk about a new era in communications and in computing.

It is, however, too early to forecast a future of global networks interoperated without regard for location or logos. Both fact and fiction are included in claims of what will be possible in the new world of open systems. Able solutions require:

- Clear goals on behalf of users on what they want to see achieved by means of open systems.
- Policies and procedures that support standardized database management functions.
- Software instruments and processes able to handle cross-network databasing and provide a prediction on performance.
- Human resources capable of comprehending and executing management functions in connection to distributed databases.

New concepts in the design, implementation, administration, and maintenance of distributed databases must be examined and the latest product advances assessed, including tools based on artificial intelligence for automating the management of database resources.

---

[3]By the International Standards Organization.

In conclusion, the open system concept involves structure, principles, and protocols. It is not just an "open sesame" approach; its implementation requires principles, steady effort, and know-how.

The architecture of the networked databases has to be studied in detail. Both current needs and growth requirements must be examined. A functional analysis should include the basic elements of the architecture as well as the concepts and tools used for integration.

2.7 Open Architectures and Interface Standards

When the need for an architecture was first recognized, vendors responded by creating proprietary solutions to distributed computing and networking. Practically every major vendor had a solution, IBM's SNA and DEC's DNA/Decnet being the better known examples.

Both SNA and DNA (as well as the other parochial vendor architectures such as DSA, XNS, and IBM's more recent SAA) are closed systems in the sense discussed in Section 2.6. By contrast, ISO/OSI is an open system and, within it, the same is true of the internet environment promoted by the Defense Advanced Research Project Agency (DARPA) of the U.S. Department of Defense.[4]

Today, persisting with a closed architecture is the best way to make our errors permanent. That is why so many companies migrate to an open architecture—in spite of vendor pressure and the fact that old systems like old politicians can be kept alive through "hormones," which is what some of the vendors are trying to do.

Making decisions about which of the available architectural alternatives should be used for networked databases means commiting the company for at least the next 10 years. It is therefore most important to keep in mind that:

- In networking, communications protocols which in the past tended to support a particular view such as master–slave or pseudo-peer now move toward *open architectures.*
- A similar feat takes place with *distributed databases,* with a trend away from half-baked solutions connected to one vendor system or DBMS and toward open interconnection standards.

A realistic estimate of the situation will reveal that, because of past practices, every major organization finds itself with a variety of incompatible database management systems and protocols.

[4]DDN architecture and TCP/IP protocol.

The fact that in the last three decades we have experienced significant growth in database applications makes the choice of standards a crucial problem. This is further underlined because of new types of implementations, the growing size and complexity of applications, increased numbers of installed database servers, and new developments in software engineering.

As database usage has grown, the desire to link and integrate separate databases and DBMS has resulted in substantial effort being directed toward the design of interconnected distributed resources. One of the major challenges of integrating diverse databases is to hide the heteroge-

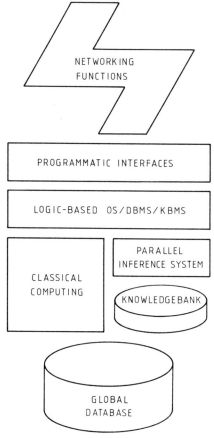

Figure 2.4 Integration of the global distributed database with the corporate network.

neity of the constituent structures from users—hence the different approaches which will be examined in the subsequent chapters.

The development and/or adoption of *interface standards* for interconnecting networked databases is indivisible from the links to be provided between networks. Not only has the trend toward distributed databases been accelerated by advances in telecommunications technology, but also realistic integration perspectives require a testbed for interface standards to be assured by the network.

As Figure 2.4 demonstrates, between the global distributed database and the corporate network there exist interface layers which help integrate the former with the latter. These include:

- Classical computing and parallel inference systems as complements or alternatives
- Distributed operating systems, DBMS, and knowledgebank management systems
- A host of programmatic interfaces assured through applications programming libraries developed over many years

The web of the networked resources becomes increasingly complex, yet our goal is both *simplicity* and *integration*. We invest in computers and communications for productivity gains, and in this connection the three most important dimensions are completeness, accuracy, and simplicity.

As far as the enduser is concerned, simplicity comprises ease of learning and ease of use. Both are heavily affected not only by the advanced tools we put at the user's disposition but also by the process of resource integration.

Integration means ease of moving between the various functions of networks, databases, and computing systems. This requires making the often diverse components appear similar to the user—typically, because they actually use *identical* front-ending standards and common formats in visualization.

A valid process of integration deals with semantic heterogeneity which may be present whether the database resources are distributed or centralized. Heterogeneity cannot be reconciled by taking the beaten path of the 1970s which, in many organizations, continued well into the 1980s. New departures are necessary in projecting, implementing, and managing the networked databases.

CHAPTER 3

Managing the Networked Database

3.1 Introduction

Sponsored by the American IEEE Computer Society and the Information Processing Society of Japan, as well as supported by Kyoto University and Keio University, a special workshop[1] aimed at exploring new technologies in database management took place in Japan. Particular emphasis was placed on:

• System-wide database integration
• Object-oriented databases and DBMS
• Virtual homogeneity in a heterogeneous environment
• Challenges with distributed databases including reliability and security

The extent of issues involved between these goals and their depth can best be appreciated by looking at the topics on which the conferences focused. These included the understanding of integration requirements of heterogeneous information systems, cognitive view mechanisms for multimedia networked databases, as well as the need for a smart data dictionary.

A new generation of data dictionaries was seen as best being approached through a knowledge- and object-oriented approach, which can be instrumental in terms of the interoperability among heterogeneous databases. We will look more closely at this subject in subsequent chapters.

Quite similarly, in the American Symposium on Parallel and Distributed Information Systems,[2] a paper by Michael Stonebraker and Wei Hong brought forward the concept that there is a dramatic drop in

---

[1]Kyoto, Japan, April 1991.
[2]Miami, Florida, December 1991.

performance when *more processes than processors* exist in the network. The reasons are:

• Partitioning schemes
• Contention
• Cycle stealing
• Systems overhead

Both events, in Miami and in Kyoto, looked at networked databases as a collection of users and servers. The users are people, but also programs, workstations, departmental computers, and other hosts. The servers perform dedicated functions to help the users. The users generate transactions and queries which, through software, are processed by various servers. Ultimately such processing provides a response which is returned to the user, but this should be done efficiently, most of the time at subsecond response time.

A focal point in technology should be to make such an approach feasible. One way discussed during the international events in reference has been a pattern-based approach for deriving approximate and intentional answers from distributed databases.

Intentional answers mean intelligent database solutions which can exploit the distributed extentional database contents. This approach is a cornerstone of the able management of networked databases. Management functions can only be automated by means of knowledge engineering, not through arcane Cobol programs.

3.2 The Need for Distributed Databases

The advent of intentional solutions was treated, at both symposia, as an integral part of the ongoing move toward interoperable database systems and the need to provide for connectivity of heterogeneous resources. As we will see in due detail, the latter can range from simpler pass-through to sophisticated access schemes, reaching databases under different and incompatible DBMS.

Pass-through can be a good approach for management applications as it helps in solving query-type data access problems. But it is not a valid solution for transaction processing which requires a virtual integration of database systems, for instance by using object orientation.

Successful companies approach the goal of virtual database integration through knowledge engineering and object orientation. Their aim has been to realize a federated information system consisting of networked databases.

As we have seen in Chapter 1, knowledgebanks are integral parts of a properly distributed database infrastructure. They look after interoperability of heterogeneous databases and bring to bear virtual integration in spite of schema discrepancies.

Intelligent heterogeneous database architectures can be developed through different strategies. This is a proactive way of thinking since it serves the recently popular server-based approaches to finding information in large scale heterogeneous database structures.

Such approaches best fit an environment of networked databases. Sure enough, databases are not the first to come into the spotlight as distributed resources. Promoted by minicomputers, the term *distributed processing* has been used since the early 1970s to describe various approaches to computer decentralization.

Over the years, however, there has been considerable confusion over the definition of distributed processing. A wide range of products represented different views of distribution, and the major disappointment has come from the fact that on-line connectivity has not always been assured.

As a result, for nearly two decades, leading companies reconsidered their concepts and goals relating to distributed processing. This phrase was successively used to describe:

1. The interconnection of independently managed minicomputers
2. Then, the network of cooperating workstations (WS) with hosts acting as servers

Both items 1 and 2 have been instrumental in bringing into perspective the need for *distributed databases*. But in the early years the distribution of databases was closely connected to the distribution of processing. Only later did the growing need for remote data access come into the picture; and only recently ANSI and ISO standardized the necessary interfaces.

Since the dynamics of implementation by each user organization are essentially different, *ad hoc* solutions which have been provided during the 1980s support a varying range of functional capabilities. The same is true of the reliability of connections as well as of standards and protocols.

As a result of *ad hoc* solutions and associated diversity, fairly incompatible approaches have been taken as the way to answer enterprise-wide database problems. The definitions of distributed processing and distributed databases still encompass a range of different competing concepts as well as technical methodologies. But the need for assuring an integrative capability has resulted in increasing interest regarding on-line access to incompatible databases.

Companies and people who tried to implement integrative approaches would appreciate that poor communications have traditionally been a major constraint in distributing functions. Today, however, networking quality is becoming less of a barrier and communications capabilities are rapidly improving. This is not necessarily true of database accesses.

Software has also been seen as a stumbling block as systems programs provided by vendors have not assured that reference data or invoked servers could be on another machine accessible through a network. As a result, the developer of a distributed application was traditionally forced to invest in basic software for reasons of:

- Reaching remote information elements or functions
- Recovering from network and file server failure
- Assuring cross-node access as well as security

Because of these shortcomings, providing for a distributed database implementation of applications and IE proved to be a time-consuming and tedious undertaking. It added considerable expense and complexity to the development of computer applications and required skills beyond those available in many user organizations.

3.3 The Growing Challenge of Long Transactions

The United Airlines/COVIA, Skandinaviska Enskilda, and Barclays Bank examples which we saw in Section 2.2, Chapter 2, have in common the growing need of handling long transactions. The complexity of applications is a business fact and information scientists are called to provide solutions—not to argue that "long transactions are not really transactions . . ." as certain vendors sometimes do.

As the implementation horizon of communications and computers further expands, from the original distributed data processing to the wider concept of distributed databases, it has become evident that clear preconditions are:

- The availability of *virtual homogeneity* which permits seamless database access and consistency in long transaction handling

• Knowledge engineering-enriched software providing effective connectivity across database facilities.

Such a concept, however, developed slowly without much thought given to integrated services spanning incompatible vendor environments. No wonder that the incompatibilities being discovered came as an aftershock.

Leading-edge organizations appreciate that true interoperability requires the support of facilities able to reach across different machine architectures, operating systems, network protocols, as well as database management systems and data structures. This means going above and beyond the heterogeneity of OS, DBMS, and their traditional sets of constraints.

One of the critical issues regarding interoperability is *response time*. With heterogeneous databases, however, the expected response time is very difficult to calculate as it is an aggregate of data communications time, the DBMS processing time, and the necessary translation time from one data structure or format into another.

Besides this, there are other prerequisites included in a dynamic competitive business environment which reflect on distributed database solutions. These include the able handling of *long transactions* to which we have made frequent reference to press the point of their growing importance. Long transactions are transactions which take a long time to complete and/or are complex in nature with each composed of many subtransactions which interleave in a commitment sense.

As several companies have discovered, the more sophisticated the models we use, the more they demand in terms of distributed databases, complex transactions, and analytical queries.

An evolving architecture, these same companies comment, is instrumental in promoting flexibility which is needed for the able handling of new products and financial instruments. There is, for example, a linkage between baseline securities and *derivative* (such as options) which has to be handled in a flexible, dynamic way to follow market trends and opportunities.

A long transaction cannot be completed unless its subtransactions are executed. At COVIA, models have been developed for long transactions, but they are very demanding in terms of cycles. Very expensive, large IBM mainframes can handle *only* 20 transactions per second due to model complexity and the search in heterogeneous databases. This does not make economic sense. By contrast, modeling on the KSR supercomputer runs at *seven times* the mainframe performance, but only at *one-*

third the mainframe cost. This means an impressive *1 to 20 ratio* in cost-effectiveness.

As another example, portfolio consolidation is a long transaction which in many banks involves a two-digit number of applications modules, some of which already exist but are heterogeneous: written in Cobol, using spreadsheets, and manipulating DBMS primitives and commands.

Some of these application modules are transaction-oriented; others aim at providing response to queries through access to distributed information elements. The more sophisticated applications use expert systems and the long transaction acts as an integrating force.

One of the basic requirements for able response to long transactions is having a polyvalent multimedia dictionary on-line. This should not be just a dictionary methodology but an active dictionary which can be remotely accessed as a whole, while subsets of it are at each distributed node.

It is also well increasingly necessary to assure both database semantics and flexibility in the usage of the distributed information elements through an object DBMS. We have seen the importance of this approach since the opening paragraphs in the introduction.

3.4 Design Principles with Distributed Databases

A number of principles must be observed in designing, implementing, and maintaining distributed database systems. These range all the way from site independence to nonstop operations for long transactions and query processing. In terms of independence from site, the following principle applies:

• Local information elements should be managed locally.
• Local IE should not be affected by other sites' conditions.
• However, local IE should be available in a global, cross-database sense.

This principle is valid all the way to independence from center site; the latter, if it exists, should have no hierarchical authority over distributed resources. All sites participating in a networked database system should be peers and therefore should not depend on one single site for command purposes.

We have spoken of centralized versus distributed databases in Chapter 2. Mainframe-based centralization of resources is like an incurable disease: It only gets worse with age. Users—whether persons, terminals, or applications—should not need to know the location of IE required for the work they are doing. All data should be handled *as if* available in the local site though in reality it may be anywhere in the networked databases.

Furthermore, even if files are partitioned and objects stored in a multiple number of sites, they should be handled logically as a single reference. As we have seen in Chapter 2, IE should be partitioned and stored in order to assure high performance—but the global database as a whole should also be capable of reconstruction.

Even if copies of information elements are reproduced, users should not need to know at which site or which data is the copy. If the objects are modified, their clones must be automatically modified as well.

Another principle to be observed in the design and implementation of networked databases is that of independence from operating system and database management system.

- Our distributed database will typically work on different hardware platforms.
- The multimedia approach we choose should run under different operating systems.
- The distributed database should be constructed from multiple DBMS, with a common interface.

Just as vital is independence from the network's primitives. The distributed system should be projected in a way to integrate a multiple number of network architectures and communication media—both local and wide area.

We have also spoken in Chapter 1 of the imperative need to assure reliability. Networked databases should work nonstop. The addition or deletion of sites and modification of database configuration must not affect the overall system. Under the worst conditions, as few sites as possible should be temporarily involved in the modification.

- Changes should be made step-by-step, not in a massive form.
- Changes should take place one at a time, only after careful testing and benchmarking.

This prudent principle is necessary in an environment of networked databases to support 24-hour per day operation, 7 days a week. Distributed transaction management as well as a steady flow of management queries make it mandatory.

Specific design principles tend to vary from one installation to the other. But no approach escapes the fact that information elements in a multiple number of sites are steadily renewed by a stream of transactions. These necessitate simultaneous update, data consistency among sites, and recovery from system failure.

All three issues should be steadily assured. And since deadlock situations may develop, they should be properly studied, predetected, and avoided in advance, not after the slowdown of the system.

The same principles characterizing transaction processing are valid regarding distributed query handling, including *ad hoc* analytical queries. In both cases, the networked databases should be seen and treated as a virtually homogeneous construct by all users, starting with the designers.

Figure 3.1 shows a knowledge engineering-assisted approach to the fulfillment of the aforementioned goals. It is an abstract of the solution

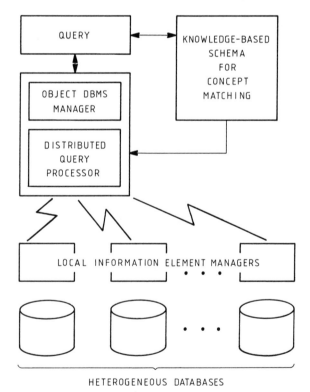

Figure 3.1 An *ad hoc* solution can be tailored to user's requirements through knowledge engineering.

implemented in a project involving the functional design of a network of real-time distributed DBMS. For nearly four years, the system has worked in a flawless manner.

These are no design and implementation activities which should take three to five years to accomplish. With driving force to handle the available skills, these activities can be completed in less than six months.

In 1982 at Merrill Lynch, Michael Blomberg pitched a system for U.S. Government bonds to an informal committee. Merrill's computer experts said they would need six months to study the practicability of such a solution.

Blomberg promised to deliver a finished product in six months—the time the systems experts wanted just to "think about it." He did it, and today his revenues are running at an annual rate of $216 million.[3]

3.5 A Two-Tier System: Common Denominator and Added Value

Due to the prevailing database heterogeneity, data access involves three significant problems. The first concerns the *specification* of desired information elements through a query language; the second, *location* of IE through a logical search mechanism followed by actual physical access; the third challenge regards the *enforcement* of security protocols that limit data access to authorized programs, terminals and people. But this becomes an actual preoccupation, provided the first and second challenges have been solved in an able manner.

How are we going to approach the problem of specification? The answer is conditioned by the technology we use. With most relational systems:

- In the case of a single database, the information elements (tuples) are stored persistently as a single unit on a single device.
- On access they are copied into a formatted block of volatile memory from which various components can be unpacked.

Different approaches are followed to make this operation cost-effective. For instance, the representation of IE in disk storage must be bit-wise identical to its representation in central memory. A valid strategy

---

[3]*Forbes* magazine, November 25, 1991.

would be to conform to the encoding conventions of the host language, operating system, and hardware.

Even supposing the query language which we are using effectively answers our requirements, to access the same disk-based IE from foreign hosts customarily requires considerable data reformatting. Hence the need for a relatively simple, consistent way of handling such reformatting requirements.

This is the minimum a short-term solution should do, and it is possible. Typically, it is achieved through drivers, as is the case with Data-Lens—the Lotus Development commodity software which is able to access 20 heterogeneous databases from the 1-2-3 spreadsheet.

The simple passthrough solution which DataLens follows is the lower layer of the short term approach which we will be discussing in the appropriate chapter. It provides a client interface for internetworking, which is the boundary between the *client* workstation and the database *server*, as Figure 3.2 suggests.

Typically implemented through drivers resident at workstation level, and assisted through a data dictionary, pass-throughs make no claim to database integration. Their objective is limited; it is one of assuring direct access to a variety of data structures and DBMS with a translation facility also at a workstation (WS) site.

Even within this simple pass-through solution which features workstation driver-to-server interface, there are options, and therefore decisions to be made. Interfaces from application development tools to incompatible data sources have traditionally taken one of two roads.

- The *common denominator* (or low road) assumes that only the functionality common to all sources can be relied on.

This may be workable, as Dr. David Reiner once said,[4] but it fails to take advantage of advanced features possessed by a particular database server. Hence, from a longer term point of view it is counterproductive.

- The opposite is *added value* (or high road). It assumes that a rich set of functionalities should be used, including selections, relational joins, catalogs and so on.

The high road eases the task of interfacing, but it is not always realistic. Even when feasible, it sets too high a standard for implementing driver

---

[4]In the symposium on large, complex databases which took place in Kyoto, Japan, April 8 and 9, 1991.

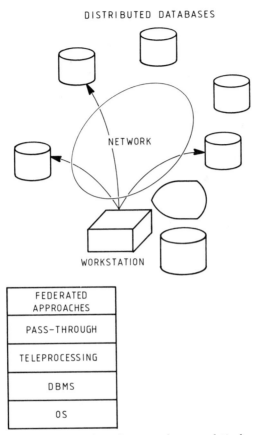

Figure 3.2 Pass-through approaches are relatively simple and can answer query requirements.

solutions. Hence, it tends to exclude other, simpler, nonrelational data-bases.

Given these relative advantages and disadvantages of the better known alternatives, another option in design is that of a *middle road*. Its interface is divided into *basics*, (that is *required functions*) and *optional functions*, depending on the features of the accessed DBMS.

With this in mind, the database pass-through application can rely on the presence of all *basic* function calls and capabilities. These are *the minimum needed* to bring information elements residing in incompatible networked databases into a given application.

This approach can be further enriched through a message-passing paradigm within the heterogeneous database environment, as we will see in Section 3.7. In principle, the higher the level of reference to which we address our efforts, the more we need to use knowledge engineering. If we try to do the needed job through classical methods, we will be confronted with severe performance limitations imposed by both hardware and software.

While in the past such limitations were taken as being part of life, we now have concepts and tools to deal with them. Our approach must see to it that computers can function as more than just information storage, retrieval, computation, and display systems. Operating in a seamless manner, they must:

- Supplement the human ability for using general knowledge to respond effectively in real time
- Emulate and follow different human reasoning processes, as necessary
- Acquire and apply knowledge, eventually including the manipulation and communication of ideas
- Focus attention on relevant information and knowledge through very fast processing power

Existing software methods are limited to relatively uniform processing of information elements, and they respond only to specific inputs and situations that have been included in the program design. New approaches must confront the challenges resulting from the fact that the *solution space* has increased and keeps on expanding.

3.6 Distributed Data Management beyond the Simple Pass-Through

While the simple pass-through solution is the simplest way to interconnect distributed heterogeneous databases, other approaches aim at the integration of database operations. These are much more demanding in terms of organizational work, as we will see in the following example of twelve independent companies which aim to bring together their database resources.

No company can afford to look at it database operations in a freeze-frame manner. Therefore, the project in reference has been undertaken with the aim to implement a top management decision to move from a country-by-country basis of activities to a customer- and product-centered solution.

Both the customer- and the product-focus, company management decided, had to be integrative, able to provide the infrastructure for looking at product demand by region.

Databases were not the only key subject. If anything, it was the derivative of an earlier management decision aiming at optimizing the location of factories and warehouses. This called for the ability to bring together both centralized and distributed resources by replacing all core transaction processing systems, which were too diverse, with one well-studied solution.

In a technical sense, the adopted approach accounts for the fact that across the many operating units of the corporation a variety of architectural requirements existed. There are differences in:

• Business organization
• Size of operations
• Scope of business lead
• Needed computer systems
• Supported databases

With regard to organization, the situation was complicated by the fact that business factors drive operating units toward markedly different approaches with respect to the degree of functional integration or decoupling. There has also been variation in terms of the number and capacity of individual processing locations.

For these reasons it was decided at corporate level to proceed with a basic study, keeping in mind the fact that very few of the twelve independent companies could afford financially to replace their organizational procedures. This reference included the investments made in:

• Customer handling
• Financial planning and control
• Product management
• Sales and marketing
• Production planning
• Billing and receivables
• Stocks and movements

One of the high points of the study in reference was the opportunity for changing from mainframe-based systems to a fully distributed, networked environment. This was projected to be based on workstations and file servers—from local area networking to long haul.

In a corporate-wide sense, such goals underlined the need for an architectural strategy able to hide distributed computing complexities both from the user and from the applications programmer. The information technology aspect of this strategy focused on:

- Database placement, answering the queries: "Where?" and "What?"
- Network-wide data access: "Why?" and "How?"
- Network-wide transfer, involving protocols and capacity planning

Part and parcel of the study has been the establishment of an *information element replication system* (IERS) which acts as an interface, facilitating the task of replacing all transaction processing chores with one integrative solution. The conceptual approach is shown in Figure 3.3.

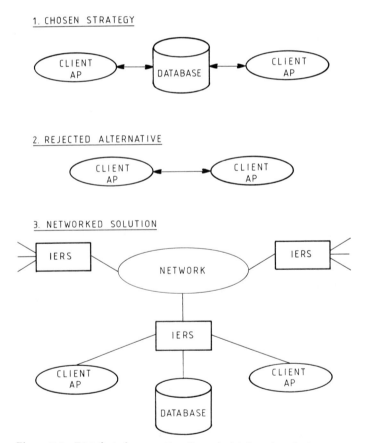

Figure 3.3 Distributed computing through database interfacing.

The basic strategy which has been chosen in integrating a variety of centralized and distributed databases is that of *decoupling*, by assuring an application-to-application data transfer through database interfacing.

- The IERS architecture does not dictate the degree of distribution a given implementation must have.
- It can be configured to support varying degrees of terminalization.

Such degree of flexibility is being achieved by isolating the program logic necessary for architecturing from the core business functionality.

Enduser applications which were written around a single centralized database could be carried to the new solution. Along with application specific exits, IERS is responsible for enabling a flexible configuration by location with the implementation environment designed in a manner which can be split up through:

- The addition of new IERS
- Application specific exits supporting a particular function

Such an approach is enabled through the adoption of a single, unified database definition composed of the union of all database requirements. This was found to be instrumental in eliminating unwanted duplications.

From a single database view, logical fault lines were drawn to support varying degrees of decoupling. This has been done on the premise that it is much easier to divide a unified database design than to piece together disparate and overlapping independent designs at a later time.[5]

As the reasons given in the preceding paragraphs help document, the chosen approach is pragmatic, providing manageable units of networked databases matching up related business functions with associated information requirements. According to the system designers, this has a significant amount of flexibility:

- Permitting a single set of applications to be installed in a network-wide sense
- Implementing varying degrees of database distribution
- Hiding distributed computing complexities at local implementation level

[5]See also the discussion on vertical and horizontal database partitioning in Chapter 2.

Systems renewal sees to it that the newly developed applications are not running on mainframes but on rather inexpensive Unix database servers and Windows-based workstations. Quite significantly, the overall strategy led to a network of deductive databases which kicks off operations on the basis of messages which it receives.

3.7 What Is the Added Value of Message Passing?

Message passing is a level of sophistication above the simple pass-through solution. It provides for effective interoperability in distributed databases and applications, hence promoting a new departure in information technology.

Solutions like the one of the twelve companies' holding which we saw in Section 3.6 are expected to shift the balance of power *to users*—that is, away from the software and hardware vendors. They will be loosening the vendors' grip on company budgets for information technology and also assuring that what is done responds to ongoing operating needs.

Message passing interoperability, like that supported by IERS, is a good method by which applications are being connected together intelligently. Such approach makes it feasible to add functionality in a network-wide sense.

Interoperability through message passing depends on high-quality networks and protocols for communications purposes, reaching every corner of the organization. However, this is no major constraint as every dynamic enterprise today has a need for first class communications solutions all of the time. They are needed because they allow the business to function properly in an ever-demanding marketplace.

Sure enough, there are a number of other technical issues underpinning the message-passing strategy. Foremost among these is the use of messages for downloading and up-line transfer—hence for job-oriented placement of IE. Such solutions provide location autonomy which can guarantee improved response and resiliency, assure local data access, and reduce peak rate communications costs.

Experimentation within this applications environment has demonstrated the wisdom to store only the required data per location—with all locations sharing an identical core information element definition. "We cannot do a global schema solution. It is too much of a luxury," said a cognizant executive. "Neither can we steadily provide transparent schema translation."

In the case study we just saw, the designers also provided a consistent blueprint by which all applications can be coded. It serves in the interapplication message definition without centralized controls which slow down productivity and create bottlenecks.

Any solution along this frame of reference has to account for the facts of organizational life which prevail. For instance, the companies integrating into the IERS network were independent, with very different programming approaches and data structures.

Local management independence has been reflected in the adopted data access principle: All accesses to the networked databases are executed only in connection to local database resources. For distributed queries and distributed transactions, a *Collect Ahead* model working in real-enough time was instituted.

In an effort to avoid rewriting a large inventory of old applications, the Collect Ahead model accumulates overnight all data necessary for a location to process its business-critical tasks. By contrast, real-time operations are executed in a network-wide landscape for all new applications.

Adding to the flexibility of the solution, within this environment both database and application functions can easily be split along work group boundaries if management so chooses. But information elements shared across the split maintain the appearance of a single database to the application.

Quite important as well is the fact that chosen architectural supports are open to evolution, by allowing work groups to join later without application modifications. Logical splitting and joining facilitates the use of networked database servers connected within a LAN environment by:

- Supporting a flexible number of users
- Providing a degree of fault tolerance
- Isolating one functionally distinct group of users to keep them from impacting another

Data transfer is based on a store and forward mechanism. Access to information elements is combined with IERS, this solution provides location autonomy with resiliency and fast response as already stated. A two-layer technology has been adopted in respect to the IERS dictionary:

- Metadata
- Configuration data

Metadata includes definitions, scope of relevance, update strategy, frequency and identification of accesses, and the metarules of the transfer mechanism. Components of the configuration data are the different location memberships such as:

- Topology by business stream
- Reference to work groups
- Relative product scope

Among the responsibilities of the data replication system is that of building distribution lists, detecting updates, propagating and applying such updates, as well as handling interactive reporting failures.

The adopted strategy sees to it that functions can be centralized or decoupled without change to the implementation logic. And while applications developers are shielded from database distribution complexities, they can make full use of the power of a networked database system.

CHAPTER 4

Treating the Networked Database as a Corporate Resource

4.1 Introduction

Rapid developments in technology have increased the types and complexity of information elements used in the office environment. Applications tend to establish their own specific data types, but to improve the usefulness and integrative ability of these applications we have to work with common formats.

Typically, application programmers use database management systems to reduce the task of sharing database contents among programs. For years, one of the key queries has been which DBMS to choose—but this is no more the number one problem, although it is still a challenge.

As we have seen in the preceding three chapters through a number of first-hand examples, the number one issue today is how to *network* the corporate databases in a manner which is both effective and seamless for the enduser. A valid solution has to account for the following facts:

- In our distributed landscape there are plenty of heterogeneous DBMS.
- Whether centralized or distributed, our databases feature incompatible data structures.
- By and large these same databases conform to local requirements of independent business units.

Historically, the usage of DBMS started with mainly hierarchical structures which slowly became greatly inflexible. A similar statement can be made of the Codasyl model, and during the last 10 years experience has demonstrated that while the relational database has ease of use, it does not contribute the power of semantics representation.

Different data models and methods have been proposed to enhance a database's semantics ability. The contribution of the object-oriented approaches is now recognized, but in a complex environment no valid approach can be found along any single axis of reference shown in Figure 4.1.

While performance, autonomy, and globality are necessary elements in a database context, we need a truly multidimensional approach where semantics play a crucial role in the choices we have to make. The solution to networked databases lies in a simple sentence: *optimize* between autonomy, globality, and better performance.

For reasons of optimization, a valid design will accept some constraints in globality, if this really helps in achieving greater performance as well as the ability to retain existing local databases without upsetting the code structure of our software. A similar statement can be made regarding the avoidance of fully altering information elements and existing records for minor performance enhancements.

Object-oriented solutions are gaining prominence because they are seen as contributing to our ability to observe the optimization principles which have just been outlined. By placing emphasis on semantics and their associated models, all IE are treated as objects according to their representation in the real world. Objects are handled in a consistent way, so application programmers can use them with one common interface—no matter in which local database they belong.

With this conceptual approach, it is possible to represent different relationships between objects such as generalization and specialization

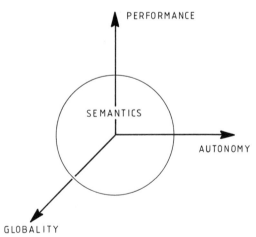

Figure 4.1   Trade-offs between performance, autonomy, and globality.

or aggregation in the real world. Furthermore, the semantics of the database can be reflected much better than with relational approaches, or for that matter Codasyl, inverted files, and the aging hierarchical approaches.

The common ground underpinning optimization, local autonomy, globality, and better performance is the need to treat the networked databases as a corporate resource. No chain is better than the weakest of its links, and network databases are a crucial link to which less than the proper attention has been paid so far.

4.2 Optimizing Our Database Perspectives and Action Plans

Optimization can be effectively done through the use of modern, computer-based tools, not by means of wishful thinking. We have to build simulators, map into them our database environment, and develop analogical reasoning perspectives.

Once we have cleared our goals, new types of basic software can be instrumental in the modeling process just described. Projects designed along this line of reference can be broadly classified into two groups:

1. One approach is that of changing the infrastructure, for instance, incorporating the new DBMS with object-oriented capabilities.
2. The other approach is to use a programming language as a superstructure, with the goal of enhancing existing DBMS to handle networked solutions.

While these two approaches are different, their common goal is to manage various data types more effectively, supporting the basic characteristics of a relatively flexible approach to the environment of networked databases.

Besides this, a joint approach involving both items is desirable because not everything can be done by means of a new generation DBMS, even in the unlikely case that this is the most perfect. To assure seamless access to distributed heterogeneous databases:

• The first and foremost requirement is to take stock of what we have available, not simply in a descriptive but in a thoroughly detailed fashion.
• Then, we must study the incompatibilities with which we are confronted and choose among the alternative strategies for cross-database access, which are considered in Section 4.3.

Properly projected and administered object-oriented databases can represent a significant increase in the ability of their users to capture the semantics of the information elements which they contain. If the solution we now have is satisfactory, such change toward object models may not be necessary. But are we really happy with what has been provided so far?

The interest in object databases has arisen from application areas where traditional DBMS fail to meet the growing requirements of endusers. Since these requirements continue to expand, the resulting new application areas require an enhancement of the currently available implementation concepts.

One of the key queries a manager poses to himself is: "What are my alternatives?" One of these alternatives is to continue the old way; another alternative is technological change. Every company has to study its alternatives and establish in a valid manner which really best fits its current and future requirements.

The avoidance of the beaten path, which is synonymous to the introduction of new solutions, is no easy way out. One major obstacle is *cultural*; it takes effort to drop past habits. Another obstacle lies in the existence of very significant investments in old technologies, most particularly in terms of programming libraries and database usage.

The message to be retained from these references is that when we attempt to optimize our database perspectives and action plans, we cannot forget about the installed base and focus only on the newer issues. Both old and new issues have to be considered together with their constraints and the way they affect the goals we wish to reach.

One of the vital elements in a strategic decision of this nature is the *human capital* at our disposal. Other critical elements are budgets, timetables and tools available within the perspectives, and requirements of the job we aim to accomplish. We can raise our resources to reach our goals if, and only if, we clearly know what we want.

The advice is valid both for financial institutions and for manufacturing companies. All major organizations face the problem of managing large and sprawling databases distributed on different machines and locations and run under different operating systems and DBMS—but some handle this job much better than others.

In complex environments, optimization studies have shown that virtual homogeneity can be served through a *metalayer* (higher up) of reference which provides the capability of logical integration. The metalayer concept can be instrumental in the creation of a federation of databases, as Chapter 1 suggested with reference to the way the Swiss Confederation works:

- Every Canton preciously preserves its independence, its laws, and local customs
- But all of them unite under a central government when federation problems must be handled

An alternative to the federation is to try to do the necessary integration work through a unique, universal schema. However, by all available evidence, this approach so far has not given commendable results. We will see why this is true in Chapter 6.

4.3 Evolving Goals in a Dynamic Organization

By definition, a dynamic organization evolves over time. This influences the way data is managed and it impacts application requirements, particularly at the managerial and the professional levels.

Changes taking place over time in the way an organization is run and/ or in the technology of the different applications cause that organization to end up having several heterogeneous database management systems as well as incompatible data structures. In other cases the choice of different DBMS is dictated by other reasons.

- To provide adequate performance it may be necessary to maintain the data in different databases with different capabilities.
- It may be that not all the data sources belong to the organization using them, and multiple sourcing poses constraints.
- The use of public databases sees to it that a user firm does not have control on how information elements are organized, managed, and presented.

As a result, applications needing IE from several repositories have to bridge the gap among various incompatible systems with different data models, query languages, authorization routines, recovery procedures, and concurrency control.

As we have seen in a number of cases, far from being an exception, database heterogeneity is becoming the rule of the day. Even *if* it were possible today to make all our information resources homogeneous (and this strictly is not possible), we will still be faced by a growing heterogeneity some years down the road.

In a dynamic organization, this is amplified by the fact that there is a huge difference between information systems support provided in the past and what is presently necessary. In the past, computer services have been conceived and developed largely monolithically—as if they were based on a hard-wired systems design.

There was little or no flexibility to interoperate or adapt to specific requirements; and the introduction of a piece of basic software by the leading vendor compounded the effects of an ossified design. Yet, new developments in enduser requests, enhanced through knowledge engineering, now call for much greater flexibility and adaptability in design.

The tools we now have available offer the possibility that the configuration of service elements can be determined by the enduser, with evident aftermaths on databases.

A dynamic and highly competitive business environment calls for the nbability to *metacommunicate* about a situation (that is, to communicate about communicating, which usually is necessary to get from an old framework into a new one for an issue or client need). This cannot be done unassisted.

In the past, a major impediment to the introduction of advanced applications was the difficulty in determining the users' needs and wants and then interpreting and mapping them into operational requirements. Today, a range of sophisticated facilities can potentially be provided, based on the logical mapping powers of knowledge engineering. Prototyping approaches make it easier for users to express their requirements, and they help provide a level of confidence in expression and satisfaction of ongoing needs.

Refinement in the definition of user-oriented applications can often be effected through the simulation of an environment, employing advanced computers and communications capabilities. Prototypes are vital because the determination of users' requests is increasingly a problem of complexity and is therefore a limiting factor.

Supposing that able answers will be provided (and can be provided), the next limiting factor is that of access to a growing number of databases where the corporate resources lie. Many applications exist today which are not properly supported in a cross-database sense. Others are even unfeasible because the needed databases are not effectively exploited.

In many cases, the applications interfaces are substandard and/or data transfer is done in a rather primitive manner with little or no exchange between local databases. A *database architecture* is needed and it should provide for cooperation between:

- Multimedia storage managers distributed in a network-wide sense
- Applications which preserve their functional autonomy but must cooperate within a global environment

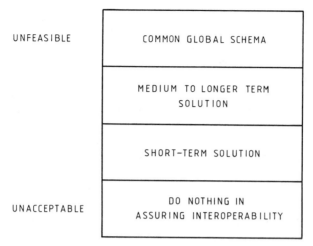

Figure 4.2   Four options with networked databases.

Altogether, the database architect is faced with the four options shown in Figure 4.2. The one at the bottom of the graph is to do nothing in providing cross-database support, leaving the corporate databases to continue growing like wild cacti. Clearly, such policy would be unacceptable. Yet, this is what many companies are presently doing.

What many people have so far considered as being the ideal solution is to provide a common global schema able to cover all databases. For nearly 10 years this approach has been tried by a variety of organizations (from vendors to users) and proved to be unfeasible. As Section 4.2 concluded, it is unwise to continue along this path.

This leaves two alternatives: short-term solutions and medium- to longer term solutions; the latter are the more sophisticated. There is no unique approach to recommend, but the cross-database job is feasible as demonstrated by a number of practical examples, whether the high, middle, or low road has been chosen.

4.4 Avoiding the Beaten Path and the Data Propagator

Once implemented in a given technology, databases are rarely if ever replaced. Even if new applications are written using different approaches to programming and novel DBMS, pragmatically it is necessary for the new applications to have access to data stored in existing databases. This poses a number of problems.

To get temporary relief from pressing issues, many companies tend to rely on a vendor offering such as a relational database to be added to the inventory of tools. In doing so, however, they forget that as long as other key issues remain ossified, the benefits from new investments will be minimal.

Rational solutions to database problems, for example, are handicapped by the fact that most applications today are host-based with dumb 3270 terminal protocols. Only the minority is on workstations connected through a LAN to file servers. By contrast, effective solutions require intelligent workstations with knowledge engineering support and object orientation.

Application designers find themselves much better off in an environment where they have a free choice in implementing advanced solutions. Key to these approaches is the implementation of an open architecture, whose functionality has been presented in Chapter 2.

Expert systems can be effectively used to exploit the advantages presented by an open architecture. Figure 4.3 gives a snapshot of a knowledge engineering-enriched solution. The user interfaces in interactive work with the distributed database through a layer of intelligence supported through metadata. Other contributing modules address database selection, query transformation, response integration, and evaluation of accuracy.

This advanced approach to database interactivity sharply contrasts with the beaten path of IMS DB/DC which for many years has nearly been the bible. Today, a number of IMS installations are beginning to ask themselves how they can take advantage of new technology for their applications because they realize that IMS is an obsolete and nearsighted procedure.

But cooperation between hierarchical and relational DBMS is not that easy, even if they come from the same vendor. A significant problem is how to feed DB2 applications with data stored mainly in IMS databases, particularly when it is not sufficient or acceptable to periodically copy/extract data from IMS and load it into DB2.

One of the early half-measures envisaged by some vendors in this connection has been the use of extraction routines, typically employed during the night run after batch, to carry information elements from the transactional database.[1] A more recent half-baked solution is the so-called *data propagation*.

On paper, data propagation aims to maintain the consistency between two or more IE copies by propagating the updates of one copy to the

---

[1]Through the DXT program.

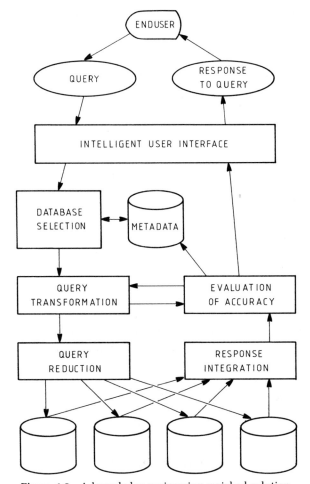

Figure 4.3 A knowledge engineering-enriched solution.

other copy or copies. When applied to a combined IMS/DB2 environment, data propagation can be used to maintain the consistency of an IMS copy and a DB2 copy of the same IE. This is supposed to enable the coexistence of IMS and DB2 applications regarding the same IE. This can be done in two ways:

- Accessing the IMS data copy through the IMS DL/I call interface.
- Accessing the DB2 copy of the same IE through the DB2 SQL interface.

In theory, such propagation can be implemented with application program logic. In practice, such an approach is maintenance-intensive, can be error prone, may require changes to a lot of applications programs, and does not provide system-controlled data consistency.

Besides this, the IBM Data Propagator (DPROP) is a one-way programming product supporting only propagation from IMS to DB2.[2] This is essentially a reincarnation of the DXT routine of a dozen years ago. Even the procedure is similar. The process of IMS to DB2 propagation with DPROP requires a copy or extract of the IMS data and a subsequent load into DB2 tables, which is DXT work.

Low technology software of this and similar types is neither evolutionary nor granular, no matter what the vendor says. It is nothing more than old stuff without any added value, and users who think granular conversion of programs will become possible when DPROP supports DB2 to IMS propagation will be deceived.

By contrast to these very limited approaches, full scale automation assumes *a priori* systems modeling of the totality of relevant networked databases and their dynamics. It calls for advanced knowledge representation and planning methods and requires a great deal of confidence about all of the systems to be used and their attributes.

An effective solution to cross-database problems requires progress in a number of areas, including the integration of data received from a wide variety of input sources dispersed over large geographical areas. It also receives inputs from sources of knowledge, including the execution and monitoring of plans involving dispersed database actors with a variety of capabilities.

4.5 New or Old Database Technology?

The transitions which have taken place so far in database management demonstrate that new technology is rarely used to displace the current one(s) in existing applications. Instead, the emerging technology and the tools which it brings are used to develop and deploy new applications. By and large, these new applications would be difficult or impossible to build using the previous technology. This has happened in the past. For instance, in the migration to relational database management systems, rare has been the case of existing Codasyl or hierarchical type applications that were effectively transferred. Instead, new applications in which improved flexibility, direct enduser access, or higher program-

[2]In Release 1 which is becoming available.

mer productivity were the goal. These were only timidly approached with elder DBMS and were executed through relational solutions. It was discovered as well, by the majority of business and industrial firms, that different levels of data purity can be found in database structures.

The information elements in the database are either background (facts) or situational (values). Background information is developed at the same time as the rules contained, for instance, in the knowledgebank. It constitutes the basic information needed by the system to represent the domain of its problems, including definition of entities, operating characteristics, and relationships between objects.

All of this is too complex to be done through patchwork and obsolete approaches like the Data Propagator. Database management systems are more efficient when they are state of the art.

Intelligent databases are equipped with several kinds of analysis and diagnosis tools assisted by embedded expert systems. Knowledge-based approaches use inference procedures to solve database-related problems that are difficult enough to require significant human expertise.

This capability to specialize distinguishes a knowledge-oriented DBMS from all the others and sets the stage of computer-based solutions for the 1990s. It is rewarding to enrich through knowledge the primary activities of a computer-based system—that is, the processing of incoming information, the handling of user input/output, and actual analysis of a situation, by applying the rules in the knowledgebank.

As far as the level of data manipulation is concerned, the basic references used by some organizations tend to distinguish between the following five classes:

- *Raw data.* Values obtained directly from the measurement devices, plans, reports, vouchers, and the like.
- *Calibrated data.* Typically raw values corrected with calibration operators such as range evaluation procedures or algorithms.
- *Validated data.* That is, calibrated data that has been filtered through quality assurance to increase their dependability.
- *Derived data.* Whether for scientific or for business reasons, data is aggregated, extrapolated, or simulated.
- *Interpreted data.* For instance, validated or derived but related to other data sets, company standards, existing plans, and so on.

This sequence of successively greater data handling sophistication needs not be precise in all cases. But it also indicates that the type of information elements available in the database can be highly dependent on the intended level of processing.

Moreover, information about the processing per se must also be retained and distributed with any IE, as it is vital to understanding and using the information being produced. This requires the definition of protocol machines and application service standards.

A basic assumption which concerns all databases is that no matter where they are available, information elements are subject to further analysis. Otherwise there is little reason to retain them in a computer-based form.

The nature of such subsequent analysis frequently determines what particular approach is most desirable. And the more sophisticated the data analysis we are after, the newer the database technology needs to be.

4.6 Multidatabase Requirements with Networked Resources

Since old, wornout database technology should be appealing to no one, there is no point in persisting with Data Propagators and old material under new banners. New quality programs must be initiated and seen through before real improvements can be made in the way networked databases are accessed and managed.

We said that pass-through capabilities address a number of networked environments providing the enduser with more or less seamless access to corporte resources for query reasons. This *multidatabase* approach avoids constructing a global schema and instead presents a collection of local schemata along with a commodity tool for information sharing.

The enduser is assisted in resolving conflicts in a manner particular to each application, integrating only the portions of the databases that are necessary to that work. This is an assisted approach, as contrasted to a more fully automated one which we will see with federated databases (Chapter 6) in connection to the manipulation of schemata.

The networked database to which the pass-through and message-passing solutions we have examined is applicable is typically a collection of independent databases of local importance that cooperate in sharing information elements while preserving their autonomy. Such a system needs a mechanism for:

- Providing every database with an integrated view of the multidatabase
- Supporting the exchange of IE between databases
- Maintaining the integrity of all shared information elements

Speaking in a generic sense, the process of assuring an integrative view of such a multidatabase calls for solving issues associated with limited schema integration. Subsequently, this leads toward either tightly coupled or loosely coupled systems as explained in Chapter 6.

Tightly or loosely coupled approaches, each with its own norms, strengths, and weaknesses, are necessary for cooperation among databases for processing not only queries but also transactions. These norms provide every database in the network with a mechanism which is able to:

- Support the specification of multidatabase queries
- Assure a display of information elements relative to these queries
- Make feasible the handling of transaction requirements
- Guarantee a consistent image after the transaction(s) is (are) executed

Since vendors typically make more promises than they can deliver, prior to choices, the user will be well-advised to ask about the degree of supported integration as well as the impact on the implementation issues which the user organization is confronted with.

A good deal of the answers which need to be provided by the vendor can be obtained through the study of the special software which the vendor promotes. Each DBMS, for instance, has an underlying data model used to define data structures and constraints and handle language aspects. If two representations have the same information content, it is easier to deal with the differences in the structures. But if the information content is not the same, then it may be quite difficult to bridge the respective differences.

This sounds like a simple and evident statement, yet many user organizations forget about it when the time comes for evaluation and decision. The greater the heterogeneity, for instance, hierarchical versus relational DBMS, the more knowledge engineering support is needed to create the bridge—but not many vendors offer it.

Just as crucial, from a systems viewpoint, is dealing with the inevitable incompatibility constraints within the context of a multidatabase. The same is true of differences in query languages.

Different languages are used to manipulate data represented in heterogeneous models. Even when two DBMSs support the same data model, differences in their query languages, or versions of them, can contribute to heterogeneity.

Differences in system aspects also lead to constraints due to heterogeneity. Most importantly, account should be taken of incompatibilities in semantics. These occur when there is disagreement about the meaning, interpretation, or intended use of the same or related information elements.

As has already been explained, detecting semantic heterogeneity is difficult since database management schemata typically do not provide enough semantics to consistently interpret their impact on information elements. Heterogeneity due to differences in data models also contributes to the difficulty in identification and resolution of semantics issues.

Sustained through object-oriented approaches, the reinvention of the importance of semantics comes at the right time in answering the growing database requirements. The industry is sure to require agile enduser-oriented, cross-database managers applicable at multimedia level. These must provide flexible solutions to cognitive issues as well as assist in synchronization chores regarding networked databases.

By all probability, one of the topmost synchronization challenges will be in virtual reality applications and animation which will enable modalities such as voice annotation of graphics and text and provide intelligent navigational capabilities. This service is offered by hypermedia for nonsequential document handling.

As the content of databases moves toward multimedia, there will be demands for speech command augmentation of menu selection by tablet or mouse. One way of executing touch and speech command is the put-that-there mode. Speech and gesture dynamics of put-that-there form a top-level command language, but they also require a very sophisticated database infrastructure from which to operate.

4.7 Beyond the Simplest Multidatabase Links

A simple pass-through mechanism can provide means for virtual integration of preexisting local databases but does not handle aspects regarding the management of multiple autonomous and heterogeneous databases. Within a multidatabase context, local autonomy reflects the fact that the databases in the distributed network were designed and developed independently.

Autonomy of future operations guarantees that previously developed local applications continue to be executable without modification. It also provides for better security of local databases. But the prevailing incompatibility as well as autonomy requirements have profound effects on the execution of global transactions on local databases.

As it cannot be repeated too often, a simple pass-through does not guarantee transaction execution. But it does help in determining the target DBMS, seeing to it that the application will find the appropriate database controller in the network. This provides for location transparency, also bringing global management aspects into the picture.

Lotus Development is not the only software company to provide a cross-database pass-through capability as commodity software. Apple Computers has done the same through DAL. It is, however, interesting to observe that both are vendor-limited, respectively promoted by a software and a hardware firm.

Apple suggests that its *Data Access Language* (DAL) software product delivers most of the benefits of client–server computing. Users say that it is useful in a rather narrow subset of real world client–server applications. One of the stated reasons is that given its high demand on system resources, it creates problems with downsizing objectives. Also, it provides less than acceptable performance for applications other than off-line data extraction.

As with many software products, the resultant solution requires more powerful computers to deliver users' data requirements. This however is a cost issue rather than a feasibility issue.

Through DAL's use of dynamic SQL at server level, the database server required significantly more resources than solutions based on remote procedure calls (RPC) as well as an object-oriented approaches. Still the fact that DAL operates cross-database as a gateway beyond single-platform has to be kept in mind.

As a product, this software was originally marketed by Network Innovations (NI) under the name CL/1, a PC-based decision support package for use with SQL-compliant mid-range databases. Apple acquired NI as part of a long-term host connectivity strategy and then extended the product in reference.[3]

Apple mapped a broader range of corporate cross-database requirements in its DAL 2.0 release by including software able to provide the DAL API on MS-DOS, OS/2, and Unix clients, in addition to Apple's own MacOS. With this extension, the potential market and user population includes WS applications for decision support that require relatively wide data extraction against host SQL databases. But it does not necessarily incorporate solutions to comprehensive and fairly complex client–server architectures.

The latter approach would have required going beyond the simplest database links of the type we have so far seen. This is feasible and a

---

[3]The approach is similar in concept to SQL gateways of the type marketed by Oracle and Ingres, SQL Services by DEC, as well as the SQL Access Group's Phase 1 specification.

number of examples will be given to document such a statement, but it is also true that generic approaches must be taken which are mid-range rather than short-range.

While in the case of query-type applications a DataLens and DAL approach permits the user's workstations to select the desired server during execution, transactional requirements call for a different level of integrative capabilities. For querying reasons this mode of operation is more demanding than decision support and its associated interactive exploration.

A transactional application may establish multiple connections which call for at least a message-passing paradigm capable of allowing the current connection to be changed during execution. This can allow an application to perform identical processing at multiple remote sites with a certain coherence among these sites.

A fundamental assumption regarding the autonomy of each distributed DBMS is that each is capable of managing all submitted transactions independently.

- When a DBMS fails, it should have the needed facilities for recovering, so that only the committed transactions affect the database.
- Once recovered, it must also be able to notify the transaction's submitter of its termination condition.

Since all participating databases are autonomous, they can all be recovered independently. But the global management systems should be in a position to determine which DBMS are functioning, thus assuring that only the effects of committed transactions are reflected in the networked database in a global sense.

A number of other technical issues must be settled. For instance, an application executing against a remote DBMS must have a uniform method of facing error conditions.

These requirements have been fulfilled by the rather recent multidatabase implementation for Operation Desert Storm. The message-passing paradigm has been underpinning the solution which was adopted.

CHAPTER 5

Computer Professionals and Database Challenges

5.1 Introduction

The information technology community has been searching for years for methods to simplify and improve the labor intensive and error prone processes of database management. Another field in demand for more effective solutions has been applications development.

Not surprisingly, database management and applications development are highly correlational. They are done by the same people and, to a significant extent, use the same tools. The major breakthrough with fourth generation languages (4GL) has been their close association with relational DBMS. Fifth generation languages (5GL) continued this tradition, also being enriched with knowledge engineering.

In the development, design, and maintenance of new computer-based information systems, approaches range from reusable code, programmers workbenches, and languages for prototyping, to automatic program generators and a growing range of workstation-oriented application packages. More sophisticated solutions use knowledge engineering and simulators for technical and business modeling.

This evolution at the applications development side matches what has taken place in connection to databases. Some 30 years ago, computer professionals were thinking in terms of files and records, with file management routines considered to be the best in technology. Then the need for data definitions became evident and *data dictionaries* (DD) came along. We will study the new wave of data dictionaries in Chapters 8 and 9.

Data description and manipulation languages began to be employed as the concept of a database management system took shape. As computer professionals learned to appreciate distributed database concepts, database modeling was found to be important and the function of a *database*

administrator (DBA) became institutionalized.[1] Today, a top function
is that of the *database architect.*

As this transition in our conceptual approaches and the tools at our
disposal took place, the very notion of what is and is not a database
changed. We now look at the database as a model of the real world,
designed, coordinated, and managed, as far as possible, in a uniform
way. This is done by means of:

- An overall architecture covering the company's distributed
  databases
- Design principles regulating functional, structural, and operational
  aspects
- The database administrator and database designers and their tools,
  including the data dictionary
- A database management system per machine and, recently, a
  knowledgebank management system
- Cross-database solutions able to cover a range of incompatible
  networked databases and DBMS

The better database professionals appreciate that information elements
should be projected and defined (not just described) in a coherent,
comprehensive manner. They should be accessible to all authorized
users through agile and friendly interfaces, forgiving the users' eventual
mistakes.

5.2 New Areas of Expertise for Database Professionals

The introduction outlined the main areas of attention for database professionals. Expertise in all of the domains under discussion is a must,
as during the 1990s multidatabase concepts will dominate the industry
and companies will ask for solutions having little in common with
what databases used to be.

The most vital support in the missions the four first chapters have
outlined is provided by databases which are networked. At the physical
and lower logical layers, distributed networked databases are similar to
the ISO/OSI model applied to networks, which is very helpful both for
design and for operational reasons.

---

[1]See also D. N. Chorafas *Handbook of Database Management and Distributed Relational Databases*, MacGraw-Hill/TAB Books, New York, 1989.

A layered approach to database management and the protocols being used permits us to elaborate the database and communications functionality, set up headers, call into play database access and communications mechanisms, as well as receive and reformat data. It also makes more efficient the processes of signing on to target environment, invoking fairly homogeneous modules, and setting up linkage areas.

In an environment of networked databases, information elements are not only stored in the database, they are also transmitted as messages over communications lines. A message is a file in the database or in the mailbox of the recipient. Therefore, every file should be structured as a message.

The most clear-eyed database professionals are after solutions which aim to minimize input/output (I/O) (as well as housekeeping chores at the applications end) by making the common ground of database management more powerful. As Figure 5.1 suggests, this kind of development is an ongoing trend in database technology.

With very old approaches, which practically means in the timeframe of the 1960s and part of the 1970s, a large number of companies used only some file management routine such as index sequential (ISAM).

This addressed just a small part of needed file-handling activities. Everything else, including I/O, was being done at the applications programming level. Such an approach was not only awkward but also resulted in a good deal of software having to be rewritten time and again—a sort of rediscovering the wheel.

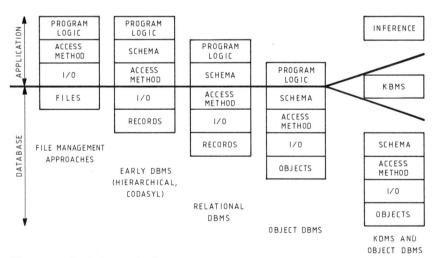

Figure 5.1 Evolution in database management concepts.

With old technology, beginning in the late 1960s/early 1970s but in a curiously large number of cases continuing until today, the I/O was handled by the hierarchical and Codasyl DBMS (IMS and IDS, respectively), but today this is plainly inadequate.

Hierarchical and Codasyl (networking, owner/member) DBMS have, however, introduced the concept of *schema*, which over a number of years provided significant assistance in database management and usage.

As we will see in the next chapter, through practice, schemata have had a very significant evolution. With this evolution the IMS and IDS approaches became progressively inadequate in facing evolving user requirements.

Relational technology relieved some of the constraints of hierarchical and Codasyl models. During the 1980s it assisted database professionals in developing more flexible and agile systems, but this approach too is reaching its limitation. Based on a concept of flat files, relational DBMS both simplified and absorbed into their mechanics the database access method. They did, however, also feature two negatives.

First, the record structure has been retained, as practiced with hierarchical and Codasyl DBMS. This is quite restrictive because in a modern implementation environment, particularly in terms of management queries and long transactions, we need to access many records in parallel—but we are interested in only a small fraction of each.

The second negative with relational models is the loss of *semantics*. This has been found to be detrimental inasmuch as managerial and professional applications need a database management mechanism which is rich in meaning. Object-oriented solutions help in correcting this deficiency.

The object-oriented approach first started with programming languages (in the late 1960s) and 20 years later (in the late 1980s) moved into the DBMS domain. Today there are a number of first class object DBMS from which to choose.[2]

Object solutions provide significant capabilities in *semantic modeling*, which is becoming an important force in software development. Semantic modeling represents the meaning of data so that external schemata can be effectively expressed, database interactivity can be more easily implemented, appropriate integrity constraints can be maintained, and inferences can be made to aid user interaction.

Representing the meaning of data in an able manner is the goal of *metadata*—that is, data about data. The use of metadata is a prerequisite

---

[2]See D. N. Chorafas and H. Steinmann *Object-Oriented Databases*, Prentice-Hall, Englewood Cliffs, NJ, 1993.

to the able implementation of networked databases which itself is one of the vital subjects of this decade. Metaconcepts are part of knowledge engineering; there is a synergy between object orientation and knowledge engineering, as we will see in the next section.

5.3 The Sense of Object-Oriented Solutions

An *object* is a callable entity, an instance of a class. A *class* is the abstraction of shared characteristics, including encapsulation, distributed consistency, attributes, referential integrity, inheritance, reusability, and network-wide behavior monitoring.

We will not be concerned with objects in the present text. But it is proper to bring into perspective that the real world mapped into the database can well be viewed as consisting of objects and object classes which:

- Exhibit properties and behavior
- Adhere to normal forms
- Help in improving integrity between databases and applications

Fertile domains for the implementation of object-oriented solutions include computer-aided design (CAD); computer-aided manufacturing (CAM); computer-integrated manufacturing (CIM); complex market-oriented operations (Forex, securities); cross-functional projects (risk management); cross-departmental projects (cost control); cartographical implementations and layouts; computer-assisted software engineering (CASE); and office automation (OA).

Objects may be real-world entities, information elements, their relationships and domains, as well as textual descriptions. Object analysis defines the unique identifier(s) of an object, its occurrence name, attributes, parent objects, and their relationships.

Object DBMS can be enriched with knowledge engineering, greatly increasing the inference capability and hence the intelligence of the database. *Idea databases* are tooled around this concept of an intentional database (IDB) layer over the extensional database (EDB) structures.

Intentional database solutions involving object orientation and knowledge engineering lead to *distributed deductive databases* (DDDB), with which the DBA and database architect should be familiar. Two strategies are available for query processing in connection to object-oriented DDDB:

- A *bottom-up* evaluation of queries is done from already known facts toward new facts.
- A *top-down* evaluation proceeds from queries to known facts.

Top-down approaches tend to provide much better performance. They have, however, the risk of entering infinite loops unless knowledge engineering constructs assure the metalayer (IDB) and therefore the contraints to limit looping.

As abstract data types, objects have associated with them operations and constraints permitting both dynamic and static aspects of the database to be represented *declaratively*. Objects have components that can themselves be objects. An object-oriented approach typically incorporates the concept of generalization. Basic concepts associated with objects are:

- Inheritance
- Message passing
- Late binding
- Overloading
- Graphical interfacing

An object has a public interface and a private implementation part. Objects also have *methods* attached to them, within their private part, specifying how certain operations are to be carried out in connection with that object. Communications with objects can only be done via the public interface, through message passing.

Currently available as commodity software American object-oriented DBMS include Ontos, Gemstone, Versant, and Object Store. The only U.S. computer vendor with an object-oriented DBMS available as a commodity is Hewlett-Packard with open ODB. By contrast, in Japan all computer and office automation vendors have an object DBMS: Hitachi, Fujitsu, NEC, NTT Data, Oki, Mitsubishi, and Ricoh.

There is a whole world of difference between the file management, hierarchical, and Codasyl approaches on one side, and the intelligence-enriched solutions of the type we have just considered on the other. If we look again at Figure 5.1:

- The two columns at the left are very low to low technology.
- The two columns at the right are high technology.
- The relational approach fits in between, sliding toward the left side.

Like hierarchical and Codasyl models, presently available relational DBMS (DB2, RDB, Ingres, Oracle, Informix, and so on) are record-oriented. As already explained, this is too coarse a structure for present-day database access requirements. Object-oriented solutions are fine-grained and therefore best fit the needs of the 1990s.

Whether we take an object view or relational view of networked databases, we deal with dynamic entities which have to be defined and managed. The record-based approach characterizes practically all developments in file management and databasing which have taken place during the last 40 years, but finally the time has come for change.

5.4 Toward Integrated Databases

The first major items to underline when we talk about global solutions in connection with networked databases is that investments should aim at *innovation*, geared toward both cutting costs and gaining competitive advantages. This policy has been adopted by leading companies after they realized that by building information technology into their products they can influence their customers and therefore the market:

- American and Japanese banks are very keen to hook their clients into their information system through fax and PC-to-mainframe or database-to-database linkage in order to maintain handholding policies and improve upon relationship management.
- American Airlines automated travel agents by developing a network which today features 160,000 attached devices—the largest network in the world. This made it easier for agents to buy seats on American Airlines flights rather than on those of competitors.
- Manufacturing companies are keen to have their databases work on-line with both their customers and their suppliers to obtain benefits from, among other things, from just-in-time (JIT) inventories.

From banking to manufacturing and merchandizing, the foremost corporations are now combining the new wave of database technology with supercomputing and knowledge engineering to support their designers, production planners, quality controllers, cost accountants, traders, and account managers in a highly competitive manner.

A competitive edge requires both a clear strategy and the newest technology. Pattern recognition is one of the foremost implementation examples concerning the second reference. In a forex application, for instance, by combining well-chosen parameters the trader is given the prevailing market pattern. A pattern reflecting market movements is in the mind of every trader, but it takes time to do it unassisted. During this time the dealing opportunity may be lost.

The new wave of database design and exploitation takes account of the information requirements of all professionals who are working at *our* firm. It also accounts for the fact that while information technology needs are extremely diverse from one company to another, at the same time there exist common guidelines which fall under five classes. Taking the banking environment as an example, we distinguish:

1. Very fast response to the company's market activities, to support operations with stringent deadlines, like trading.
2. Real-time information with less strict response time requirements, as for instance in commercial lending.
3. High volume but simple operations of the classical transaction type (debit, credit).
4. Low volume but complex and typically confidential information concerning long transactions.
5. Highly distilled information for interactive management reporting and enduser computing applications.

Each one and all of these classes call for global database access involving not only the company's own distributed operations by location but also the clients' database resources.

Beyond this common background specific requirements start, which the database professionals are called to satisfy. The best way to look at the challenge is through an approach which from the bottom up ranges from an open architecture to proprietary solutions. A layered scheme is shown in Figure 5.2.

Whether the issue concerns databases, networks, or processing gear, it is wise as a policy to follow a layered structure. The bottom layer is hardware which is necessary for any solution, but it is not enough.

Most organizations have multiple hardware platforms with hardware-specific operating systems running applications unique to these platforms. Each application generates files in a native format which often varies from system to system. This is the reason why information elements distributed throughout the network cannot be properly controlled unless specific measures are taken in their regard.

Typically, we try to remedy this situation through software. In Figure 5.2, the six layers over the hardware are divided between commodity software and in-house developments:

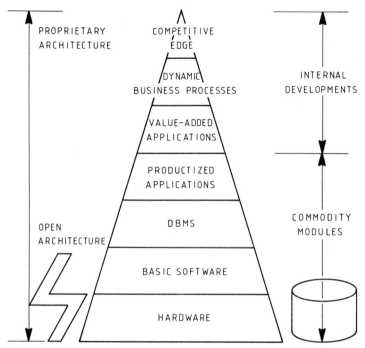

Figure 5.2 Open and proprietary parts in an environment of networked databases.

- From OS and DBMS to teleprocessing and productized applications, commodity software should abide by open architecture standards, the way we already discussed in Chapter 2.
- By contrast, value-added applications, the definition of dynamic business processes, and a competitive edge implementation will be proprietary.

A networked database environment underpinning this approach offers significant opportunities. Today, value-added applications use long transactions which are global, while simple transactions will mostly be local.

Local operations of the current accounts and saving type will be executed by location, with the exception, for instance, of customers who bank with more than one branch office. There is a large number of simple operations of the local type. Hence, in the majority of cases, access to databases is needed locally, not globally.

However, competitiveness is increasingly connected to global applications—which will be less in number but more complex. That is why we care so much to provide multidatabase solutions so that the local databases will be shared across locations.

5.5 Preparing for Database Mining

Global database access must be done while retaining the integrity and consistency of the corporate multimedia resources: data, text, graphics, image, voice—and we must be doing so at an acceptable cost. This dictates the use of an overall integrative architecture which might, for instance, dictate that while the databases are globally distributed, in some cases their contents are consolidated centrally, at least in a logical sense.

As practiced by a number of financial, commercial, and industrial organizations, central consolidation simplifies the tracking routines but also requires a complete system for managing heterogeneous information elements. This is true both for those currently used and those which are archived in active files.

In an environment of networked databases, this requires the development of a corporate standard platform for data management for both commodity and user-developed applications. It also makes the need to rationally organize and manage these IE is more critical than ever.

There is a great difference between centrally exercized control for consolidation purposes and a centralized database. Leading-edge organizations not only discovered this difference but also adopted appropriate policies to face the associated challenges. An example is the creation and exploitation of a client-centered marketing database.

The National Westminster Bank, for instance, decided to use a database computer (Teradata) for its marketing database—most specifically for the *customer information system*. As stated during our meeting: "only now our people are beginning to understand the difference between a data access goal to be implemented on a distributed basis and the failures into which centralization has led us."

Delays in vendor software and support have contributed to the downgrading of the centralized solution, leading to the decision that: "Even the global accounting application will *not* wait for DB2. Centralization cannot do the job, even if DB2 was a valid alternative."

An able response to managerial and professional requirements will be functional as well as structural. A good example is provided by corporate *Treasury*. In the typical organization, consolidated Treasury operation may involve from 15 to 20 different functional databases as well as linkages to external text and data resources, such as public databases.

Access to so many incompatible databases may sound easy to do off-line, but it is not so. Batch solutions are of no value to Treasury problems either. When the database architect looks closer at the subject of on-line access, he or she recognizes that this means reaching:

- A two-digit number of incompatible data structures
- Multiple databases run by an equal number of heterogeneous DBMS
- An aggregate of machines with different operating systems in distributed landscape

This type of heterogeneous environment is not unique to treasury operations. Marketing is another example. Active customer accounts have to be managed on-line and elements of them (orders, inventories, prices, accounting records) may be distributed among incompatible structures. Yet, *database mining* is important in:

- Evaluating customer profitability
- Measuring customer lifetime value
- Forecasting which customers will retain profitability in the long term
- Adopting different marketing approaches for different profitability segments

Database mining means the able exploitation of corporate resources which are computer-based. We aim either to derive patterns out of this operation or to explore customer relations in depth—doing so in a factual and documented manner. Patterns tell us a great deal about market trends as well as product life cycles. The analysis of customer relations reveals profit and loss figures, indicating the customers on which we may wish to focus our attention.

Both references are pertinent to the active management of any customer list. Another example of the need to exploit on-line heterogeneous networked databases through database mining is given by the recently popular approaches to reactivating dormant customer accounts by properly exploiting the corporate database resource. For instance:

- Identifying and segmenting dormant and lost customers
- Reflecting on and evaluating the probable reasons for loss of business

- Assessing the likelihood of and the means for profitably reactivating dormant customers
- Setting up successful programs to revive such dormant customer relationships

Though among themselves the databases will be largely incompatible, we can always streamline the architectural approach which we take to aid in our search for a valid technical solution. This sounds evident, but it is not necessarily so. It takes effort to achieve seamless database access for mining purposes.

5.6 Visualization Policies with Databases

Companies often take a cavalier or simply careless approach when dealing with their database problems. They struggle through a number of problems which are to a large measure their own creation—because the database environment with which they deal outlived rather than resolved multiaccess questions.

Figure 5.3 shows a good and a bad policy with a database architecture. The top diagram goes from the general to the detail as the information elements move from headquarters relevance to local usage only. This permits valid partitioning procedures.

By contrast, at the lower half of the same figure, the headquarters' database(s) and those of regional importance have developed independently of one another, without coordination. This makes integration virtually impossible; the databases have little in terms of communality over and above the other incompatibilities which may exist.

The lesson from these and many other references is that disparate, uncoordinated approaches can not and will not be effective. A more generic solution is needed to address the whole distributed database environment in an efficient, integrative manner. Because of the complexity of the problem this search for more efficient technological solutions increasingly involves knowledge engineering. The implementation itself extends well beyond what has been done in the past through the more limited data processing viewpoints.

One of the most important areas for the application of a sophisticated approach in accessing databases is the case of their vertical integration. Billions of dollars have been spent in collecting and encoding data. However, this information is generally not readily available to the people who need it.

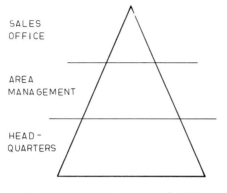

SALES OFFICE

AREA MANAGEMENT

HEAD-QUARTERS

AN INTEGRATIVE DATABASE STRUCTURE

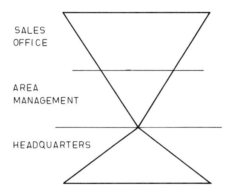

SALES OFFICE

AREA MANAGEMENT

HEADQUARTERS

INCOMPATIBLE APPROACHES WHICH CANNOT MERGE

Figure 5.3 Good and bad policies with a database architecture.

For example, variable input data from sales statistics can be treated algorithmically and heuristically to provide sales forecasts.[3] These sales forecasts can be combined with inventory levels to help in inventory planning—the goal being to minimize investments as well as the effects of obsolescence and spoilage.

Production plans can be elaborated by using inventory planning data and information on machine capacity, specialization, and occupancy.

[3]For practical examples, see D. N. Chorafas *Handbook of Management for Scientific and Technical Personnel*, McGraw-Hill/TAB Books, New York, 1990.

Cost evaluations can be done all the way from the sales function, to JIT inventory management, the production schedule, and quality control.

In all these fields, interactive evaluation and experimentation defies conventional reporting. But the implementation of knowledge engineering can be effectively combined with expertise in numerical modeling—both being supported by on-line access to networked databases.

Interactive visualization of the results is necessary and the same is true of a foundation for explanation capabilities which hide the structure, mode of operation, and dynamic behavior of the system from the enduser but provide:

• Support for conceptual modeling
• Analysis of alternative control strategies for reasoning
• Incorporation of explanation–generalization facilities

Such requirements go beyond the act of networking databases but are nonetheless fundamental in the construction of understandable and user-friendly information systems. The provision of reasoning in the interactive presentation of database contents will be of increasing importance in the 1990s, significantly improving the usability of databases.

To be accomplished in an integrative manner, such processes require know-how going well beyond the ability to access diverse, often incompatible databases. Otherwise, they cannot be done in a comprehensive manner—which is the reason why many reporting schemes today bring ambiguity into the management function rather than assisting it. By contrast, a properly architectured integrative solution will see to it that:

• No data translation demands are placed on the user, allowing him or her to focus on the problem at hand.
• Domain solutions point to needed action by capitalizing on concepts which are both comprehensive and easy to visualize.
• Planning and control tasks become quite tractable, thus enhancing the sense of responsibility and accountability.

Several research projects have suggested that a significant step in this direction would be to individualize constraints due to heterogeneity in databases as well as in query and presentation functions. The goal should be that of streamlining technical issues, thus allowing each user to consistently obtain information that is both relevant and timely with regard to immediate decision needs.

In conclusion, new techniques to promote homogeneity in information usage are required to best match system capabilities with professional characteristics. Databases should not be designed to be application-specific, but the architectural design should account for the perspectives of the applications environment as we have seen in Figure 5.3.

5.7 Cultural Change in Database Management

Want it or not, the database administrator and systems programmers are greatly involved not only in the management of information technology but also in its betterment as they proceed with their work. If nothing else, they have to work for both interactivity and visualization in connection to databases; but without change in past concepts there can be no success. By way of results, organizations:

- Need evidence that the specialists are able to overcome the inevitable technical difficulties with networked databases.
- Want such evidence to be provided through new departures in terms of managerial and technological solutions.
- Fail to appreciate that new departures, however, require a cultural change, otherwise they will be suppressed or fizzle and thus lead nowhere.

Unless the current culture of a company's own data processing and database specialists changes, little will be achieved in terms of meeting the most necessary integrative goals. This has severe consequences to the competitive position of the firm.

The statement just made is particularly true in the case of an enterprise involving a number of interrelated activities, each with a defined objective or set of objectives. A practical case has been mentioned in the preceding section with the manufacturing engineering example.

Accounting is another area where several functional resources are necessary to work together in order to provide management with the compass it needs to navigate through a fierce marketplace. Figure 5.4 outlines a two-tier system which impacts in a distributed database sense:

- The kernel represents common activities which often, but not always, are provided in a network-wide manner.
- The outer ring identifies eight operations which are often performed distinct from one another, with a proliferation of departmental computers often run on incompatible machines.

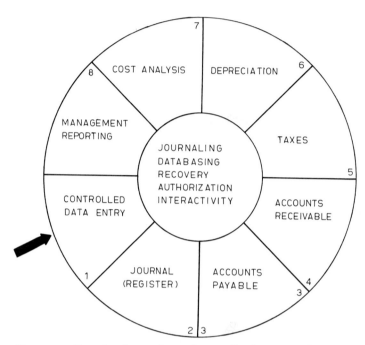

Figure 5.4   Kernel and outer layer of an application system for transaction handling.

The point often missed in connection to this schema is that even if the computers were all centralized, diversification and heterogeneity would have been the rule rather than the exception. This comes as a result of differences in operating systems, DBMS, languages, data structures, and so on.

This example is just as valid in connection to a mainframe which runs a couple of OS (e.g., VM, MVS), two or three DBMS (IMS, DB2, Adabas), and the like. In fact, this mainframe case is by far the most defective of any other alternative, as the special software ends up by consuming 80 to 90% of mainframe cycles.[4]

Taking the centralized department computers as a point of reference, one of the better known firms has been confronted precisely with this case of diversity in DBMS, OS, and equipment. Then the Board decided that there should be a new, integrative approach to assets and liabilities management. This required putting different, incompatible database solutions to work together—not one or two, but a dozen of them.

[4]As a specific benchmark with real-life (mis)application of that nature documented.

Had the old, standard centralized approach been taken, this would have been a forbidding task to work around the monolithic structures. But the chief technology officer had the background and foresight to understand that strategic applications cannot be done that way.

The same company found that, like assets and liabilities management, cost control operations must be able to access on-line many interrelated databases which contain information elements pertaining to the costs we intend to control. A cost-oriented implementation must:

- Access all cost elements in all profit centers of the organizations, no matter where they are located
- Provide data on cost consequences of decisions taken by management in directing activities and projects
- Not only overcome the fact that necessary data is distributed over large geographic distances, with distinct IE by location, but also visualize the result in a consistent and easily understood manner

There is more to this subject. The mere provision of appropriate cost data will not assure that the right control decisions are made. Since managerial needs and procedures vary with different types of projects, there is inevitably some degree of fluctuation regarding the efficiency of different operations. But the development of a networked database solution to serve cost control programs should guarantee the same comprehensive routines and presentation services all over the enterprise. This means:

- Throughout operations in the home country and abroad
- At any time the query is posed, independent of time zone
- Whatever the type of operation or project to which cost control is applied
- However management action is exercized and followed up

A common frame of reference is important for other crucial applications too, subjected to advanced analytical tools used by data-hungry algorithmic and heuristic solutions. Analytical results are crucial in maintaining the firm's profitability, and they will not come as a matter of course.

5.8 Understanding Database Contents and Requirements

One of the qualities of an efficient system solution is the ability to break down referencial complexity across departmental lines. Financial institutions and industrial companies wish to use their databases to build regular communications channels with their customers, but they are often inhibited by the fuzzy nature of database contents.

There are many practicalities and pitfalls along this line of reference. General Electric, among others, worked hard in integrating some of its databases with telephone communications because of the leverage this offers to its business. The challenges faced have been:

- How to use the database to provide a more personal service to individual customers.
- How to get appropriate data to assure an up-to-the-minute picture of customer history.
- When and how to transform single transactions into long-term relationships.
- Which should be the chosen ways and means for turning customer demands and even complaints into sales opportunities.

Whichever way the database goes so goes relationship management. But raw data held in some or all of the networked databases will not provide answers to these queries. Data filtering is necessary and this has to be done through heuristics and algorithms.

Information provided for relationship management purposes has to be smooth, predictable, consistent and comforting. *Raw* data presented to a marketing executive, for example, will not be comprehensive and may even be counterproductive. A valid solution must be able to:

- Handle different, often incompatible, sources of information
- Overcome incompatibilities in data structures and database access structures
- Massage the obtained information to really help endusers in their work
- Personalize text/data presentation in response to *ad hoc* queries

This requires, first of all, an architectural solution regarding text and databases (keeping software and hardware involvement in perspective) all the way from workstations to distributed servers and the central text and data warehouse.

The importance of the latter reference will be better appreciated if we account for the fact that documents rather than simply numerical data will be the overriding user need (and database load) in the 1990s. With this, the networked database concept takes on a new aspect, that of integrating all sorts of files already on magnetic disks, magnetic tapes, microfilm, paper, and, of course, optical disks.

The massaging of information stored in such diverse media has to be done within a fully distributed database environment which must be properly synchronized with shadow-image capabilities. This is necessary to assure 24-hour a day uninterrupted operations even if there are crashes within the networked database structure from time to time.

Transpiring through these references is the fact that the new culture in database management has to be polyvalent. As we will see when we talk of the Intelligent Database Assistant (IDA) by General Telephone and Electronics[5] (designed to answer the requirements of distributed heterogeneous databases), such polyvalence cannot be effected and maintained without knowledge engineering.

Traditional databases are considerably more rigid than the knowledgebanks which we construct through knowledge-intense approaches. Classical database structures require an *a priori* uniform definition for each entity and explicit storage allocation of facts and values. All of this implies precision and completeness and results in considerable complexity as the database size grows.

Knowledgebanks, on the other hand, represent knowledge rather than data and do so in a flexible, dynamic fashion. As intentional constructs, they not only help the on-line users in seamless searches in networked environments but also in better understanding database contents.

Stored values and facts can change; the structure and interrelationships among networked databases can also be altered. But the development and usage of a knowledgebank helps with the problem of understanding:

- When an input matches a given pattern we are after or want to see exploited.
- Which is the action by an inference rule, taking care of initiating a database update.
- Whether such action is dynamic rather than fixed in advance, accounting for messages being received.

On-line negotiation on database values is another requirement served by a knowledge-enriched database architecture. Initially, optimization subsystems were monolithic programs that had possible options embedded within them. This approach did not allow us to easily discern the

---

[5]Described in Chapter 14.

structure of a negotiation pattern and made it difficult to add new kinds of connections and interrelationships.

With a knowledge-enriched approach, the negotiation subsystem divided into two parts: an interpreter and a collection of rules written in the negotiation language. This permits us to describe the *semantics* of a node, but it also requires new approaches to the definition of what a distributed database system is—and how it should work.

Computer professionals at large, and database specialists in particular, should understand that database concepts and practices are undergoing major transformations. These are compounded by the fact that many endusers have become computer literate and some of them know more about advanced technology usage than the company's computer experts and the vendors.

PART II

Schemata, Dictionaries, and Protocols

CHAPTER 6

Schemata, Metaphors, and Distributed Databases

6.1 Introduction

Schema combines in one word view, form, and meaning. Etymologically, it means a diagrammatic representation, a scheme or outline. In logic, schema is a *syllogistic* figure bringing reflection into the picture and the formation of concept(s).

Gottfried Wilhelm Leibnitz (1646–1716) saw in schema *monadology;* the principle essential in each monad (unit), constituted of its own peculiar characteristics. Immanuel Kant (1724–1804) considered schema a medidating factor, making possible the application of categories of phenomena and their classification.

Schematism is a particular form or disposition of something, an exhibition or outline in a systematic arrangement. The formation or use of schemata often constitutes a system which in logic forms a character or figure of syllogism. In database-oriented applications,

- Schemata are descriptions of data managed by one or more DBMS.
- A schema consists of schema objects and their interrelationships.
- Typically, every DBMS has its own schema.

Schema objects are class definitions or data structure descriptions, e.g., table definitions in a relational model. They can be entity types as well and relationship types in an entity-relationship model.

Schemata can be viewed as application-specific components that define database contents and structure. This is vital to database users performing *ad hoc* operations as well as to application programs.

- Schema-to-schema mapping leads to functions that correlate schema objects to objects in another schema.

- The task of schema translation involves transforming schema X
  (describing information elements in one data model) into an
  equivalent schema Y describing the same IE in a different data
  model.
- This activity also generates the mappings that correlate schema
  objects in one DBMS to schema objects in another DBMS.

Schemata can be developed at different levels. A *conceptual schema*
describes the conceptual or logical data structures which address the
logical-level description of the database. It also reflects existing relationships among those structures.

At the same time, from the user's viewpoint the subset of the database
that may be accessed is described by an *external schema*. Since different
users may need access to different portions of the database, each one
may require a separate external schema.

The *internal schema* of a DBMS describes physical characteristics of
the logical data structures in the conceptual schema. These characteristics include information about:

- The placement of records on physical storage devices.
- Physical representation of relationships between logical records.
- The placement and type of indexes and other information
  characterizing a given DBMS.

A good deal of the description in the internal schema can be changed
without having to change the conceptual schema. Thus, it is possible to
alter a given physical representation without changing any application
program source code. This makes it feasible to fine-tune the physical
representation of the DBMS.

6.2 External Schema and Global Schema

In defining a database schema the user is producing a model of some
real-world concept or system. The goal is to create a representation
whose state *maps*, and therefore resembles, that of the real world. The
whole essence of an external schema rests in these few words.

Within a networked database environment, a *global schema* is the
integration of all local participant schemata from each site. Its aim is to
represent the global database reflecting on and normalizing the DBMS
on any one site. Such schema integration is attempted through a number

of mapping operations which aim to resolve database conflicts and specify integrated objects, properties, and relationships.

One way of looking at global schema is pictured in Figure 6.1. The global schema concept integrates a number of external schemata on the one side and a number of *subglobal* and local internal schemata in the other. Each one of the internal schemata is corresponding to a networked DBMS.

The notion of subglobal schemata essentially suggests that it is possible for multiple sites to share the same integrated schema, or different sites to have different integrated schemata. Even through such subdivision, reaching a global schema architecture represents a high level of complexity.

Citibank, which has studied this subject in depth, comments that: "Even *if* we could redo everything relating to networked databases from scratch, ending up with only one global schema, we could only handle current state of the art. This will not involve what will be dominant after 3 or 5 years." Hence, better solutions than brute force have to be found.

The problem is of course with the installed base and its diversity. "The reason God built the world in 6 days," a proverb says, "is that there was no installed base." This is hardly the case today with corporate databases.

The global schema of distributed heterogeneous databases is very difficult if not impossible to construct. Moreover, if any of the underly-

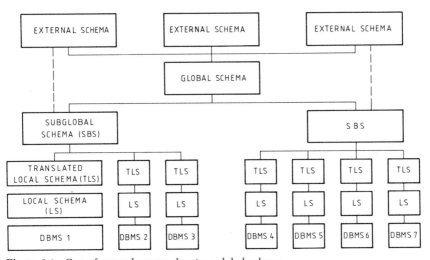

Figure 6.1 One of several approaches to a global schema.

ing local database schemata change or a new local schema is added, the integration process must be performed again.

Apart from its other technical shortcomings, this approach cedes control over the structure of existing databases to a central authority. By so doing it becomes a cumbersome, inflexible structure, over and above the fact that the interfaces so constructed can be used only if all databases needed to perform a given task are accessible on-line.

Many well-intended efforts made a frontal attack on the installed base but failed. The earliest on record is the UNCOL project by IBM—the acronym standing for Universal Computer Language.[1] The project took place between 1957 and 1959, and many people have forgotten about it in the meantime—but the evidence remains.

There were no DBMS and concepts of schemata in 1957, but there were already several heterogeneous procedure-oriented languages (POL). This posed portability and integration problems, as happens today with schemata, DBMS, and database accesses.

Central to the UNCOL idea was that processors would perform the transformations from any source POL to a universal computer model, which used ideas similar to the (then new concept of) compilers. A *decompiler* would produce object code not in a specific machine language (ML) but in UNCOL.[2] Then compilers would convert from UNCOL to ML.

This was supposed to operate in the same way which naive software specialists today talk of the global schema. It did not perform its intended functions because the whole scheme was complex and difficult and the unknowns far exceeded the factors under control.

This conceptual error has been repeated recently under many guises. One of them is IBM's heralded *Repository* reincarnating the experience of UNCOL thirty years later. People, evidently, never learn.

The skeletons of several other fruitless efforts lie along the global schema road. The trap lies in two-way convertibility between external and internal schemata through the global schema bottleneck as depicted in Figure 6.2. What UNCOL and global schema have in common is the illusion that there exists a miracle way through which a universal computer-oriented language would guarantee automatic passage from:

- Assembler to assembler
- Machine language to machine language

---

[1]See D. N. Chorafas *Programming Systems for Electronic Computers*, Butterworths, London, 1962.

[2]The same example explains why reverse engineering promoted as a cure by some vendors is illusory.

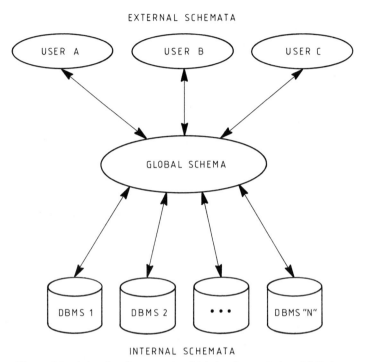

Figure 6.2 A two-level approach which has been tried and failed since 1958.

- Data structure to data structure
- DBMS schema to DBMS schema

Nothing could be more untrue. Not only is this not a simple task, but there is no evidence of it being feasible. Theoretically, it is most desirable to have such a solution, but the difference between illusion and reality also exists.

Precisely because the complexity of a global schema approach can be huge, alternatives have been devised to allow the merging of adjacent schema levels in an attempt to simplify complex situations. For instance, in the case of multiple networked sites:

- An approach to federated data modeling may serve as the external data model
- The local participant schemata may be permitted to coexist and interoperate

In some rare cases it may be possible to merge local participant and translated host schemata at a given site. This is in the background of the reference made in Figure 6.1 to translated local schemata. When we talk of tightly coupled federated databases, this concept will be in the background of our discussion.

However, it is prudent not to bet on the ability to generalize this approach. In the long run, it will be the exception rather than the rule. Hence the wisdom of having alternatives applicable to the realities of the environment in which we have to operate. This is the sense of realism—and of flexibility.

6.3 Alleviating the Problems of Heterogeneity through Export Schemata

Approaches to tightly coupled databases require support of an *export schema* in order to alleviate the problems of heterogeneity. An expert schema will be done in some common data model, subsequently defining a sort of *global-enough* schema as a union of export schemata.

Therefore, the export schema can be an important concept with networked databases. Its value lies in the fact that not all data of a component database may be available to the system and its users. The export schema represents a subset of a more general solution that is supposed to be *system-wide* available—though it may not be feasible in the first place. The purpose of defining export schemata is to facilitate the management of local autonomy. This is achieved by limiting the set of allowable operations that can be submitted on component schema(ta).

An export schema may include *access control* information regarding its use by specific users. Consequently, a federated schema can be seen as a loose integration of multiple export schemata, including information on data distribution that is generated when bringing together such export schemata.

This definition provides significant freedom and therefore adaptability to specific situations. For instance, there may be multiple federated schemata (one for each class of users) serving an expert function.

Through this approach, users are supposed to be provided with a reasonably integrated, location-transparent view of the multidatabase without having to conform their work to a global schema. This is in line with the concept advanced by many researchers nowadays that the provision of a monolithic global schema is not feasible in general, particularly when there are:

- Many databases being added or removed from the networked system
- Wide differences in the kind of information stored at different nodes
- Incomplete linguistic constructs associated to each DBMS.

This concept about possibilities and impossibilities is catching on, despite the fact that the global schema approach is still worked on by other researchers at companies and universities. The latter conveniently skip the evidence of lessons learned from the past.

Principally, but not exclusively, the global schema proponents are those who have tied themselves to the concept of centralization. As we have seen in Chapter 5, England's National Westminster Bank provided an excellent example along this line of reference.

"The situation becomes critical," the cognizant NatWest executive was to comment, "as more and more executives and professionals in the bank are asking for database-wide access and integrating information capabilities. NatWest dropped the centralization track because it does not do the necessary job and the same is true of global schema approaches.

"The global schema will not work," said both the National Westminster and County NatWest executives. "You spend time and money, and finally end up with no usable approach." Both financial institutions underlined that this is not just a technical systems problem. It is an organizational and business problem.

But the technical problem cannot be solved without providing a sound solution to the organizational and business perspectives—which is a fact that only the foremost financial institutions and industrial companies have understood.

The same leading-edge companies and their technologists also appreciate that when it comes to the manipulation of schemata and cross-database solutions to be provided the size of the networked database does not really matter. What matters is their homogeneity and its negation, their diversity. Diversity may sound like a technical issue, and to a large measure this is true. But in reality, the background factors are business, organizational, even political—as explained in the preceding paragraphs.

As it cannot be repeated too often, sound solutions see to it that organizational and technical aspects are indivisible. The National Westminster Bank brought up as an example the work done by GDAU, its Group Data Architecture Unit. In this, six to eight people have been working for three years creating a data definition and logical data model.

This project focused on two applications: One with IBM's DB2; the other with Link of Unisys. The latter has addressed the vital problem of handling major corporate customers.

"We cannot even define customers the same way," said the cognizant executive, "particularly for large customers and the partnership definitions." The project ended up with profiles which were completely different from one system to another—hardly a usable result. "You may let the group continue but you don't let them influence anybody anymore," was suggested.

Other organizations, too, who tried to rationalize the end points, took the global schema road and failed. One of them said in the course of the research that in the early 1980s it undertook a bank-wide model with basically centralization and global schema ideas in mind. Nothing came out of it and it was abandoned because the concept was not particularly coherent; the software was largely wanting; and the hardware could not support such an ambitious undertaking.

Hence the decision was made to be pragmatic in the future; no more "all data concentrated" in one place. From then on, emphasis was placed on enduser needs and requirements, not on the whims of the data processors.

Addressing systems solutions starts with the query: *"What do the users like?"* In the case of the National Westminster Bank, the users said to the internal research which took place: "We like a blackbox which no matter what we ask will be able to deliver." "That's the whole idea of MIS and of *ad hoc* analytical queries," said the responsible executive, adding that "For fast response, we need not only schemata but also parallel handling of data."

6.4 Driving for Schema Compatibility through Object Orientation

What is meant by being *schema compatible?* There is no unique answer to this query. Schemata change as we massage record structures. But schema compatibility can be better supported through an object orientation, manipulating syllogistic information at atomic level. In Chapter 5, we made reference to the benefits which an object approach provides.

The opposite of schema compatibility is *schema mismatch.* It arises with diversity but also when similar concepts are expressed differently in the schema. Depending on the model, schema elements which can be compatible or alternatively mismatched are such things as:

- Relations and attributes
- Types and functions
- Entities and relationships
- Classes and methods

In many instances, schema mismatch is really the result of domain mismatch problems, with some of the domains being in the schema instead of in the data. Besides this, networked databases may use different identifier lengths, formats, and other properties which are maintained locally and are noncompatible in a global sense.

This brings up strategic, tactical, and operational issues connected to the chosen architecture for networked databases. Basically, the architecture of a database system is primarily determined by:

- Which schemata are present
- How they are arranged
- How they are constructed

The process of creating schema compatibility can take different forms. In a loosely coupled federation of autonomous databases, it typically leads to the definition of an *import schema*. Export schemata and import schemata have much in common as the former lead to the latter.

In developing federated solutions in a loosely coupled system, each user is the administrator of his or her own schema or schemata. Typically, the user:

- Looks at the available export schema(ta) to determine which one(s) describe data he or she would like to access.
- Defines the notion of federated schema by importing the export schema objects through an interface.
- Employs a language to make reference to export and import schema objects suitable to the application.

With this approach, the user is responsible for understanding the semantics of the objects in the export schemata. Component DBMS dictionaries need to be consulted for definitions, links, and other information. Data dictionaries play a very important role in networked databases, as we will see in Chapters 8 and 9.

The administrator of the database system defines and manages a federated schema and the external schemata related to it. In a loosely coupled distributed solution, however, federated schemata are defined and maintained primarily by the users and only secondarily (in a coordination sense) by a system-assigned administrator.

Database architects and database administrators worth their salt are able to appreciate that in a networked database structure the local schemata, including the user-defined types and function specifications, have to be respected. In a federated solution, when a user accesses another database, its schema is imported into the interface and becomes part of the local schema. The imported schema may be viewed as a local cache of an external schema, but importing a schema into the user's database raises interesting problems, particularly within an object orientation.

We have seen in Chapter 5 the fundamental notions behind an object orientation.[3] One of the axioms of an object database is that a subtype inherits all functions such as attributes of its supertypes. This is an important contribution of objects to schema manipulation.

If a type in the networked database becomes a subtype of a certain type in the local type hierarchy, then it must inherit all of the functions of its supertype. However, while this is the theoretical principle, it may not hold in the general case for databases that have evolved autonomously.

Hence, some integrative object-oriented DBMS choose other strategies in approaching this problem. For instance, Hewlett-Packard's Pegasus deals with the problem of importing types in two ways:

- If a user does not specify any relationship between the local and imported schemata, the imported schema defines a new type hierarchy in the default database—in parallel to the existing local schema.
- If a user specifies supertype/subtype relationships between the types of local and imported schemata, Pegasus propagates all existing functions over a type to its subtypes using internal or user-defined rules.

Pegasus is an object-oriented DBMS specifically designed for cross-database access. The general idea behind this construct is shown in Figure 6.3. This figure represents an ideal case of object-oriented coverage of diverse schemata and does not mean that Pegasus is able to support the whole range of alternatives which is shown.

---

[3]For details see D. N. Chorafas and H. Steinmann *Object-Oriented Databases*, Prentice-Hall, Englewood Cliffs, NJ, 1993.

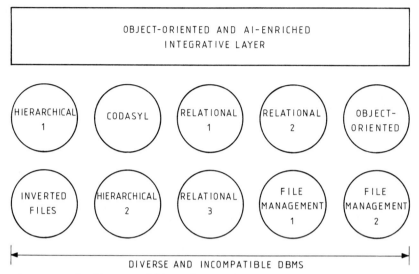

Figure 6.3 Flexible, expandable, and open solutions to distributed heterogeneous databases.

Different alternatives are being examined in a design sense. For instance, an internal rule may assume that the implementation of a function already defined on a type overrides the implementation of a function with the same name defined on the imported supertype. Such flexible merging of type hierarchies is useful for databases that have evolved independently but now have to work in a cooperative manner.

6.5 Metaphors and User Profiles

Many people fail to appreciate that a major issue facing the introduction of interactive networked databases is the ability of users and potential users to grasp the impact and importance of new methods of operation. Any mode of working that allows man–machine interactions to be thoroughly investigated is highly beneficial. Able approaches embrace both:

• Simulation and emulation techniques oriented toward queries and transactions in a distributed sense
• The adoption of laboratory (hence, restricted infrastructure) experiments based on new technologies

The concept and usage of schemata is key to this approach. Though necessary and important, schema definition and manipulation is not the whole thing. A very important layer interfacing between external and internal schemata is that of *metaphors*.

A metaphor is a reference to a known real-world situation that the enduser (or the system designer) tries to invoke. This permits us to relate the right conceptual models to a given task while projecting and subsequently employing the artifact. Figure 6.4 gives in a nutshell the meaning of this reference.

1. Multimedia information constitutes the bottom layer.
2. Above this comes the functionality supported by the DBMS.
3. The internal schema is a *metalayer* over the DBMS.
4. The metaphor interfaces between external and internal schema.
5. The external schema stands over the internal schema and the metaphor.
6. The concept is in the user's mind, the way the user reflects on the world and on the problem.

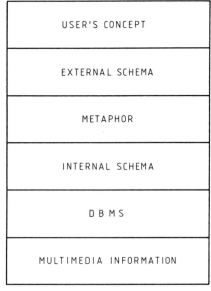

Figure 6.4   A layered view of enduser interactivity with databased resources— from metaphor to multimedia information.

The user will typically translate the concept into one or more external schemata. This is done while moving from an abstract, idealized world view to a more concrete demand tooled around what is expected in terms of knowledge or information. This is what really is reflected in the external schema.

The strength of the metaphor is that it presents its contents in a form which machines can understand, as contrasted to what people understand. Etymologically, however, metaphors were written for people—as for instance the way they are used in the Bible. Their goal was to explain things in a way common people can understand.

Both in a people-to-people and people-to-machines sense, the role of a metaphor is a *better explanation* largely made in an indirect way. Hence, a prerequisite notion is understanding the user's metaphors and therefore the external schema(ta).

Metaphors can effectively assist in providing the needed bridges to the heterogeneous databases. Under appropriate conditions, they help in correlating the external and internal schemata—a facility which has not yet been exploited in its full strength.

In order to provide appropriate connectivity; user-to-machine and machine-to-user metaphors should be embodied in the *human window* (man–machine interfaces, MMI). This practice can be particularly beneficial with applications addressed to networked databases and designed for graphical representation and effective means of dialogue.

Ideally, a metaphor should be tailored to specific needs. However, merely grafting databasing and communication processes onto a general computing practices is inadequate. Endusers will be served in a better way when the concepts of metaphors and human windows are enriched with:

- Knowledge engineering tools
- Intelligent dictionary capabilities
- High-speed access to databases
- Real-time man–machine interaction
- High-quality communications
- Navigational aids used after the appropriate reference is found
- Personalized presentation processes to fit the user's decision style

Through knowledge engineering we should exploit the fact that the metaphor interfaces between the external and internal schemata, essentially translating the user's conceptual model through the semantic content of a linguistic structure. This is why it was stated in preceding paragraphs that a metaphor's message is what machines understand, as contrasted to the conceptual model which is better understood by people.

This reference helps in identifying the reasons why, in order to improve the mapping of sophisticated applications into computers, more work is needed on both *mental models* and metaphors. The language we use forms our mind and should also express our concepts in an efficient manner.

Mental models, metaphors, and schemata enhance the information scientist's ability to deliver information services to the endusers. Several worthwhile applications have approached this subject through knowledge-based technology by:

- Effectively assisting users in an environment of distributed heterogeneous databases
- Supporting people with special needs, *ad hoc*, as these needs develop rather than in a stereotyped predefined manner

Users, particularly those who are computer literate, are demanding greater flexibility in the way they interface for their daily operations with different incompatible databases. Though the use of metaphors is still in its infancy and there are major issues to be studied relating to access aspects,[4] their usage is indeed recommended practice.

In terms of linguistics, metaphors can be effectively described by object-oriented expert systems shells. The semantics which they involve are, however, the visible outcome in whose foundations we find user profiles.

A *user profile* is a description of the relevant characteristics of the enduser for the purpose of designing and operating networked database services. Profiling helps in channeling, in an accurate manner, these services to the user's problems. The elements of a profile will vary depending on the user who is involved. Examples of profile dimensions in a system design sense are:

- Decision style of the user
- The user's presentation priorities and mode(s)
- Language favored by the user
- Databases the user needs to access
- Specifics regarding the user's employment of the database services
- Numerical computation, text processing, and logical constructs

---

[4]See also Chapters 10 and 11 on ISO's remote data access (RDA).

- Authorization and authentication
- Other options and choices

The user profile needs to be distributed over many databases, connected to the various services with which the user is involved. In itself, this user profile may be employed for different purposes, essentially becoming a design constraint.

6.6 Enduser Control and External Schemata

In old times, solutions were developed—or at least attempted—in a way to fit the needs of everybody. This approach has led to many horrors: By shooting for the 100%, project failures have become legend, and when they succeeded the user had to adapt to the system rather than the system adapting to the user, as the case should have been.

The awkward mentality behind this approach lasted for over three decades and dictated that information service was designed in an awkward, ossified way aimed to fit the full range of all users—but none of them precisely.

Special attention was in fact paid to the least responsive users who were fed with lots of printed output—rather than the proactive ones who had truly special needs and wanted to work on-line in a flexible way.

Slowly, topmost organizations have changed their approach in this regard. Today, parametrically expressed design characteristics and constraints help to personalize the system to each of its users, providing a basis for dynamically adapting the service provided by networked databases in an interactive way.

Citibank's Quotron, which is one of the better known information providers, has gained a competitive advantage by integrating a user profile expert system into its network. This enables information provider services to know the subscriber's characteristics and preferences at the moment he or she signs on.

In this and similar cases, user control is exercised through metaphors which the system can understand. This provides a valid way for reconfiguring existing generic services to make them more suitable for a new set of users, or the same user at different instances and professional functions.

Through the contribution of knowledge engineering user profiles, metaphors and external schemata impact the way information systems present their results. They assure effective means of providing the user with control over applications as well as access to networked databases.

The term *user-control* refers to flexible configuration and reconfiguration of information services which become increasingly user-oriented. This does not mean that all endusers will necessarily have equal flexibility or control over the networked databases. The important point is that the possibility of providing user options is recognized to be an essential design requirement.

A special form of user control arises in connection with *ad hoc* service creation—not just *ad hoc* response to queries. In classical data processing, *ad hoc* solutions are impossible and, even planned ones:

- Typically are very lengthy to materialize
- Require a carefully managed progression in terms of software development
- Address the distributed database structure as a monolithic entity rather than a flexible proposition

Modern approaches promote enduser control and work in antithesis to all these three points, but they also require a considerable degree of cultural change. They also call for tools which permit production of new services in a very short time frame.

Companies which have tried this approach know by experience that metaphors and external schema oriented solutions dominate the new system design culture which leads to greater efficiency. Greater efficiency is highly necessary today because of:

- The fast evolution of user requirements in a networked database access sense
- The fact that it is not possible to foresee all of the potential uses of the IE we have in storage

User control and knowledge-enriched support for external schemata are not only compatible processes but also complementary. They both fit well into a functional architecture of networked databases, provided the tools at its disposal are adequate. At the technical side, such overall functional architecture must provide:

- An agreed, high-level, conceptual framework for all database services which are already envisaged *or might be envisaged* over the whole range of enduser interactivity

- A context within which more specific applications perspectives can be developed, built upon the best of current practices and in a knowledge-engineering intense manner

Once properly architectured, a valid approach will proceed building block by building block, assuring properly engineered relationships between components. Rules that constrain the way components may be interconnected will be detailed and the same is true of principles that suggest useful compositions of these building blocks to meet evolving needs.

The able manipulation of schemata, the way it has been discussed in this chapter, sees to it that all database networks developed from now on should be highly flexible. This also requires knowledge-enriched guidelines explaining:

- How the components and rules can be applied to meet steadily evolving requirements of a fast-growing user population.
- When and how interactive database services should be personalized, and under what criteria.
- Why constraints in design, though necessary, must be dynamic in terms of their evolution.

Metaphors, schemata, and user control fit well in this architectural perspective whose implementation is an essential part of an integrative solution regarding the database resources, both private and public.

Building blocks that are designed and constructed separately but obey a common architecture can be assembled together into a system more easily than if there were no such common architecture in sight. Once such a policy is adopted, it becomes possible to obtain a wider choice of components which are cheaper and more generally available. It also will be possible to instantaneously specialize networked resources to evolving enduser requirements.

CHAPTER 7

Can We Solve Cross-Database Problems through Schemata?

7.1 Introduction

When in the early 1980s the problem of integrating diverse heterogeneous databases first came up, it involved classical transactional repositories and their applications. The then developing decision support and
management information systems (MIS) needed to access some of the
contents of transactional databases but not in an *as is* fashion.

To answer the requirements of ten years ago, some vendors came
around with an approach based on off-line extract routines. IBM's DXT
linking DB2 to IMS is an example of this fire-brigade approach which
was supposed to be only an interim until more elegant solutions could
be developed.[1]

Not only vendors but also user organizations develop data extraction
programs to feed their separate an distinct information center database.[2]
Valid ten or twelve years ago, this approach no longer satisfies management requirements.

Data extract done in a batch form during night runs has been a solution
admissible on the short run, but it became increasingly inefficient and
counterproductive. As a result, other vendors, particularly small software companies,[3] promoted the idea of a *global schema* within a heterogeneous database environment.

User organizations, too, moved in this direction of a global database
schema, and a number of ambitious projects have been started with its
implementation as the goal. As we have seen in the preceding chapter,

---

[1]We have already spoken of the same vendor's Data Propagator which essentially
propagates a bad solution *ad infinitum* into the future.

[2]See also in D. N. Chorafas *Interactive Message Systems*, McGraw-Hill, New York,
1984, the editor utility and closed user group implementation developed for a group of
Italian banks.

[3]Like Computer Corporation of America, Cambridge, Massachusetts.

after years of trying and lavish money spent on such projects, none has succeeded.

These negative experiences saw to it that attention has now been focused on a family of solutions; all of them use the notions of external and internal schemata. Each has its own *strengths* and *weaknesses* as well as *opportunities* and *limitations*.

The better thought-out approaches have in common the premise that a good way of looking at any resource other than the *local* resources in an environment of networked databases is as a *foreign* resource. Many of these foreign databases will be supported through a DBMS with its own schema.

To preserve the full autonomy of the local resource, only that part of the foreign database which is exported is visible in a system-wide sense. This assures a sort of globality default without global schema constraints.

In most of the models which we will consider in this chapter, the local database has its native schema which remains valid through the communication established with other databases. *Registration* introduces a foreign schema to the local system, making future cross-database interaction possible.

7.2 Multidatabase Approaches during the Last Decade

One of the earlier efforts in terms of a new departure for cross-database solutions was the project *Multibase*, which took place in the early to mid-1980s. It addressed multiple heterogeneous database structures of Codasyl and relational type using a high-level query language.

- The concept of type generalization was used in connection with an extensive *view definition* facility.
- A multibase query processor was designed to decompose a global query into subqueries against the local schemas.
- A local database interface translated queries received from the query processor into queries expressed in the local data manipulation language (DML).

The query language of Multibase is DAPLEX. It provides certain procedural constructs like iteration with the data model, based on a functional paradigm.

In the mid-1980s, another effort in a similar direction was the Amoco Distributed Database System (ADDS). It used an extended relational data model to integrate relational, network, and hierarchical databases. ADDS generated an equivalent description of different local databases in connection to the ADDS data model, using an extended relational algebra with joins, natural joins, outer joins, intersection, and selects.

The ADDS approach differed from the functional one taken in Multibase. Its developers characterized their solution as extended relational, but as they progressed in their work they found it necessary to implement a composite global schema.

Still another effort, *Mermaid,* started as a research project at Unisys and has been marketed by System Development Corporation. Mermaid allows the user to manipulate the IE stored under various relational DBMS running on different machines using SQL and a common language called Ariel.

- The SQL or Ariel queries get translated into a distributed intermediate language (DIL).
- For each DBMS, there are driver processes at the local site.
- The driver translates DIL subqueries to the local DBMS query language.

All information about schemata, databases, users, host computers, and the network is contained in a data dictionary/directory. Mermaid software provides data translation from local to global representation and vice versa.

Using knowledge engineering, the General Telephone and Electronics (GTE) laboratories developed in 1988 the *Intelligent Database Assistant* (IDA). This is the most sophisticated of custom-made, cross-database efforts so far. IDA is a shell. Its first practical implementation took place with the California operations of GTE. Known as CALIDA, this application addresses hierarchical, relational, and file management systems.

The focal point of CALIDA concerned access to different distributed databases containing customer files, service (connect) times, and accounts. We will study IDA/CALIDA in significant detail in Chapter 14.

Dataplex is a heterogeneous distributed database management system developed in the late 1980s at General Motors Research Laboratories. Like in other approaches, the data definitions of all participating databases are transformed to an equivalent relational data definition. Contributions of Dataplex are:

- The mapping of nonrelational data structures—such as IMS—to relational schemas

• Translation of relational subqueries to equivalent nonrelational
  queries

The *ShareBase* project at the University of Southern California (USC)
is focused on an approach oriented to the controlled sharing and exchange of information among autonomous, heterogeneous databases. It
emphasizes the identification and resolution of various types of heterogeneity at the *metadata* and specific fact levels, including objects and
representations.

A sophisticated construct, ShareBase provides for a heuristic-based
agent that attempts to assist nonexpert database users in establishing
and dynamically refining shared patterns. The approach properly
underlines interoperability issues; heuristics helps in determining
shared patterns.

IISS is a cross-database effort following the entity-relationship model
and addressing Codasyl as well as relational DBMS. It provides a forms-
based user interface, but queries must be compiled in advance.

Another entity-relational model is *SCOOP*. Developed in the early
1980s, it predates many other examples and attempts to cover a domain
characterized by hierarchical, Codasyl, and relational DBMS.

Also addressed to an environment of Codasyl and relational DBMS is
DDTS. The approach which it takes is relational and includes checking
for integrity constraints, local query optimization, and local and wide
area user communications.

Still another early project is *Sirus–Delta*. Basically relational in nature, it addresses Codasyl and relational DBMS. By contrast, *MRDSM*
(which is also relational) operates only across incompatible relational
DBMS. It features a multidatabase language dealing with multiple semantic interpretations.

An extended relational model, *Omnibase* also operates in heterogeneous relational environments. It handles query processing but more or
less limits itself to DEC installations. A late 1980s construct hooked to
IBM, Omnibase aims to cover hierarchical, Codasyl and relational
DBMS, attempting to do so through the use of auxiliary schemata.

7.3 Reflecting on the Major Classes of Cross-Database Solutions

As the cross-database examples we reviewed in the preceding section
help document, there can be a great variety of approaches in facing the

operability challenges presented by networked databases. Solutions are being searched for in either a loosely coupled or tightly coupled manner.

CALIDA, MRDSM, and Omnibase are loosely coupled structures. These are more flexible and relatively easier to develop and implement, but they address themselves more to query handling than to transaction processing.

ADDS, DDTS, Mermaid, and Multibase feature a variable degree of tight coupling. There may also be intermediate cases, for instance, IISS. No general rule can be set stating that one approach is better than the other. All have their strengths and their weaknesses.

Neither should approaches simpler than the project references we briefly reviewed in this chapter be forgotten. For instance, in Part I we have spoken of actual implementations based on message exchange and simple pass-through.

With message exchange, the code is executed locally and the switching of messages takes place among local databases. Solutions can be based either on the pipes approach as used in Unix or on the blackboard adopted and employed in knowledge engineering.

In terms of cross-database solutions simpler than message passing, we have spoken of the pass-through software to a variety of incompatible DBMS (for instance, DataLens by Lotus Development and DAL by Apple Computers).

The introduction to this chapter also spoke of a process of system level registration. The concept of system level registration is better carried out with the local DBMS reference in mind. This practice tends to describe such things as:

• DBMS schema and functions
• Data structure(s) being used
• Network protocols
• Operating system characteristics
• Constraint by computer types

The functions being executed are the manifestations of operations. Properties, relationships, and computations on, say, objects are expressed in terms of functions which lead from arguments to results.

This is the general model toward which researchers orient their efforts. But while necessary it is not enough. To successfully set the stage for useful work in a cross-database sense, we must carefully consider:

1. Specific database models utilized by our computer systems
2. Type of real-time applications that we execute or have to execute

3. Prevailing mix between transaction-type and query-type applications, including long transactions
4. Size of ongoing applications and their interactivity
5. Time interval required to incorporate changes in system features
6. Required time and cost for dynamically expanding feature sets
7. Quality issues encountered during the process of cross-database operations

All seven items impact the solution option we should choose among what is feasible and the specific technical characteristics such an option should have. No doubt, another major factor is the human capital available to do the needed job. But if we are wise enough, we will not take this as a constraint; we will build the human capital to the level of wanted expertise. This is the better approach to problems connected to the interoperability of networked databases.

7.4 Capitalizing on the Use of Schemata

One thing the different approaches we have considered have in common is the extensive use of *schemata*. Their plurality, however, suggests the need for putting some order to this broad landscape. Can we cast them into classes which permit dealing with them more effectively?

Figure 7.1 classifies in a layered mode the four more dominant current approaches. Top to bottom, this structure goes from the more complex in terms of design and implementation to the simpler; it ranges from medium and longer term solutions to approaches offering themselves for immediate implementation.

Tight coupling is the nearest thing to a global schema, while trying to avoid its limitations. If the distributed databases in the network have a certain semi-homogeneity, for instance:

- All relational: Ingres, Oracle, Sybase
- Coming from the same vendor: DB2, IMS
- Being on-line for the same well-defined application: CAD/ concurrent engineering

And if the involved database diversity is measured in a low one-digit number, then tight coupling databases can be attempted. There is no assurance that it can succeed, but it might.

However, let's make sure that contrary to global schema solutions which try to force a unique discipline on diverse and incompatible data

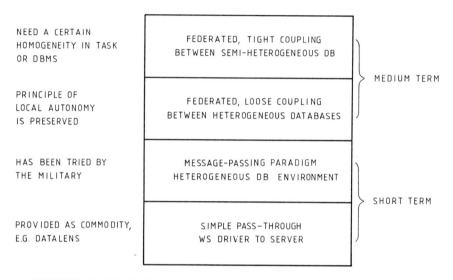

FEDERATED SOLUTIONS REQUIRE OBJECT ORIENTATION AND KNOWLEDGE ENGINEERING

Figure 7.1   Approaches taken in distributed database environments.

structures and DBMS, tight coupling executed in a federated sense permits them to maintain their locality. This is positive but also sees to it that some constraints need to be implied—which for some implementations could be restrictive.

Applied to an environment of federated databases, tight coupling can also be seen as addressing a subset of a larger population. The prerequisite is that some communality exists among these databases and it is well understood. This prerequisite is necessary to permit building a rule-based expert system.

A different way of making the foregoing statement is that since no two organizations have the same requirements, a tightly coupled database solution must be more or less custom-made. Therefore, it is a medium to longer term approach, requiring information technology specialists who:

• Are versatile both in knowledge engineering and in object-oriented approaches
• Have a good grasp of all schemata and their primitives in the DBMS to be tightly coupled
• Are able to choose and employ strong and powerful tools, which may not always be easy to understand in terms of their facilities

DBMS schemata are evidently at the core of the tight coupling approach. The simpler (though not very simple) way to handle them is in a freeze-frame manner which makes the solution rather static. But for transaction handling reasons this *might* be acceptable, depending on the requirements posed by the applications.

With reference to Figure 7.1, the second layer from the top represents a fully heterogeneous environment with a realistic cross-database goal being development of a loosely coupled system. Like the examples we have seen in Section 2, this will help provide "any-to-any" access if at the same time a good deal of emphasis is placed on the development of human windows (agile man–machine interfaces).

The contribution necessary from knowledge engineering for that approach depends on the level of sophistication of the applications running on the networked databases. Both current and future projects must be considered, assuring that the solution being provided can continue to be valid in the longer run.

- An open architecture should dominate conceptual characteristics and protocols.
- An integrative perspective should be properly chosen and implemented.
- The possibility should be kept open for using more sophisticated methods and tools as a result of gaining better experience with the model.

In this case, too, DBMS schemata are the cornerstone of a valid solution. Any integrative approach would rest on schema import/export as discussed in Chapter 6.

In fact, the *mapping of schemata* is the background principle characterizing the top two layers of Figure 7.1, a procedure underpinning the federation of databases. But there is also a difference in terms of what each layer supports. While the loosely federated solution is easier to implement than tight coupling, it also has its limitations. It can be quite efficient for cross-database queries, including analytical queries to heterogeneous networked databases participating in the federation. However, it is not necessarily recommended for transactional type applications and updates, due to the cross-database consistency which updates must demonstrate, as well as for security enforcement reasons.

Different approaches have been tried to remedy these shortcomings. But such remedies typically lead towards the topmost layer in Figure 7.1, that is, tightly coupled systems whose strengths and limits have already been considered.

The positive aspect is that mapping schemata within an environment of networked databases does away with the restrictions of a centralized database approach containing all of an organization's information elements. Users can access the local databases from anywhere in the network without needing to know the physical locations of files, operating system, syntax, or the networking protocol commands. And they can work with the metaphors best fitting their decision styles as well as their work.

7.5 How Far Can Message Passing Go?

Message passing—of which we already spoke in general terms—is simpler than the two federated alternatives examined so far in connection to Figure 7.1. It requires the least coupling among the networked heterogeneous databases, simplifying by so much the interconnection effort.

Starting with the fundamentals, a federation of databases necessarily addresses the issue of semantic data structures. It also accounts for the facts that:

- Relations and attributes have to be chosen for performance or design reasons, or both
- Aggregation toward composite objects among the networked databases has to be technically sustained

The simple coupling procedures required for message exchange pose no tough prerequisites. Hence, they impact in the least possible manner on man–machine interfaces as well as on data access procedures.

If we take an historical look at the way the third layer in Figure 7.1 has evolved, we will see that the concept of message-based systems for cross-database access began in the domain of military applications. Typically, format definition precedes the protocol which has to be set.

Format definition is a prerequisite to database interconnection through message-passing routines. More precisely, formats and standards must be valued against data models; but there may be other prerequisites.

For instance, message translation may be necessary. In this connection a number of different centralized solutions to the translation problem have been tried on the wrong premise that a data dictionary can do some minor miracles—which is simply not true.

Even a huge data dictionary cannot do all the work which is required in a highly heterogeneous environment. The data dictionary provides directory and data definitions, but as the networked databases environment expands:

- Local database A risks not knowing how to approach local database B, mapping into it the translated message.
- Though an intelligent database A knows that it could subset the problem and send a message to B, it may be unaware of some of the constraints.

Conceptually, this can be solved in either of two ways. One leads to a more restrictive approach requiring relatively homogeneous schemata, for instance, all relational.

The alternative is more flexible and moves out of a centralized translator toward a distributed solution. Figure 7.2 shows this decentralization translation approach, suggesting between the lines of the block diagram that:

- A distributed translation process should account for the fact that the database environment and its heterogeneity will expand
- It is also wise to keep the node translator small, rather than letting it become too big and unmanageable

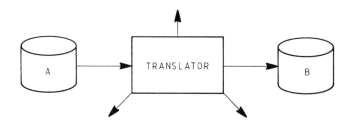

Figure 7.2   A transition in schema translation.

The good news is that in message passing the problem of complexity can be resolved by subsetting. This simplifies the message-passing/translation issue and permits flexible solutions, capitalizing on new technology to answer new user requests in an able manner.

A properly designed message-passing strategy must account for the fact that different applications have different requirements. Experienced systems engineers appreciate that it is not possible to generalize while we try to solve the problem of exchanging information. The best architectural solution is that which permits us to make the system extendable and personalized.

Personalization is necessary to respond to the growing demand for technological solutions which can emulate the work done by managers and professionals, as well as their decision styles. This contrasts to what the EDPiers have been doing for nearly 40 years with their slowness in grasping the change in the world of information technology and user demands.

We have often underlined the importance of *expandability*. Technically, it is the simplest at the bottom layer of Figure 7.1. Here, the approach rests on a relatively simple pass-through actuated by:

- An application programming interface (API) at the human window level
- DBMS-specific drivers at the interconnection level whose inventory can increase as we address more databases

As previously mentioned, one of the best examples of this solution is DataLens by Lotus Development. It permits the user of the 1-2-3 spreadsheet to access some twenty different DBMS and file structures—one driver at the DataLens level for each one of the supported data structures.

This and similar approaches are excellent in the short term. Though closely linked to one vendor's products, they can be used effectively to solve a problem which has defied many large corporations—mainframe vendors and user organizations alike.

This, however, does not mean that pass-through should be adopted in the longer run as a corporate standard platform for data management in an environment of networked databases. But it does mean that over the shorter term the flexibility of the method and the facilities supported by pass-through for query purposes can be impressive.

Because the drivers do not open the files they access, they can access any type of file, including graphics files, word processing files, ASCII files, and even the obsolete EBCDIC files. Pass-through can also help managers to think globally, in a networked databases sense.

Within limits, this solution can be quite helpful to companies who need data integration but have a distributed, heterogeneous database network that requires the management of a large volume of information in an able manner. Eventually, this approach can be made more sophisticated by adding workflow process control, user customization, an activity log, and data organization standards.

In conclusion, each one of the alternatives in Figure 7.1 has its advantages and its limitations. No solution is or can be ideal; we should always look for compromises. But all four alternatives are feasible and which one to choose depends on the particular situation, the resources which are available, the timetable, the budget, and the goals.

7.6 Proceeding with Schema Integration

Schema integration refers to the process of trying to put different existing but incompatible schemata under a sort of common schema. This should not be confused with the global schema of which we have spoken as being unfeasible. The idea is to create a *virtual* rather than a real common schema. Figure 7.3 should be interpreted in this light.

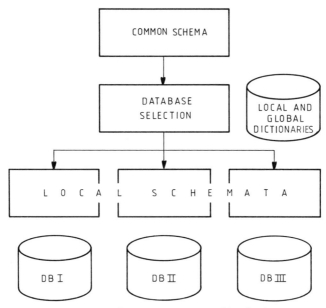

Figure 7.3 Mappings between common and local schemata.

The fact that, more or less, we are after a virtual solution should not be seen as making our mission so much simpler. Virtual integration requires *schema analysis* which involves two activities:

- Studying and comparing the schemata to be integrated, including identification of naming conflicts (homonyms, synonyms), value types, structural differences, constraint conflicts, etc.
- Specifying interrelationships among the schema objects, assuring that related information is represented in a similar form though it belongs to different schemata

Only when the schemata are represented by means of the same model is analyzing and comparing their objects feasible. Comparison of the schema objects is primarily guided by their semantics, not by their syntax. In contrast, *view integration* refers to the process of combining multiple user views into a single schema.

Most people look at schema integration as a way of merging existing databases into a unified family of schemata. This is only half true. Proposed approaches are mainly classified into two groups, depending on the data model being used:

- One is based on the relational model, the way we have used it over the last fifteen years.
- The other is a semantic, object-oriented solution which will be prevalent in the mid-1990s.

Although relational views can define virtual relations, they are not powerful enough to deal with integration aspects of information elements such as those sought after through generalization. Relational views are restricted to a single database, but knowledge engineering rules can support generalization of multiple databases (and derivation), also allowing aggregate operations.

Semantic models provide a richer set of abstractions which can be used in designing the conceptual structure of databases. This is particularly useful with a top-down design approach which permits us to take a global look at the networked databases prior to starting with the details of each.

However, several problems exist by way of realization. One of them is the rather heavy overhead incurred for schema integration. The overhead for mapping the different record-oriented data models onto semantic models or vice versa can be high. Therefore, even though work on schema integration may be elegant from a theoretical viewpoint, it is expensive and difficult to apply to real-life implementations. Another technical difficulty comes from the fact that while semantic data models are expressive and helpful in specifying data definitions, for many of them the query languages being used are still procedural, hence retrograde.

The lack of *metalevel* concepts and tools is particularly felt because when various databases are integrated, emphasis is placed on *constraints*. Different types of constraints are required to specify the relationship between a generalized entity and its constituents. Constraints which cannot be captured in structural constructs are expressed as laying outside of the data model but still being present. They must be defined explicitly in the data model implementation language.

Through knowledge engineering, formal and informal semantics of data integration can be treated uniformly in first-order logic without much loss of generality. Knowledge formulated in terms of logic is easily mapped within this context assisted by underlying formalisms.

As the whole approach under discussion is in full evolution, it is appropriate to notice the positive fact that current integration methodologies are driven by semantic considerations. This permits the handling of objects from both their semantic and their structural aspects.

Object orientation permits us to bypass the classical approach to integration which has been based on the principle that if two classes are to be integrated, a common superclass should exist or be created.[4] In many cases, experience shows that it is impossible to find such a common superclass if the two classes to be integrated have semantics heterogeneity.

7.7 The Semantics of Schema Integration

An essential feature in schema integration is an understanding of the real semantics of the distributed information elements. This is just as important in trying to integrate heterogeneous networked databases as it is in providing interoperability in connection to incompatible computer systems.

By understanding the semantics of entities, attributes, and relationships we improve our ability to reason in a cross-database sense. Real meaning of attributes can be captured using common concepts, concept hierarchies, and aggregate concepts.

[4]This is the concept underpinning the global schema.

Each attribute can be characterized by one or more common concepts representing properties as well as characteristics possessed by certain objects—whether physical or logical. These concepts, however, must not be application dependent.

The establishment of relationships among attributes can take different forms. One approach is outlined in Figure 7.4. Names from different databases help determine relationships leading to a classification along the line of reference: synonyms, homonyms, aggregates, supersets and subsets, or other relations.

The drawback of this approach is that the concept hierarchies must be manually constructed—though only once for each domain. However, a knowledge-engineering construct could be built to help in classification, doing part of the job by establishing a taxonomy through defined attributes. Subsequently, relationships could be worked out automatically and tested by another expert system. This can be done by capitalizing on logical and structural properties of attributes, through the use of descriptors.

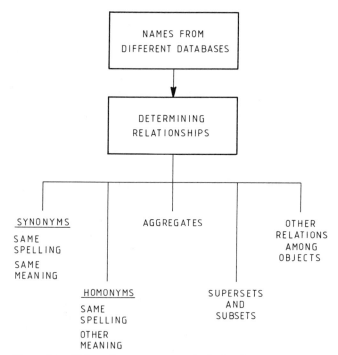

Figure 7.4   Elaborating on names and relationships among attributes.

A more powerful approach is to capture aggregate relationships between attributes. Equivalence can be elaborated on a higher level, that of an aggregate which consists of a set of attributes. There are many situations where attribute equivalence cannot really be sorted out on the basis of individual attributes, while there may be an equivalence among aggregate attributes.

A key step in automating part of this work is keyword matching with synomym dictionaries. An intelligent data dictionary, like the one we consider in Chapter 8, can be an instrumental tool and the same is true of equilibration and feedforward approaches.

They both help the researcher and/or developer to avoid committing the same type of error again. In the background of these references lies the fact that the virtual integration of views and schemata is an increasingly important part of database design. It is vital in terms of systems evolution to support complex and multiple applications sharing databases which are networked, retaining their local autonomy but subjecting them to aggregation factors.

In conclusion, view and schema integration methodologies proposed and used to date are driven almost purely by semantic considerations. They permit integration of objects, but such an approach has to be valid from both semantic and structural view points. A semantic data model can be used to:

- Help in forming global conceptual schemata which are common and globally valid in a virtual sense
- Represent the metadata embedded in a schema or schemata through a self-describing approach
- Map the metadata of local schemata as well as the mapping between local and common schemata

This approach will not automatically do away with the semantic barriers which currently exist due to differences in data models, database management systems, and supported data types. But it will ease them. Providing a way to integrative solutions is important because such differences cause difficulty in network-wide cross-database query processing, the formation of common views, as well as the execution of update operations on views which should be globally valid. For these reasons, researchers in the field tend to distinguish some key aspects in addressing semantic heterogeneity. Top of the list among them are:

- The need to know and master the prevailing semantic differences in the networked database environment.

- The ability to reason about semantics in various database activities, in a more or less homogeneous sense.

Hence, methods are required for making the semantics of each data model explicit so that it is possible to build intelligent environments which are full of meaning. In turn, these can be instrumental in our effort to manage heterogeneous databases—on which a great deal of our competitiveness in the 1990s depends.

CHAPTER 8

The Increasingly Sophisticated Data Dictionary

8.1 Introduction

A *data dictionary* (DD) system is a key computer software tool for the management of information resources. It provides facilities for recording, storing, and processing descriptions of an organization's technology investments, as well as a connection to the linkages between information elements and processes, metalevel concepts, control, and security issues.

A dictionary represents various levels of knowledge related to data and words as well as the concepts behind them. It may contain schemata, metaphors, definitions, and semantics, represented therefore in a form understood by people and computers. Relations between concepts may also be provided as metainformation, such as constraints and controls.

The basic functions of a data dictionary are developed over time, as we will see in Section 8.2. Because of these functions, its able usage can lead to simplified software development through the provision of a comprehensive and consistent documentation. DD services also help in increasing the portability of available systems skills, resulting in reduced personnel training costs.

Both data and word dictionaries are a vital part of modern databases. The existence and implementation of powerful on-line dictionary facilities is also crucial to the development of intelligent databases. Japanese researchers distinguish between three kinds of DD:

1. *Electronic word dictionaries*, each constituting a nested relation and having some hundred thousand words.
2. *Concept dictionaries* characterized by a classification hierarchy of relations with several hundred thousand concepts.

129

3. *Thesauruses* in the form of semantic networks. This is an intermediate form between a word dictionary and a concept dictionary.

The importance of computer-based dictionaries is increasing as there is a definite need for massive multimedia collections of text, data, graphics, image, voice, and other on-line information elements. Recent efforts see to it that large subsets of text are tagged and annotated with structural features and characteristics.

Just as important is the evolution of efficiency tools for text management—particularly those able to handle increasingly larger and more detailed machine-readable thesauruses of concepts and multimedia references, as well as directory assistance.

Lexical databases and knowledgebanks need to be established to serve the growing requirement of man–machine interactivity. DDs will also need to be provided with powerful tools for their on-line access, consultation, and manipulation.

Computer-based dictionaries must describe their contents in a comprehensive manner. These should be fully understandable to men and machines by the knowledge and information contained in the dictionary alone, as contrasted to conventional dictionaries for humans which often omit procedural elements.

Organizations which exploit such facilities in a steady manner have found that it is not easy to identify and implement the ideal data dictionary. At the World Bank, there is an information systems specialist who searched for the ideal DD for 10 years and still did not come up with a concrete answer.

Precisely because commercially available DDs leave much to be desired, the Japanese decided to develop an electronic dictionary from scratch, as a nationwide effort. One of the goals is to fit not only the present but also the evolving requirements which are demanding an increasing sophistication.

8.2 Evolving Nature of a Data Dictionary

While we continue to talk of *data dictionaries,* we increasingly mean *multimedia* facilities. This is no different than the use of the word *database.* The information elements which a database contains are increasingly multimedia (i.e., text, image, graphics, data, and voice) rather than just data.

In its basics, a data dictionary is a software package which helps us in defining data objects and other entities stored in our databases. At the very beginning, DD contents merely focused on directory services and data definitions, but this has expanded considerably.

Dictionaries do not depend on a specific system or algorithm, and once developed they should be applicable in many areas. Hence, they should be polyvalent and endowed with functions able to support their utilization from general purpose implementation to the creation of customized subsystems when necessary.

While the services offered by an on-line dictionary facility can be wide-ranging, the language portion itself constitutes a knowledgebank rather than a database.

- An ordinary database has some creative aspects in collecting and storing data.
- However, the ordinary database does not require intelligence embedded in an individual piece of software.
- Data is created by a mechanically simple operation though it represents an intellectual fragment.

By contrast, many items in a modern data dictionary differ greatly from this simple way of representation, being created and described by specialists who have great knowledge. However, knowledge evolves over time and this adds to a dictionary's impact and contents. As a result, a DD must be:

- Dynamically kept up to date, hence corrected
- Steadily evaluated in regard to its value
- Visualized at every request by a user entity—whether a person, computer, or program

All this must be achieved on-line with the assistance of computer-based tools. When executed in an able manner, such processes greatly enhance the quality of the database contents, leading to the characteristics of a knowledgebank.

Because the volume of modern databases can become enormous, it is necessary to establish the technology that can handle this vast, complex mass of information. A data dictionary for networked databases can be created by a limited number of people, but this impact is most significant on a great number of users.

In an environment of networked databases, the data dictionary will need to be both central—as a *corporate repository*—and distributed.

This is shown in Figure 8.1, which suggests that many users will be accessing the data dictionary facilities in reference. Among them:

• Database architects
• Database administrators
• Software developers
• A myriad of endusers

All of them should be able to access the central repository which integrates the contents of the distributed DD, plus other elements whose access is infrequent and therefore makes no sense to distribute. But there also should be linkage to the distributed DD resources which will be used most frequently by the applications programs running locally and the local DBMS themselves.

Within the now growing perspective of interactive implementation, whether they are global or local data,dictionaries are getting enriched with *metadata*—that is, data about data. They need metadata interfaced between the DBMS, distributed databases, and the runtime applications.

Metadata contents also become indispensable due to the growing workstation environments, interactive use of software, and spreading

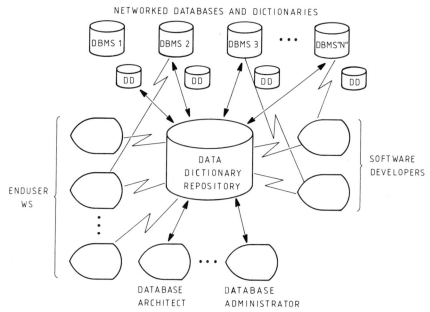

Figure 8.1 Data dictionary facilities should be both central and distributed.

access to public databases. Also promoting the utilization of metadata is the existence of incompatible networked DBMS which, by and large, lack the facilities to:

• Dynamically define changes in the information elements landscape, in a networked sense
• Aid endusers in understanding and in accessing the multimedia information they need
• Doing both functions directly and interactively during ongoing operations

Therefore, besides using the data dictionary as passive storage to capture interrelationships among schemata, information elements, and data formats, leading-edge organizations start looking toward an active role for them.

An active role for DD calls for the use of knowledge-engineering techniques together with distributed query processing. It can best be served through an object-oriented programming environment—which in turn demands an increasingly active and intelligent data dictionary.

Because of the reasons which have just been outlined, the services a data dictionary offers have grown significantly from the original directory, data definitions, and links to applications programs. A 10-fold approach to the functionality of a data dictionary can be projected in the following terms:

1. Directory services
2. Quick index and redundancy screening
3. Thesaurus of multimedia definitions
4. Concept and schema classification
5. Semantic meaning of information elements
6. Constraints, metadata, and metarules
7. Controls, range, and synchronization
8. Links to programming modules and other objects
9. Security, authorization, and authentication
10. Metalevel structure in an "any-to-any" networked databases sense

During the research which led to this text, one of the database experts commented that: "There is too much in this list of dictionary facilities. The users always want everything, but a dictionary should not try to do everything. It should be the most stripped-down item in the whole system." There is, however, no unanimous opinion regarding the point just made. To the contrary, other database experts suggested the wisdom to add at least three more items:

- Hypermedia
- Dynamic data ownership
- Version management

One database expert advised to include *timestamp* criteria. Others disagreed, saying that the timestamp is part of the schema model not of the DD. Some added that "Just to say you have a DD is not enough. You have to specify the standard in which you keep the data dictionary."

This evidently poses other problems in the sense that every major vendor has their own DD which is far from satisfying even one-third of the functionality which the majority of database experts see as necessary. Furthermore, networked dictionaries (in the sense presented in Figure 8.1) must have specific standards associated with them, different than those of the more classical stand-alone and centralized DD.

8.3 Looking at the Data Dictionary from a Systems Viewpoint

If we look at the DD from a systems viewpoint, we will see that each of the networked databases which should be served may have different requirements. Other differences grow out of the implementation work being done. While a data dictionary should be in principle applications-independent, every type of implementation poses specific needs which should serve to enrich the dictionary endowment:

- The real-time world has different DD needs than batch processing, where the dictionary plays a minor role.
- The virtual user interface calls for adding source-to-target intelligence, which is not necessarily required in other environments.
- Commercial applications require somewhat more polyvalence than scientific ones, where there is a rather consistent reference framework.

Have these perspectives been taken into account in the development of commercially available data dictionaries? The answer is negative: No software or hardware vendor has truly targeted specific markets for DD services or really tried to provide valid answers for each one of them. Yet, there is a market demand for such services.

The careful researcher of dictionary facilities which have been supported during the 1980s until today will also discover another major systems gap. Three very important issues to the able use of the data dictionary have *not* been addressed in a factual and documented manner, as should have been the case. They are:

• Integrity
• Reliability
• Timeliness

Even today, most efforts in connection with these three factors are still too sporadic and uncoordinated. All this badly serves applications with networked databases which require data dictionary assistance in, among other domains, *system catalog* tables—a sort of Bill of Materials.

In the majority of cases, every database server has differences in the information which it contains in tables, columns, and other database objects. Therefore, quite often, generic client applications that query the system catalog for metadata do not function properly in a cross-database mode unless the on-line data dictionary supports them.

What the typical user wants to do with a data dictionary is to look up a name, definition, reference, or address. But the more sophisticated user may wish to also look up a class or an instance.

In the case of *instance*, the user may wish to identify the class to which it belongs. Both the more sophisticated and the less sophisticated users need the ability to browse the DD. It is not an absolute requirement that this is in the DD itself, but a process that employs it—such as hypermedia—must be on hand.

All the outlined supporting functions must be provided in a seamless, computer-based sense. Unlike humans, computers cannot yet perform intelligent processing such as analogical inference with common-sense knowledge. The lack of imaginative capabilities at the computer side sees to it that not a single reference to information elements should be omitted in a dictionary.

One way to face this challenge is to collect as many examples as possible in the dictionary development process, extracting usage profiles from the examples that are entered into the dictionary. Also, automatically compiling and verifying dictionary contents is necessary.

If the design process is executed in a thoughtful manner, at runtime the computer will be able to extract various kinds of elements to supplement the contents of its data dictionary. For instance, through knowledge engineering it can enrich its word dictionary with:

- Unregistered words
- Statistics of word usage
- Observed co-occurrence of pairs of words, data, or concepts

Extraction can be made from examples through some intelligent mechanisms. Selected information elements can not only be used as reference to revise contents of the dictionary but also registered in the DD in the form of automatically compiled entries.

All this goes well beyond the classical view of a data dictionary whose mission is to provide both definition and description of data structures, including references to their use. This transition to current DD perspectives and requirements has been made through:

- Incremental additions and modifications made to the already contained data definitions
- The implementation of a conceptual data structure and associated functions which has been facilitated through mapping
- Richer directory services provided to help interactive users, runtime applications programs, and the DBMS

As the sophistication of the contents of the data dictionary has increased, the database has been enabled not only to contain but also to manipulate metadata about the information elements stored and retrieved during the different DD applications.

Due to its increasingly enriched features, the data dictionary has come to be viewed as a centralized repository of information. Data descriptions have gone beyond the "data" reference to include issues such as:

- Meaning
- Relationships
- Usage
- Format

Each one of these added-value contributions helps support the planning and control of the information resources at our disposal assisting in the work of both the database architect and the database administrator. It also serves to enhance the development of new applications and, as well, it is invaluable to endusers as a reference source.

8.4 The Japanese Electronic Dictionary[1]

The Japanese Electronic Dictionary Research Institute (EDR) was established in April 1986, with an initial endowment of 5 billion yen to be raised to 14 billion yen by the end of 1994. Seventy percent of the budget is contributed by the government. The other sponsors are the Japan Key Technology Center, Fujitsu, Hitachi, Matsushita, Mitsubishi, Oki, Sharp, and Toshiba.

The goal of the EDR Institute is to produce computer software: a dictionary, application programs, and a modern database structure. The latter would be the result of the outgrowth of research into systems utilizing sophisticated dictionary facilities. The institute licenses the products it produces as well as its know-how.

In a nutshell, the effort put together by the EDR Institute is shown in Figure 8.2: The electronic dictionary is seen as the prerequisite to crossing two other milestones:

• Semantics-oriented compound electronic document processing

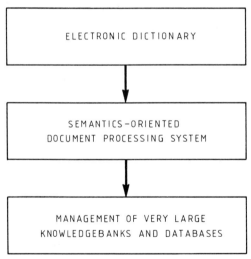

Figure 8.2 Milestones to be met by the Japanese electronic dictionary project.

[1]This and the following sections are based on a personal meeting in Tokyo with Dr. Toshio Yokoi, General Manager of EDR.

- The need to manage large knowledgebanks and very large databases

Such goals require new types of software and reusable software policies.[2] As shown in Figure 8.3, another aim to be reached through the ongoing research at EDR is semantic extraction from compound electronic documents.

Dr. Yokoi stated during our meeting that EDR has coined the term *electronic dictionary* to underline the fact that it is a dictionary on computers and for computers. All dictionary facilities being developed can be:

- Processed and recompiled by computers
- Stored on magnetic or optical media
- Adapted to diverse applications

While machine readability is a basic requirement for electronic dictionaries, this is not enough. The same is true of natural language processing. A fully integrated development support environment must be provided to achieve the performance needed in the 1990s and beyond.

Correctly, EDR works on a large scale text database able to provide references necessary to check and upgrade the whole system of net-

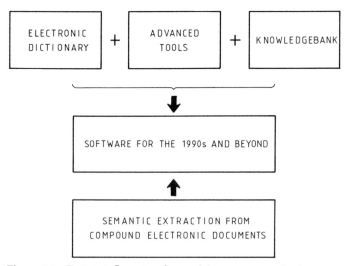

Figure 8.3   Factors influencing the need for new types of software.

[2]See also Section 8.6.

worked databases. Part and parcel of this effort is the semantic extractor from document contents, one of the pillars of the Japanese approach to the dictionary issue.

In other terms, an electronic dictionary is no more a rather mechanical version of a conventional dictionary, but a rich *knowledgebank* which contains all the *metaphors* and associated information computers require for understanding the work to be done. EDR tries to extract concepts out of large volumes of data and automatically build up conceptual networks.

One of the basic premises characterizing this effort is that the proposed extraction technique would be most effective when used for verifying conceptual networks, as well as in helping in the understanding of a number of natural languages by computers.

At the core of the approach chosen at EDR is the fact that the increasingly diversified applications to which computers are addressing themselves require a technology which enables them not only to process natural languages but to comprehend them. Solutions along this line of reference will:

- Improve the way human interfaces are made
- Expand the range of applications
- Form a basis for smooth exchange of information between people and machines, as well as among humans themselves

During the second half of the 1990s, multinatural language processing technology[3] will be at the center of both information processing and knowledge engineering. The Japanese look at natural language processing technology not as an application domain but as a basic and common background needed in many fields.

Work in process at EDR and other laboratories suggests that it should be feasible to find the meaning of words through the intelligence incorporated in a knowledge-enriched dictionary. But to do so, users (human beings or machines) need to understand word definitions. They should utilize the dictionary's examples in conjunction with their own store of accumulated knowledge. They should also interactively employ the electronic dictionary as a dual tool: for interrogation and to implant knowledge into the computer.

Since the extent of human knowledge is extremely broad and diverse, EDR set for itself the goal to develop from a linguistic standpoint a

---

[3]As opposed to shot-by-shot natural language approaches which characterized the 1980s.

common-sense database. The aim is to make a general dictionary specification, development method, and support system without being affected by specific languages and applications. The terms currently handled by the EDR project are:

- 200,000 general words in Japanese and an equal number in English
- Some 500,000 concepts derived therefrom and most useful in on-
  line exploitation

At the present time, the functions of these words are limited to those
required for correct expression and information conveyance. Further
extensions are possible.

One of the functions to be supported is automatic indexing and classification. For automatic indexing, a program parses a document, then
associates the pertinent concepts which will be exploited during the
research phase further on. In a similar manner, we can automatically
parse a query in natural language through the concepts which help in
indexing the document(s).

A primary concern in intelligent query handling is how to establish
a practical technique for semantics processing. The dictionary can play
a major role in this quest, though in regard to most queries no common
understanding may exist on theories, representation forms, or processing methods.

8.5 Word and Concept Dictionaries

Electronic dictionaries must include the meanings of words, their concepts, grammatical features, as well as knowledge that will enable computers to understand the concepts and metaphors in question. The
sense of this particular reference is not different than that supported by
metaphors for data.

The role *word dictionary* must fulfill in response to the prerequisites
just described is to handle grammatical features enabling computers to
comprehend in a semantical sense the existing syntactic structure. Part
of this requirement is the ability to map word concepts. A single word
can represent more than one concept. Frequently used words *de facto*
contain multiple concepts.

When analyzing sentences, we have to identify the concepts of words
within each sentence. That is why it is vital for electronic dictionaries
to properly describe word concepts.

Morphological, syntactic, and semantic information is an integral part of the word dictionary. *Morphological* information consists of headwords or morphemes and between-word adjacency with attributive data.

Typically, headwords are used as a stepping stone of sentence analysis for primary dictionary reference. They also assist in morphological generation in the final stage of sentence research or construction.

The first process of work done on morphological characteristics is sentence analysis. The output is used for looking up words in the dictionary, generating headwords and their adjacency thus leading to the study of sentences. The dictionary should allow the parser to dispose of all the information that can be linked to a word:

- *Morphologic,* including phonetic and conjugated forms
- *Pragmatic,* applicative-type information
- *Syntactic* and *semantic*

Syntactic information consists of grammatical features: parts of speech such as nouns, verbs, adjectives, or adverbs, and data of syntactic structure. This is governed by words and is employed in syntactic analysis to parse sentences as well as for syntactic generation.

Semantic information clarifies word meaning. Therefore, word dictionaries must contain descriptions of word concepts to be described in a simple sentence. At the EDR Institute, head concepts are used to index the concept dictionaries.

Head concepts are identifiers of each word's meaning, providing an interface to the concept dictionary. In this sense, a word dictionary will contain two levels of reference:

- Surface level information to be described independent of any specific application system or algorithm
- Deep semantic information, which is generic and stored in the concept section

Semantic information is distinguished through its representation by means of concept relations. An object orientation serves this purpose and helps in semantic manipulation. It also assists in other functions of a head concept which, as defined by EDR include:

- Symbol explanation, used to discriminate one concept from the others

- New entries in concept dictionary, as well as descriptions of concepts
- Interfaces to other sets of information to find possible equivalences

The concept dictionary can be divided into concept *descriptions* and concept *classifications* by type or relation. Both have a major role to play in terms of on-line functions.

Concept descriptions provide a variety of useful relations. Concept classifications assure a hierarchy of concepts, created to reduce the needed volume of knowledge by enabling knowledge inheritance from superconcepts to subconcepts. This process is shown in Figure 8.4.

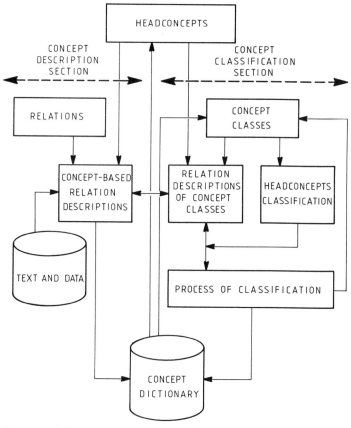

Figure 8.4   Infrastructure of a concept dictionary and its component parts.

Based on descriptive knowledge, a properly organized concept-oriented dictionary can enable computers to understand concepts that are described in word dictionaries. Concept-relation representation is created to map the internal structure of a concept. It is essentially a semantic representation which should be kept as general and flexible as possible.

The basic structure of concept relation can be mapped onto a hyper-semantic network through its nodes. A networked structure is applicable to a wide range of objects: words, sentences, paragraphs, as well as situations.

A sophisticated inference capability will further require other characteristics, some of which may seem to be controversial (for instance, sacrificing generality and flexibility).

Inference rules can be written in representation formats similar to those of adaptive logic systems. An embedded inference engine can be employed at the user's discretion in the way which best fits the actual requirements:

- Humans understand sentences based on their accumulated knowledge.
- Computers require knowledge for sentence comprehension stored in a concept dictionary.

The definitions of concepts contained as descriptions in the knowledgebank must also deal with links and relationships between concepts. This is necessary inasmuch as concepts are often defined by their reference or relationship to other concepts.

Valuable assistance can be rendered by a concept hierarchy in which descriptions can be deduced by an inheritance mechanism. In such a hierarchy, a concept is represented by a set of properties with a property reflecting relations between concepts.

Concept categories can be extracted by examining the differences among sets of concept descriptions between nouns and verbs. Concept relations among the concept categories must be defined within a designed framework, in which a set of properties shared by some concept categories are located as their superconcepts.

The results need to be analyzed, with corresponding hierarchy and relations easy to modify on the basis of requirements presented by an ongoing application, as they develop. This means the ability to handle *ephemeral* hierarchies, created and dropped in a dynamic sense—the way object-oriented systems work.

An ephemeral hierarchy can be enriched through experience. Concept categories can be selected to group elements which share the same properties. Head concepts can be defined and classified, the same being true of concept properties and prevailing relations among them. Thus a hierarchy can be constructed above the concept categories based on:

- The relations of properties
- Their definition
- The results of their classification

In conclusion, we have to think of tomorrow's data and word dictionaries as well as their requirements as being in full evolution. The foremost developments are interdisciplinary, precisely the way large networked databases are developing. Therefore, we need an increasing amount of knowledge engineering support, as underlined throughout this chapter.

8.6 Placing Emphasis on Reusable Software

We have spoken about the importance Japanese researchers are placing on *reusable software*. This preoccupation finds its counterpart in America. We have to implement reusable software policies since the future of the services we derive from computers and communications depends on them; but there are prerequisites to be met.

One of the basic requirements is to assure that the range of facilities provided by a data dictionary can be used throughout the software life cycle. Programming languages make use of the data dictionary as a software development tool.

- Procedural language programmers can interface their code and also extract file, record, and database descriptions.
- Logic programmers can use dictionary facilities to maintain order in program development and execution.
- Users can address the DD for control reasons, e.g., to assure that they enter the correct number of arguments or for authorization purposes to information access.

The concept of metadata is implicit to all three of these references. The description of how an object, or its method, can be used is similar to the concept of how an information element can be employed by referencing its metadata.

Through the appropriate facilities, semantic information can be added to support a user interface by extracting metadata. This can be instrumental in terms of how:

- Queries are constructed
- Retrieval is made
- Consistency checking takes place

The use of metadata provides a powerful tool for reusable software purposes. This is particularly true when metadata is stored in the DD and used in a proactive manner, controlling roles and driving all the interactions among the various system components as well as those between the system and the outside world.

If the reusable software goal is seen in a network-wide sense as it should be, then another dictionary service to be provided is between different parts of a network or among independent interconnected networks. Such a facility can also be instrumental in interfacing multiple databases.

What the more forward thinking systems architects would like to have is a metalanguage able to represent dictionary information that could be translated into whatever usage comes along. We do not have available today valid tools for that sort of metarepresentation in data dictionaries that will be common to different classes of utilization, but some research projects aim to make it feasible.

In other terms, metarepresentation is a problem which is beginning to be seriously addressed at least at laboratory level. From an applications viewpoint in concurrent engineering, for example, systems designers would like to have:

1. The ability to handle multiframeworks and their anomalies

The leading thinking is that such solutions must include implicit and explicit methodologies, incorporating structural ways of dealing with frame progression.

2. Flexible extension capabilities, not just design extensibility but also semantics

This is necessary to help users to semantically generate schemas, including the ability to capture the sense of data with full meaning.

3. Management and housekeeping of the distributed repository facility

Under item number 3 comes a whole range of issues. One of the less intricate of these is how to deal with the *least common denominator*. The more intricate include the possibility (or impossibility) of reverse engineering, deductive and inductive extensions, as well as providing for co-existence of different schemata and methodologies.

An object-oriented environment can help in reaching such goals but we must recall that there are presently no available clean methods on how to deal with complex networked database systems and their data dictionaries. Yet without such facilities we will not be able to face the oncoming challenges in information technology.

Systems experts with experience in this domain suggest the need to address *process* models and not only the *data* models. What is intended by this approach is to assist in:

- Engineering different views advanced by a variety of users
- Taking account of user profiles, through expert systems
- Modeling user profiles and making them available for network-wide use

All this is way ahead of the more classical manner in which networked databases and their data dictionaries are approached today. But if we wish to develop newer and better systems, we have to think of more advanced solutions—always reflecting on the impact and implications of the oncoming changes on the investments already made and the further work to be done.

CHAPTER 9

Information Resource Dictionary System (IRDS)

9.1 Introduction

The National Institute of Standards and Technology (NIST) originally adopted the Information Resource Dictionary System (IRDS) of the American National Standard Institute (ANSI) as a Federal Information Processing Standard (FIPS PUB 156). Subsequently, as the designers themselves were not satisfied with the first set of norms, a new effort done at NIST, ANSI, and ECMA[1] led to NIST Special Publication 500–201, whose object is generally known as IRDS II. This publication:

- Specifies computer software providing facilities for recording, storing, and processing descriptions
- Focuses on resources significant to an organization in terms of information elements and data processing routines concerned with such descriptions

Though ANSI X3H4 and the NIST used different titles (respectively, "Information Resource Dictionary System" and "Federal Information Processing Standard for Data Dictionary Systems"), the two groups practically have identical goals and a similar development approach. ISO has also been involved in this effort.

The specifications of *IRDS II* are currently under development. They are object-oriented and based on the following components:

1. EIA/CDIF (CASE database interchange format) by the Electronics Industry Association[2]

[1]European Computer Manufacturers Association (ECMA), of which most American computer vendors are members.

[2]Notice that the information technology industry is recently characterized by a new confusion. The terms *CASE Database*, *Development Database*, and *Repository*, are more or less synonymous—the latter being the term preferred in marketing. They all presuppose a first class data dictionary, and tend to merge with dictionary concepts.

2. PCTE (Portable Common Tool Environment) by ECMA, an object construct
3. ATIS (A Tool Integration System) by DEC, also object-based
4. AD/Cycle and RM/MVS by IBM

Numbers 1, 2, and 3 are the main inputs. In the background there is also the original IRDS already approved by ISO, but in all likelihood this will change to IRDS II when it becomes available.

As far as IRDS II is concerned, its syntax is based on static semantics. The next goal is dynamic semantics as well as state transition. Connection between the different lower-level models being supported is done through a metamodel and meta-metamodel—with knowledge engineering entering the standardization business. The three information models followed by IRDS II are:

• Entity-relation (ER)
• Data flow diagram (DFD)
• "Core"—including text and document handling

It is quite proper, however, to underline that the proposed norms of IRDS II are not yet completed and therefore are still far from being accepted as American and international standards. Only conceptually can they be discussed in a meaningful sense, and this is the goal of the present chapter.

9.2 A Reference Model That Might Become Repository Norm

Along the line of data dictionary concepts which have been outlined in the preceding chapter, the ANSI/NIST normalization effort primarily addresses the functions performed by data dictionaries. By contrast, ECMA leans toward CASE tools.

Let's start by underlining that at this stage IRDS[3] is *not* an information repository in the sense of an enhanced data dictionary productized[4]

---

[3]From this point onward, the reference will be to the IRDS effort at large rather than distinguishing the fine print between IRDS I and IRDS II, which would be senseless since the IRDS II effort is still in process.

[4]The term *productization* had been introduced into computer literature a couple of years ago. It means that a certain concept, norm, or standard is not just explained on paper but it has been endowed with necessary supports (usually software) to be *turned into a product*.

with software support. Rather, it is a methodology which data dictionaries and CASE tools would be expected to follow in terms of addressing:

- Elements, records, file definitions, tables, columns, and index definitions
- Modules, from programming routines to larger software applications
- User-oriented issues and organizational facilities, including location definitions

This makes IRDS an all-inclusive approach to the standardization of different systems methodologies. Another aim is to take a shot at the normalization of plans regarding information strategies, rules, policies, processes, and products in relation to computer handling requirements.

ECMA created the Reference Model for CASE Environment Frameworks, also referred to as the ECMA Reference Model. Shown in Figure 9.1, it constitutes a recommendation for the set of services required to support a CASE environment, describing features each service set provides. For instance:

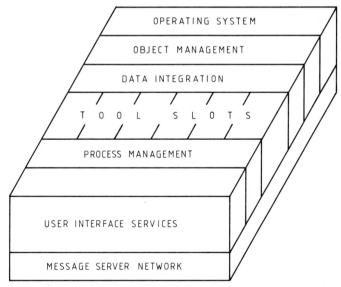

Figure 9.1   The ECMA reference model—for what it may be worth.

- Data repository services, such as object storage and naming
- Data integration services, like version and configuration

The ECMA Portable Common Tool Environment norms describe a set of services and their interfaces aiming to provide an infrastructure for tools environments, particularly those supporting systems engineering projects. PCTE includes an Object Management System (OMS) that serves as the repository of the information used by the tools.

Another characteristic of PCTE is the description of schema management services to build and administer an information model for the repository. The PCTE information model can be tailored for individual tools. Such tailoring enables each tool version to map its own information model into the global model.

Object management system contributions have been provided by the Object Management Group (OMG). This is a consortium of software vendors with a shared goal of developing and using integrated software services employing object-oriented technology.

The CASE Data Interchange Format technical committee of the Electronic Industries Association (EIA)—which has representatives from third-party software and hardware vendors, users, and academia—advanced norms to permit interchange of CASE models and information among tools. CDIF supports the exchange of semantic information and presentation chores and provides an extensive framework which permits design of flexible systems.

For its part, ANSI has created standards specific to IRDS and continues to work on these standards.[5] ANSI is currently elaborating on the next version of the norms, referred to as ANSI IRDS II.

Digital Equipment's A Tools Integration System proposal to the ANSI X3H4 committee is looked on as a possible standard for the services interface in IRDS II. This proposal led to the decision that ATIS will serve as a foundation for services interface. However, the ANSI committee is evaluating needed changes before the interface in reference (of the IRDS standard) is approved.

The ATIS proposal describes the services interface of an object-oriented repository in terms of both functionality and the basic information model. As a foundation for the services interface of the IRDS standard, ATIS is relevant to aspects of the information model regarding certain repository functionalities like versioning.[6]

---

[5]See ANSI X3.138 Information Resource Dictionary System Standard and ANSI X3H4 Information Resource Dictionary System Requirements Document.

[6]Explained in Section 9.5.

ISO has created standards specific to an Information Resources Dictionary System.[7] For this work, it adopted the ANSI X3H4 IRDS reference model whose matrix depicts a layered partitioning of functions, interfaces, and services of an environment.

The ISO reference model is intended to describe IRDS technology used to manage the information resources in support of the engineering, operation, and management of heterogeneous databases. The associated norms specify a software aggregate that can be used to describe and potentially control the information resources of an enterprise.

The ISO model defines the structure and, to some extent, the contents of the information to be maintained in the IRDS. It also elaborates on the services to be provided for maintaining and retrieving information from the repository.

Among the original FIPS PUB 156 primary objectives had been that of improving identification of existing (rather than only future) valuable information resources which have to be shared. At the same time, the IRDS effort aims to simplify the conversion of software and data as well as to increase the portability of acquired skills.

But over a period of time, as the number of different contributors multiplied, so did the norms being brought forward. Ironically, there is at this moment no true grand design accepted by all standards institutes. To the contrary, there are too many of both of them (institutes and designs). Yet the effort is not totally fruitless.

The furthermost goal of all these efforts is that of making possible the correlation of all information resources in a normalized, vendor-independent *open information system* with a data dictionary being the focal point. The intentions are indeed noble, but the diversity which is included—not to mention confusion between many standards—does not really answer universal homogeneity requirements.

To properly appreciate the work currently being done and the difficulties it encounters, it is important to keep in mind that no methodology, including IRDS, is performing miracles. It is up to the user organization to face its responsibilities and proceed with the:

- Standardization of its information elements, records, reports, and forms

[7]See ISO Information Resource Dictionary System Framework; ANSI X3H4 Information Resource Dictionary System Reference Model; and ISO Information Resource Dictionary System Services Interface.

- Elaboration of needed schema and subschema definitions for sound database management

A user organization may set up and organize one or more information resource dictionaries. What IRDS may eventually provide is the methodology for facilities required in doing so. That will be helpful in maintaining an association between dictionary objects and the organization of the corporate data dictionary, which constitutes the kernel of the IRDS schema.

9.3 Basic Notions about IRDS

Among the basic goals of the IRDS effort is an improved way to assure the proper identification of existing, valuable information resources that can be shared within the same organization or, for that matter, with other organizations. At NIST and ANSI, a well-structured data dictionary is correctly seen as also being instrumental in a policy of reusable software.

American and Japanese efforts in the development of a new generation of DD have at least this in common. They do their best to provide powerful tools which can be instrumental in reducing unnecessary development of computer programs when suitable modules already exist in the company's applications library.

Though the methodology standard advanced by ANSI/NIST does not require an organization to use a dictionary system in a precisely prescribed manner, IRDS concepts can be employed to:

- Aid development, modification, and maintenance of manual and automated software production all the way through its life cycle
- Support a normalization program for information elements defined by an organization for its own use
- Streamline files, records, reports, and forms management in a whole range of applications— from nonautomated to fully automated environments

This is accomplished by providing a common framework and terminology able to specify required dictionary capabilities. Another facet of the same effort is that of helping to evaluate different vendor offerings.

In developing the specifications for an IRDS standard, recognition was correctly given to the fact that dictionary technology is evolving and that its use is expanding. Hence, the developers adopted a modular approach, including specifications for:

1. A kernel dictionary functionality containing two user interfaces: one of a menu-panel nature; the other featuring a common language interface
2. Five additional modules presently available
3. The possibility of more modules to come[8]

Taken together, the six initial components of IRDS constitute the base-level standard for which the outlined two-tier approach has been adopted. The kernel specifications are intended for implementation on the more powerful microprocessors available today (such as RISC and i846), as well as upwards from these.

The defined five functional modules interface with the kernel and can act in unison or independently from one another. Hence, a user organization can choose which one to acquire to fit its ongoing needs. Contained in the five modules in reference are specs for:

- A starter set of dictionary data structures
- An IRDS-defined security facility
- Procedural definition for IRDS commands
- Functions supporting an organization's life-cycle management methodology
- Application program interfaces along the evolving API standard

A basic (or standard) and an extended mode of operation constitute the two alternatives for an IRDS component. This distinction is necessary because the basic mode allows no extensions or modifications to IRDS functionality. In contrast, under the extended mode IRDS accepts additions to its functionality.

The user organization has an option to operate in standard mode or provide extensions, but it must use the IRDS standard command language and a panel interface. The latter is designed to support interactive processing, particularly for inexperienced users, specified in terms of entities, relationships, and attributes.

- An IRDS entity represents and/or describes a real-world concept, person, event, or quantity.
- Such an entity is not the information elements actually existing in a database.
- A relationship is an association between two or more IRDS entities.
- Attributes represent properties of an entity or relationship.

[8]X3H4 and ISO TC97/SC21/WG3 are developing three additional modules and some more are under consideration.

A key concept of IRDS is *type*. Attributes of a specific type typically apply to some of the entities, accounting for the fact that, in the general case, different attributes have different meanings. The concept of type is also applicable to relationships.

Relationships can have attributes as well. There exist ordered sets of attributes known as attribute groups. Entities, relationships, attributes, and attribute groups are referred to as the *instance* of the respective type—basically an object-oriented concept.

Relationships in IRDS are binary, denoting an association existing between two entities. The reason for this choice is that the vast majority of current implementations use binary relationships which, besides everything else, are simple enough. It remains to be seen whether this will hold in the future.

As a standard, IRDS does not dictate a specific implementation approach. While users see entities, relationships, and attributes, the model of a database can be object-oriented, relational, Codasyl, or other types of DBMS. A similar reference can be made to the nature of software implementation, which more or less is left up to the user organization.

9.4 A Four-Layered Approach to IRDS Architecture

One of the goals of the IRDS normalization effort has been to guarantee performance of operations across databases without being hampered by the constraints of proprietary data dictionaries. To serve this purpose, the work along the lines of standardizing information elements as far as possible started at the level of NAMING facilities.

LINKS were the next issue being addressed. The IRDS dictionary can be set up to include cross-references to applications, with information elements, forms, and records not only standardized but also cross-referenced. This means the ability to initiate and sustain:

• Definition and enforcement of business policies on data—such as classification of value to the organization
• The concept of an *IRDS schema* as a critical reference to the whole implementation of a dictionary facility

Figure 9.2 shows a four-layered structure focused on the IRDS schema. It demonstrates the relationship between IRDS processes and IRDS data. It also illustrates the ANSI/NIST standard's self-describing nature as well as the utility of using the same descriptive technique for both IRDS and its schemata.

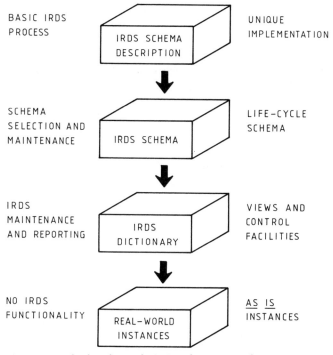

Figure 9.2 The four-layered IRDS architecture and its characteristic features.

The chosen structure of IRDS sees to it that where entities, relationships, attributes, and attribute groups exist, an IRDS schema will contain the corresponding:

• Entity type
• Relationship type
• Attribute type
• Attribute group type

These types are organized into the minimal common denominator schema of Module 1 and the *basic functional schema* of Module 2. Both will be discussed in subsequent paragraphs.

As already mentioned, a user organization can add additional entity types, relationship types, attribute types, and attribute group types to satisfy its particular requirements. IRDS specifications include facilities that enable the user organization to extend and customize the minimal schema and basic functional schema in a way dictated by its requirements.

According to NIST and ANSI, such an extended approach provides the needed mechanism to define and develop additional IRDS functions and control procedures. This is quite important when developing new applications within a networked database environment. Typically:

1. *Data entity* types will include documents, files, records, and other information elements.

Documents will contain instances of data collections readable by humans. Files may describe instances of an organization's data collections. Records address themselves to logically associated information elements that belong to an organization, as well as instances of data belonging to that organization.

2. *Process entity* types will be organized into system, program, module, and user entity.

The system entity describes instances of collectioning processes and data. The program entity addresses instances of automated processes that must either be logical subdivisions of program entities or independent processes called by program entities.

User entities can address issues connected to individuals or organizational components. A collection of relationship types provided by the basic functional schema collection includes virtually all the connections between basic functional entity types that might prove useful to most organizations most of the time.

The majority of these relationship types are grouped into relationship class types. Here again the basic concepts reflect thinking along object-oriented lines with inheritance, metalevel functionality, and runtime instantiation.

In an implementation sense, a software package conforming to the IRDS specifications includes the minimal schema and other descriptors which are necessary to establish controls over and ensure the integrity of the IRDS schema. The contents of the schema description layer are outlined in Figure 9.3.

It is important to keep in perspective that Module 2 of IRDS supports intra- and interorganization communication about information resources. It also defines a starter set of IRDS entity types, relationship types, and attribute types reflecting agreements reached by members of X3H4 and attendees at user workshops sponsored by NIST.

METAENTITY TYPES	ENTITY TYPES	RELATIONSHIP TYPES	ATTRIBUTE TYPES	ATTRIBUTE-GROUP TYPES

Figure 9.3 Schema description layer of the information resource dictionary system (IRDS).

Since it is not feasible to identify all entity types, relationship types, and attribute types that might be useful, a user organization can augment the basic functional schema using facilities connected to the aforementioned IRDS extensibility features. Organizations that have networked databases may want to add additional entity types to the basic functional schema. The same is true of organizations currently facing data conversion and migration problems.

Data conversion and migration is challenging because of the lack of appropriate documentation and the need to know the impact of change on business users, functions, applications, and databases. We need appropriate tools to help standardize and document the current configurations and the interdependencies between business functions and information resources.

In the case of IRDS, cross-reference analysis can be of help in studying the impact of changes prior to being committed to them. IRDS can also be of assistance in software design and development by providing a standard dictionary facility for access by different media:

- Tools at the same design level
- A variety of downstream tools

One of the projected benefits is the ability to use names for design objects, employing the organization's standards to be developed rather than parochial naming facilities. This is an important subject to many user organizations, as ANSI/NIST have found out and the following section documents.

9.5 Handling Entity Names

To ease the task of network-wide name handling, IRDS contains a generalized facility enabling users to assign different kinds of names to an entity. These different names may serve distinct purposes and conventions exist regarding their issue as well as their coordination. Such conventions are served by a distinction made between access names descriptive names, and alternative names.

It is important to perceive the conceptual difference prevailing between these three classes in order to understand the IRDS effort as a whole. Most important for an entity is its *access name*.[9]

The access name acts as a given entity's primary identifier on which the structure of most commands and panels is based. In many cases, it also serves as a means for saving time and reducing the potential for error. An access name has two parts: assigned access name and version identifier.

In current practice, most often a user is responsible for specifying the assigned access name of an entity. A better option is to have IRDS generate it through a standard algorithm.

This automatic generation facilitates cross-database handling by allowing a user to enter new entities into IRDS through a system-generated name option. This may even be a temporary name to be waived once the correct names of the entities are known. After this is done, the user can modify the system-generated access names and then move the entities by employing functions available in the interface facility.

Terse access names, NIST and ANSI suggest, have the disadvantage of not conveying the meaning of the object represented by the entity. Hence, terseness can cause problems, particularly in dealing with non-technical users, that is, managers and professionals unfamiliar with the contents of a database.

A parallel classification–identification scheme helps in relieving this constraint by reflecting on known families, groups, and classes—as well as on basic codes. This way, it permits us to build scenarios of business strategies, missions, processes, products, and services within a context of networked databases. A methodology that is very specific to the organization can thus be used without being encumbered by predefined business planning software by "this" or "that" vendor.

Alternatively, IRDS allows users to assign a *descriptive name* to an entity. This will typically be longer and more meaningful than the access name. The structure of the descriptive name is the same as that of the access name, but for semantic purposes there is also an assigned version identifier.

Versioning is an important consideration in modern database management and is also a concept being used with object-oriented approaches.

---

[9]This serves as a *basic code*. See also D.N. Chorafas *Handbook of Databases and Relational DBMS*, McGraw-Hill/TAB, New York, 1989.

As the real-world object changes, the corresponding entity will have to be altered as well.

The kernel of IRDS functionality makes it feasible for a user to track such changes by revision numbers. These represent the chronology of the entity and hence the chronology of the object the entity describes.

- The highest revision number corresponds to the most recent version of the entity.
- Each revision is stored as a distinct entity in IRDS repository.

A related concept is the desirability of identifying *multiple variations* of an entity. Variations are denoted by a variation name, creating a specific string that must begin with an alphabetic character. One of the facilities provided by IRDS helps in controlling valid variation names for each entity type.

As the foregoing paragraphs demonstrate, so far the handling of entity names by IRDS has been rather straightforward. There are, however, clauses which make difficult, if not outright impossible, the implementation of this methodology in an environment of distributed heterogeneous databases. For example, for the normalization process to hold, access names and descriptive names must be unique throughout an IRDS implementation. But particular features characterizing "this" or "that" DBMS could make the application of such a principle difficult, if not outright impossible.

Therefore, the uniqueness of access names and descriptive names has been one of the most debated features. Plenty of arguments have been made in both ways.

During the development of IRDS specifications, for instance, members of Technical Committee X3H4 and attendees at a user workshop sponsored by NIST voted for name uniqueness throughout an entire IRDS. This contrasted to name uniqueness only within a given entity type as some technical specialists had suggested. The choice which has been made means that a user cannot, for example, have a FILE entity with an access name "Inventory" and a RECORD entity also called "Inventory."

One of the main reasons for this choice is that uniqueness of assigned access names and assigned descriptive names in the context of networked databases simplifies the command language and panel interfaces.

This is of significant advantage in architecturing the distributed database structure and in its subsequent operation, but it poses other problems. The unique name choice increases the challenges during the actual creation of new entities. To face this problem, IRDS incorporates clauses which permit us to immediately recognize the type of every entity whose name is included in a command or panel.

Thanks to this facility, the user is not repeatedly forced to be specific on an entity's type. However, the leeway was left so that organizations that want to use assigned access names or descriptive names that are unique only within an entity type could adopt their own, to employ self-naming conventions.

While such an approach makes sense, the problem arises that editing entity names in huge distributed databases is no easy matter. Neither is the currently prevailing design of files, records, and other information elements able to accommodate one or more extra characters. This can mean significant manual interventions.

Other IRDS features are relatively easy to handle, in addition to the assigned access name and the descriptive name of an entity. By applying the basic functional schema, a user may specify alternative names for a given entity. This permits the handling of the difficult problem of synonyms and aliases.

9.6 Customizing and Maintaining IRDS

A number of facilities, over and above what has been described so far, have been projected to create and delete entities and relationships in IRDS. Existing entities and relationships can also be modified by changing their attributes.

Users can modify assigned access names and descriptive names as well as copy an entity to create a new entity. This new entity will have the same attributes as the original one, including relationships with the same entities to which the original entity was related.

- Versioning approaches can be used to distinguish between the copies.
- A general output function helps in producing reports and preparing query responses on specified IRDS entities.
- The same approach permits the handling of relationships and their associated attributes.

The precise format of IRDS reports can be defined by implementors. The standard describes facilities that enable users to specify, among other issues, the:

- Contents of a query or report, including the entities, attributes, and relationships that should appear
- Kinds of names to be displayed on a request basis by IRDS users
- Sequence(s) of information elements in the networked database, at origin as well as destination

Such customization capability enables IRDS users to vary the contents of a report, depending on its intended employment. This makes the approach flexible enough and fit for on-line queries.

An entity list can be named and will remain available to the user who created it for the duration of an IRDS session. If an entity list is not named by the user, it will become so by default. A current unnamed list is retained until:

- Another unnamed list is created
- The latter overwrites the old list
- The current list is named
- The IRDS session ends

For every entity, relationship, attribute, as well as attribute group that can exist in IRDS, the schema will contain a description of the corresponding entity type, and so on. The IRDS schema itself is also described in terms of entities, relationships, and attributes.

Because of the potential for misunderstanding that could occur in discussions on the IRDS schema versus IRDS itself, similar yet distinct terminologies for schema and system are used in the specifications. Typically, the IRDS schema contains:

- Entities called *metaentities*
- Relationships between metaentities specified as *metarelationships*
- Attributes known as *metaattributes*
- Attribute groups, called *metaattribute groups*

A user can investigate as well report on the contents of an IRDS schema. The output's format can be tailored by specifying the metaentities that should be displayed by name or type, as well as metaattributes and metarelationships to be displayed in connection to metaentities.

ANSI/NIST procedures foresee that user organizations can build an IRDS Dictionary that documents and manages their network of computers, databases, local area networks, wide area networks, modems, terminals, and cabling plant. They can employ primitives to relate each of these elements to their business as they see fit.

Solutions can be made to account for applications software, systems software, and specific users' requests. The impact of change scenarios can be analyzed by employing some of the facilities embedded in IRDS. For maintenance purposes, for instance, the system's kernel contains facilities that are important in reporting on contents:

- Versioning
- Life-cycle phases
- Quality indicators
- IRDS views
- Security

We have spoken of versioning. The notion of IRDS *life-cycle phases* has been introduced to support the methodology which a given organization employs. The user can document in IRDS the life-cycle phase in which, for instance, a given entity exists.

An extensible life-cycle phase module extends the corresponding facilities of the kernel IRDS by implementing integrity rules and customization features needed to control the movement of entities through the life cycle. The structure of the life cycle itself can be adapted to match the preferred methodology of an organization.

Life-cycle partitioning helps in maintaining a set of compartments within the dictionary, thus separating objects being controlled from those that can be modified freely. It also provides facilities for moving objects from one partition to another.

Quality indicators are an important concept promoted for reasons of both software robustness and software portability. Quality indicators can help system developers and users in learning to think globally in a sense of networked databases and cross-system software usage.

However, there may be many overlapping *IRDS views* acting as windows into a given life-cycle phase. Entities in such a life-cycle phase may appear in several IRDS views. For example, the phase supporting requirements analysis may include multiple IRD views for one or more project teams. However, the norms specify that all entities in a designated view must be in the same life-cycle phase.

The IRDS *security* module defines an access control facility that allows organizations to restrict access to schema, schema content, and functionality. Such facility supports two levels of access control.

The global entity level is based on functionality, type, and view. Access can be controlled at the global entity level, for instance, by granting read-only permission to access IRDS or a given schema which it contains.

A finer grained entity level security controls access to individual entities. This feature operates as an additional layer of security beyond the global security perspective:

- An organization using fine-grained entity level security can assign IRDS users READ and/or WRITE privileges for specific entities.
- For users not having the appropriate READ permission, for instance, any entity with the additional security is treated as though it does not exist in the view in which the user is working.
- For users having READ but not WRITE permission, secured entities can be examined but not modified or deleted.

Finally, an application program interface provides linkages through which commands and resulting output can be passed between the IRDS and programming languages that have a CALL feature. IRDS can also be treated by the user-developed application as a subroutine.

9.7 Adding to IRDS Capabilities

The data dictionary methodology which we have examined seems sound enough and therefore worthy of detailed study. There are, however, two reservations which need to be made in the sense of the foregoing positive statement.

The first reservation is tooled around the difference which exists between a DD definition (as well as its corresponding prescribed methodology) and its *productization* into a functioning data dictionary. IRDS is a methodology normalized by the standards bodies, but it is not yet productized. Hence it is not available in the market as commodity software.

There may be many claims by this or that vendor that their products conform to IRDS, but these cannot be taken at face value. We have the experience with false claims from the ISO/OSI model.

Among the funny claims being made in this connection, for instance, is one by the company marketing a repository product which it advertises as "IRDS-compliant." This company suggests that the wares it peddles are an *open architecture* which conforms to IBM's AD/CYCLE mainframe repository as well as to IBM's SAA and CUA guidelines. It would be difficult to find an approach more "open" than that.[10]

---

[10]False claims and even ridiculous ones are nothing new in information technology. Hence, one has to be very, very careful.

The other shortcoming of IRDS lies in the absence of projected facilities and associated methodology for the handling of compound electronic documents. Yet, this is an area of great importance for the 1990s and beyond.

There is need for a document-oriented dictionary management system subdivided into development support and operations. This should not only consist of specifications but should also include basic software, setting the stage for subsequent practical use.

Such a system should be particularly addressed to high-performance workstations as well as networked, large-capacity databases. It should feature truly sophisticated software with programs tooled toward a document-oriented dictionary development—including verification and operation.

Figure 9.4 presents an approach to this challenging issue based on the extension of current studies in connection to the development, testing, and operation of a word dictionary. While emphasis is placed on feedback at the top of the graph, just as important is an evaluation module to help estimate the way a document dictionary will help users in:

* Processing a significant range of applications
* Testing the document dictionary's utility and completeness as a product

Document dictionaries will be particularly important for intelligent systems, featuring machine readable masters with hundreds of thousands of entities per application. An integral part of an able solution is a *concept classification* facility with a general thesaurus as well as advanced software for concept description.

A knowledgebank, for instance, can contain semantic descriptors of hundreds of thousands of concepts. Another basic ingredient is an object-oriented deductive database.

In Japan, for example, both the Electronic Dictionary Research (EDR) Institute and the New Generation Computer Project Institute (ICOT) believe that deductive databases are the most stable mechanism available so far for knowledgebank development. They also postulate that the best way to start from the document processing end is by:

* Extracting knowledge from on-line documents step-by-step, including words and pictures—whatever comes into natural language.

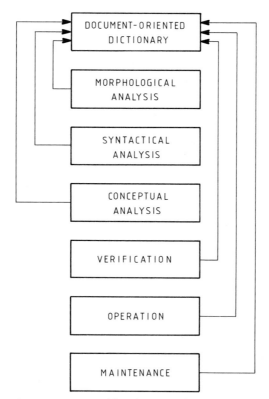

Figure 9.4 A possible solution to the
development and operation of a document-
oriented dictionary.

• Using the natural language approach as the fundamental
  mechanism for full document understanding.

Such work requires a large, sophisticated as well as high-quality electronic dictionary. This is the domain where EDR addresses its efforts
the way we have seen in the preceding chapter.

"One of the challenges," Dr. Yokoi[11] was to underline, "is the extraction process needed to understand document content and semantics."
ISO's Open Document Architecture (ODA) works well with simple documents, but complex documents require much more in terms of what
needs to be embedded in the knowledgebank.

[11]General manager of EDR.

To help provide the methodology and procedures necessary for document understanding, EDR evaluates memory-based reasoning (MBR).[12] It considers MBR as a very important concept available to the document dictionary domain. Some aspects of MBR are used in Japan in connection with case-based reasoning. It is, however, important to underline that the knowledge in a dictionary is *not episodic*; it is basically a semantic memory and hence the need for an extended semantic network approach.

In connection to the document-oriented work being described, EDR is currently busy in developing an editor and tools for document dictionary purposes. The editor is based on *hypermedia*. The maintenance system, also under development, is enriched with knowledge engineering and its utilities include a dictionary converter.

EDR's development is an intelligence-enriched converter able to apply itself to grammatical information as well as syntactic theory support. Knowledge engineering routines embedded in the converter help in restructuring syntactic theory according to user's choice.

The message to be retained from this discussion is that electronic document dictionaries are still at laboratory level, but ongoing work is expected to give tangible results. The specifications under development for the IRDS dictionary methodology will do well not only to account for the document-oriented work in reference but also to incorporate it in a normalized sense.

---

[12]See D.N. Chorafas and H. Steinmann *Supercomputers*, McGraw-Hill, New York, 1990.

CHAPTER 10

ANSI SQL and the SQL Access Group

10.1 Introduction

In the mid-1980s the American National Standards Institute (ANSI) and the International Standards Organization (ISO) began taking steps toward resolving some database heterogeneity problems. The chosen approach was to adopt a standard able to make the languages and formats of database communications as compatible as possible.

- The Structured Query Language (SQL) was chosen as the format used by applications to retrieve data from databases.
- This choice rested on the premise that with SQL, applications could be written which were able to access data in multiple databases, in a multivendor environment.

But then, reasonably quickly, two things were discovered: The productization effort was missing; and SQL as it stood could *not* respond to the new interactive, *ad hoc* cross-database access needs—nor to transaction handling, project orientation, the growing graphics requirements, and multimedia.

As a result of the first challenge, a consortium called *SQL Access Group* (SAG) was founded in 1989 as a nonprofit corporation.[1] Its membership is open to all parties as either producers, reviewers, or users of database access technology.[2] SAG currently has 42 members.

The second challenge led to the development of new SQL standards which were not necessarily compatible with the original SQL which is now being referred to as SQL1:

[1] By leading hardware and software vendors, as well as user organizations working on the interoperability and portability of SQL-oriented applications.

[2] Though only DuPont has been, as a user organization, among the early sponsors of the SQL Access Group and its Access Technical Specification.

167

- *SQL2* addresses itself to transactions which are not supported by the original SQL version.
- *SQL3* extends the SQL2 transactional characteristics and handles triggers, graphics, multimedia, and object-oriented constructs.

SQL2 and SQL3 are worked out by ANSI and will be productized by SAG. There are also a number of other SQL efforts, such as SQLX for user-friendly handling, OSQL for object orientation, the recent distinction between dynamic and static SQL, and so on.

There seems to be no way to stop the proliferation of incompatible SQL versions, and this evidently does away with the benefits of a standard.[3] But at the same time it is true that the original SQL has aged. It is too restrictive and in no way responds to current and coming requirements.

10.2 A Family of SQL Standards

We said that agreeing on a given standard is one thing; making it available to users is another. The goal of the SQL Access Group (the abbreviation to the acronym SAG is rather unfortunate) is to productize ANSI SQL versions as they develop:

- SQL1 started with the 1986–1987 agreement (SQL87) and w revamped in 1989 (SQL89)
- SQL2, also known as SQL92, as stated, incorporates transaction processing
- SQL3 is in the process of normalization by ANSI and ISO and may be available in 1995

Designed in a flexible manner, the remote data access (RDA) norms elaborated by ISO and productized by the SQL Access Group describe which variants of SQL must be used throughout a distributed environment. But we already said that while the original intent was to have one common SQL dialect throughout the system, variants have been specified, such as SQL87, SQL89, and entry-level SQL2.

This, ANSI and ISO suggest, was necessary because SQL89 improved upon SQL87 but neither of them addressed transactions, objects, and graphics. As a result, in an implementation sense, the level of SQL has

---

[3]Regarding the history of SQL, IBM made available the commercial version in 1979. The first SQL standard by ANSI was published in 1986–1987.

to be negotiated at the time the application dialogue is created. So much for international norms.

Of course, all versions of the Structured Query Language specify data definition, data manipulation, and integrity checking. They also identify components supporting access control and programming language interfaces. *Data definition* includes declaring the name of tables, data types, and constraints and granting table manipulation privileges to database users.

Data manipulation operations may be invoked through query specification or by means of a cursor. SQL includes predicates for comparison and string matching, quantifiers, summary operations for max/min, and so on. Each view is a specification of database operations that would produce a desired table as output.

SQL2, the upward compatible enhancement of the original SQL standard, is intended to be a superset of SQL89 that replaced the elder SQL87. SQL2 standardizes a number of features not included in the original specification. It also includes substantial additional means for schema manipulation, dynamic SQL operation, exception handling, enhanced integrity constraints, transaction management, and data administration.

In parallel to this development, specifications for access to remote heterogeneous sites are part and parcel of the emerging ISO/RDA standard. Though some of the norms for distributed database management are still under development, RDA already:

- Provides protocols for establishing remote connections between database clients and servers
- Supports an environment with conforming SQL servers at each remote node in a communications network

In preparation for a further enhancement to SQL functionality, tools for object-oriented data management are currently being elaborated. They include triggers, assertions, user-defined data types, domain and table hierarchies, as well as stored procedures. These constitute the SQL3 standard with publication expected about 1995.

Among other features, SQL3 will support a sophisticated mechanism for efficient *data abstraction*. Data abstraction embedded in SQL89 has a rather elaborate view approach which, while improved in SQL92, still needs further enhancement. The projected SQL95 version will quite likely incorporate current proposals for user-defined data types, applications-specific null values, and optimal strong type checking in domains.

Along object-oriented features, the new SQL will support *inheritance*. It will allow hierarchical classification of data objects with the ability for one class to acquire characteristics from another.

Furthermore, a recursive union facility in SQL95 will provide a generic tool for specifying queries of a bill-of-materials type: "Compile an expanded list of all parts needed to manufacture machine A; locate all subassemblies containing part B as a component."

Other features of the new SQL will be enhanced existential and universal qualifiers (already introduced with SQL89) and data security beyond declaring and managing database access control—which has already been featured with SQL89.[4]

SQL3 will define an enhanced facility for database security management able to build upon the existing security model to include roles in addition to objects, actions, and users. A *role* is a named collection of authorized actions on objects. Role hierarchies can be established to facilitate granting and revoking application privileges.

The SQL3 proposal further specifies advanced capabilities to manage substransactions, permitting their potential rollback. Classically, a transaction either commits or fails; but this binary condition is not acceptable with complex transactions.

The projected SQL95 features currently studied by ANSI make feasible greater flexibility in managing subtransactions. The latter are defined and administered through *savepoints* to which a substransaction or long transaction can be rolled back. Releasing a savepoint is equivalent to precommitting operations executed subsequent to this savepoint.

As these evolutionary steps help document, we are essentially talking of a "non-SQL SQL." The passing prominence of the original SQL started when the hypothesis was disproved that because of the trend toward relational database models, as well as standardization efforts, the evolution of databases will be more or less frozen. The market voted otherwise.

At the same time, while the original SQL[5] no longer responds to current and coming needs, using the improved Structured Query Language versions (SQL2, SQL3) can be an advantage in the distributed landscape of information technology. This is supported by the facts that SQL:

- Proves to be a dynamic, evolving norm to which both vendors and users contribute

---

[4]There is in fact another superset of the original SQL, and therefore of API, introduced by Microsoft. Known as ODBC, it has been adopted by different vendors.

[5]IBM in 1979 and ANSI in 1986–1987 succeeded in making SQL the foremost of "non standard standards."

- Features an English-like syntax for writing database applications that reach across networks
- Has a number of options that give programmers some freedom to design and enhance their products

ANSI and ISO standards (as well as SQL Access Group productization) are important inasmuch as parochial dialects of SQL supposedly projected to "better" exploit different features can, and usually do, box SQL applications into a particular vendor's own database management system.

Just because there are so many SQL versions, what a user company decides to do is evidently a challenge. In this and in the next chapters, we will be looking into the way the chips may fall.

10.3 Standardization Efforts with the Relational Model

The relational model was introduced in 1969, and SQL was developed and timidly marketed by IBM about 10 years later. Its object was to provide a relational-oriented query facility able to access data within a more or less centralized database, based on the primitive command: "SELECT . . . FROM . . . WHERE . . . ."

Originally created to serve the IBM environment, SQL has been implemented by most of the relational database vendors—for IBM compatibility reasons. Each vendor has its "improved" version, but even within IBM there are SQL dialects, a great deal of them being incompatible. Hence, while several vendors say that "they support SQL," implementations are not necessarily homogeneous.

There are, as well, significant application domains which are not being addressed at all by SQL. For instance, transaction processing and graphics—though, as stated, this is corrected with SQL2 and SQL3. Furthermore, today users are requesting access to distributed relational databases which are not homogeneous or compatible, and SQL cannot help in this task.

1. Users would like to write applications that execute on one computer but access data on another computer.

The overriding demand is for interoperable solutions. As Figure 10.1 suggests, networked databases must be accessed by their users in a seamless manner. Since heterogeneity is a fact of life, this can be achieved only through the establishment of an observance of solutions along the lines already described. If SQL does *not* really support cross-

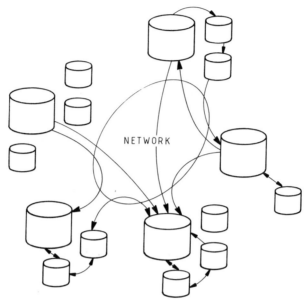

Figure 10.1 Networked databases accessed by their users
in a seamless manner through interfaces.

database access functions, other software has to do so. We will talk of
this issue.

2. Users also want to have extended functionality, covering
   analytical queries which need input from different platforms.

The SQL Access Group is addressing these problems by productizing
a new set of standards under ISO's remote data access. This is done in
conjunction with the productization of improved versions of SQL which
are normalized by ANSI and ISO.

3. The more sophisticated users face a fast growing need for
   handling long transactions and complex queries. This need is
   propelled by demands from their clients and they simply cannot
   afford to discard it.

Competitiveness calls for able answers to customer requests. To say
that these do not find response in any version of SQL—current or
projected—is to state the obvious. Hence, new solutions have to be

found. SAG is not working on such solutions. The SQL Access Group came into existence because its original founding members decided that any SQL language extensions and database access procedures must be committed to the official ANSI and ISO standardization process.

Work currently done by the SQL Access Group aims to contribute to the compliance process. The organization publishes specifications for users that would permit *practical interoperability* as the official standards are finalized and adopted.

One of SAG's aims is to remedy the fact that existing ANSI standards lack many necessary features because they were not written for application developers. This is part and parcel of the ongoing productization work—but at the same time, different interpretation by different vendors and/or semistandards outfits leads to divergences.

To help in a coordination sense, the SQL Access Group and X/Open have formed a cooperative agreement in the area of data management. The *X/Open Portability Guide* has been selected as a user documentation base because it defines existing practices, including extensions to SQL89, and reflects research on existing implementations while defining further extensions to support *dynamic SQL*.[6]

Members of the SQL Access Group are active in the following information technology standards and consortia: ANSI and ISO SQL2, ISO/RDA, X/Open, and Open Systems Foundation (OSF).

Both standardization and improvements are in the different organizations' agendas—though admittedly they are conflicting requirements. Extensions made through the productizing effort by the SQL Access Group to the X/Open definition aim to:

- Support the *client–server* model in the implementation of distributed heterogeneous databases
- Provide session management for all remote connections
- Handle dynamic SQL capabilities as well as the newer ANSI SQL versions
- Enrich the SQL structure by additional data types commonly found in existing products
- Improve error-handling procedures in on-line implementation
- Provide applications with a uniform description of the database structure

In these areas, work underway on the proposed ANSI/ISO *replacement standard for SQL* served as the base for future development references.

---

[6]Discussed in Section 10.6.

Along the same line of reasoning, the SQL Access Group adopted a preliminary specification for SQL embedded in the C programming language.

10.4 The Complex Task of Database Access

In spite of the rather widespread usage of SQL for all these years, no standard method exists by which all users can communicate with servers from different vendors. There is not only heterogeneity in DBMS and data structures but also protocol incompatibility creating major technical barriers which have for many years prevented cross-database access by SQL or anything else.[7] This has been aggravated by:

1. The fact that each vendor's brand of SQL is "better" and therefore slightly different
2. The prevailing conditions whereby message formats and communication protocols vary from one vendor to another
3. The backwardness of some protocols which cancel benefits to be obtained from the relational model

Nowhere is item number 3 more valid than in the IBM world, with the awkward and inefficient 3270 protocol. Because of 3270, even the best relational DBMS is subutilized, and let's not speak of the investment made in workstations which are used *as if* they were nothing more than dumb terminals.

While the main fault is with backwards oriented substandard protocols, SQL is not above blame for inefficient database access either. Let's not forget that IBM's Structured Query Language was originally developed at a time of nonintelligent terminals, low bandwidth connections, relatively small databases, and centralized resources. SQL shows many scars due to each of these limiting factors.

It makes practically no difference that in the mid-1980s SQL replaced the Relational Data Language as the ANSI X3H2 database standard. Nor does it change anything that subsequently it was adopted by the International Standards Organization's Open Systems Interconnect (OSI) committee. SQL's limitations are widely visible.

Originally projected to serve as a relational query level over a hierarchical DBMS (IBM's IMS), the functions and infrastructure of SQL include:

[7]DataLens, DAL, CALIDA, MIA, and other approaches are relatively recent efforts and they are not yet widespread.

- Data definition language (DDL), which defines data structures and relationships
- Data manipulation language (DML), which moves and updates data
- A data control mechanism, which defines access and security constraints

This is what is practically supported by other query languages, but the three aforementioned items—while necessary—are no longer enough. A golden hoard of other functions is needed in an interactive distributed database environment, where *ad hoc* queries and multimedia dominate, and these *ad hoc* queries become analytical as well as polyvalent, addressing incompatible databases.

Although vendors have claimed that the goal of application portability motivates their support of SQL, proprietary SQL implementations from these same vendors have prevented such a goal from being reached. Yet, as we will see in the next sections, portability is an absolutely necessary characteristic.

One of the problems in all this is that even though ANSI sets standards, such "standards" are *described* rather than *defined*. This means that many areas of ANSI SQL are left up to the vendor to define. Given a different communication protocol, one vendor's SQL client cannot connect to other vendors SQL servers across the local area network because of different client–server protocols and client–server message formats.

This shows the reason why SQL users have not been able to operate with more than one heterogeneous relational DBMS at a time. Hence the need to develop a truly standard SQL server interface to accomplish the interoperability of relational DBMS and application tools. Such a feat has been attempted by:

- Mapping SQL statements to RDA services (discussed in Chapter 11)
- Encoding SQL data and encapsulating them
- Including dynamic SQL capabilities
- Providing for authentication and access control
- Handling diagnostic messages

By addressing itself to the aforementioned functions, the SQL Access Group specification now aims to achieve the interoperability goal. It is based on emerging standards such as the ISO/RDA and guidelines from the X/Open consortium, such as remote procedure calls (RPC).

- SAG's application programming interface (API), a part of the specification, expands the syntax definitions of ISO/ANSI SQL to include support for remote database calls.
- SAG's formats and protocols (FAP) and its specifications determine standard message and reply formats as well as server communications.

The SQL Access Group's specifications are essentially an application programming interface for distributed databases. As such, it includes enhancements to the existing standards, some of which focus on:

- Standardized system catalog names
- Diagnostic messages
- A way for communicating databases to respond to whichever level of SQL the other one uses

Such enhancements, in turn, have been adopted by standards organizations for inclusion in the next releases of their respective SQL-oriented standards.

However, one of the limitations of the SQL Access Group specifications is that they are strictly relational DBMS oriented. SAG's specifications do not take into account any of the older database architectures, such as hierarchical and Codasyl, or for that matter the new wave of object-oriented DBMS.

Another major pitfall is that no particular thought has been given to seamless programming portability in view of changes advanced by the new standards and similar developments. As a result, some of the users' existing relational applications may need to be reworked to function with the SAG specifications.

Communications protocols are also issues in need of better definition. The software of SQL Access Phase 1 (which was demonstrated in New York in July 1991) uses the OSI networking protocols. Phase 2 will add support for TCP/IP and possibly other networks such as Novell NetWare. Phase 1 of the technical specification closely follows the ISO/ANSI standards for the SQL query language and defines a syntax for embedded SQL regarding Cobol and C programs.

Phase 2 will include a call-level interface, which is an alternative technique for handling SQL commands in an application. This type of interface is popular among vendors of front-end machines. Some people predict completion of Phase 2 by mid-1993—but there are always delays with software.

10.5 Interoperability and Portability

The fact that the outcome of Phase 1 has been successfully demonstrated with a relatively restricted application does not mean that it works in a perfect manner. The shortcut which the July 1991 demonstration took to reach results was to decouple clients from servers. According to this strategy, users should be able to:

• Buy their client software and front-end development tools from one vendor
• Procure the database server(s) they need from another vendor

This is supposed to happen without having to also buy a gateway program that translates one vendor's protocol into the other's. Such gateways are relatively expensive and often constitute a weak link in a network.

In the New York demonstration, front ends were as varied as the servers and their applications: spreadsheets, menu-based character forms, graphics-based maps, and other interfaces. Several clients collected data from more than one server, but the demo was highly controlled—which is not what happens in a typical implementation environment with plenty of endusers.

This limitation may be corrected when products are developed based on the SQL access specification. It can be reasonably expected that such products will provide users with a real multivendor cross-database *interoperability* and up to a certain level of program *portability*. The two terms should not be confused. Any work aimed to solve problems inherent in multivendor environments must have three goals:

• Interoperability
• Portability
• Distributive capability

Reflected in SAG Version 1.0, the primary objective is interoperability aiming to achieve a standard level of data exchange between heterogeneous relational databases.

• *Interoperability* provides the ability to write an application on one platform that accesses data on other platforms.

Many issues can complicate the interoperable use of data (for instance, difference in SQL language syntax, semantic behavior of statements, schema definition, data types, transaction semantics, error handling, and reporting). Because of diversity, it is difficult for a user to write a single application that can access more than one vendor's database without modification.

- *Portability* refers to the ability to write an application for one vendor environment and use that application on other platforms without reprogramming.

The goal of the portability effort is to allow users access to a *virtually* single set of resources which they can universally reach. Portability will see to it that the same piece of software run on different platforms can manipulate information elements in any SQL access server. It is important to notice that for any practical purpose:

- These goals are followed by a number of cross-database projects, though the approach which they take is different.
- The better projects in this field utilize and incorporate a great deal of knowledge-engineering work—but not necessarily ISO and ANSI standards.

A radical approach to the portability issue is the one which takes the proverbial long hard look in examining the available options. The call for *open systems* is part and parcel of this reference, but most people fail to realize that open architectures do not start at the top layer but at the bottom—specifically the *operating system* (OS) level.

This is the goal which NTT's Multivendor Integration Architecture (MIA) has set to achieve. The first goal, which underpins Version 1, has been that of establishing a universal *software standard* to which the operating systems of five different vendors have to adapt.

Portability in regard to DBMS and data structures comes thereafter. For instance, the provision of distributed database services within NTT's Multivendor Integration Architecture is RDA-oriented as far as remote access to distributed heterogeneous databases is concerned.

The third goal the SQL Access Group and other efforts have set for themselves is *distributive capability*. Solutions under development will allow a single SQL access application to simultaneously interoperate with multiple SQL access file servers and the relational DBMS running them.

A major difference with MIA is that this work concentrates on relational structures while MIA Version 2 will include nonrelational DBMS as well. Let's also take notice that DataLens by Lotus already addresses relational and nonrelational heterogeneous databases, but only for interfacing to the spreadsheet.

While keeping these differences in mind, we can look at the work done by the SQL Access Group as that of productizing a comprehensive specification for relational database connectivity and, therefore, interoperability. As it matures, it will most likely provide a method for application programs to access data from multiple relational DBMS vendors, running on different platforms through a standard programming interface.

When implemented in a reasonably sophisticated manner, this approach may allow a single SQL access application to interoperate with multiple SQL access servers simultaneously, according to the model shown in Figure 10.2. Such an effort does not have much to do with software portability in the more classical sense of the term. The primary emphasis is placed on interoperability.

Though desirable, particularly for the organizations which are intensive users of computers and communications, software portability in

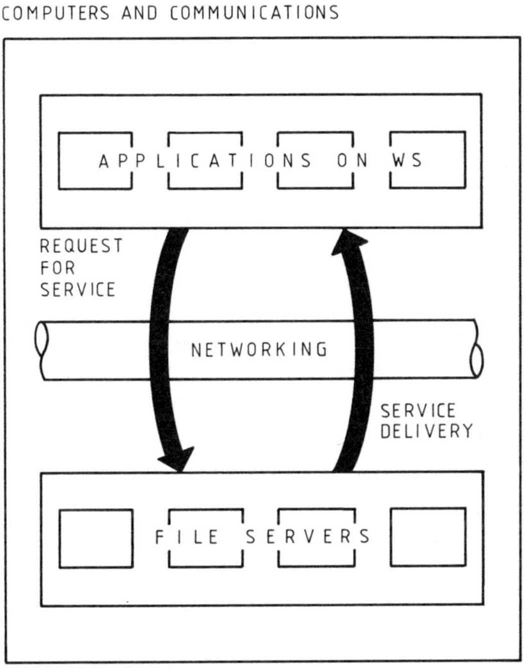

Figure 10.2 Interoperability in a client–server model.

the dual computing and networking sense is still some time away. To be achieved, many current practices will have to change. For instance, today, even in regard to ISO and ANSI standards, more than 50% of each vendor's implementation consists of proprietary enhancements. Standards are taken by most as really reflecting the lowest common denominator on which vendors can build their wares.

For these reasons, it is simply illusory to state that the $100 billion or so of development money spent each year throughout the United States, Western Europe, and Japan on applications software can benefit from true portability. It would have been great to invest such money on portable rather than parochial code, but this is not for tomorrow. Yet even the more limited scope of user interoperability is a worthy goal to pursue.

10.6 Dynamic versus Static SQL

Today, many gateways and other database coexistence tools use dynamic SQL statements. In this sense, *dynamic* SQL is another name for the better known classical SQL, which must be interpreted and optimized with every statement. The term *dynamic* was coined to contrast the approach to a more recent SQL variation known as *static SQL*. Dynamic SQL interprets and optimizes each statement every time such a statement is submitted. Run-time interpretation is necessary for the handling of *ad hoc* queries, but it consumes a good deal of cycles.

Query optimization is, however, a CPU-intensive process in which the SQL processor decomposes a complex statement to speed up data retrieval. In terms of total execution time, this is the most costly part of database processing. This turns out to be disastrous with mainframes, for which SQL was designed, but can be acceptable with workstations.

Since interpretation acts as a cycle sponge, optimization approaches are necessary. *Restriction* and *projection* are two common techniques for expediting relational DBMS searches. One basic principle that can be applied to both techniques is that of data transitivity.

- Restriction reduces the number of rows, which represent entities.
- Projection limits the number of columns, which represent attributes.

Let's recall that the way SQL operates can be described as "SELECT . . . . FROM . . .WHERE . ." If within the logic of a query's "WHERE" clause, attribute X is greater than attribute Y, and attribute Y is greater than Z, then it can be deduced that attribute X is greater than Z.

The underlying premise in this simple logic statement is that if the database's SQL optimizer makes that sort of a deduction, it could reduce the complexity of a query. This can be achieved by projecting the scope of the query onto attribute X alone, while restricting the search to only those rows in which attribute X is greater than Z.

By contrast to this optimization procedure which improves upon cycle usage but not in a radical sense, static SQL is designed to expedite applications that require fast responses to repetitive, standard search requests. This offers faster execution time than optimized dynamic SQL because it does not interpret each query every time that query is submitted.

Since static SQL queries are written, interpreted, and optimized in advance, they can typically be lifted from a report program. In this manner, this approach avoids the performance problems created with dynamic SQL in an operating environment characterized by intensive, interactive applications—but queries are not *ad hoc*.

The static approach is more recent than the dynamic, however, there are penalties associated with it. The elder dynamic SQL is flexible because it can provide a general-purpose connection to query what tables and columns are in a database. This can be achieved by dynamic SQL without having to know the names of the tables.

With static SQL users lose flexibility because they can only apply this technology in applications where enquiries are predictable. It can happen, but this is not really the way to bet. Nevertheless, static SQL too has optimization possibilities.

Remote procedure call (RPC) technology can be used in conjunction with packaged static SQL statements. Some systems specialists think that static SQL and RPCs can play a valid role in predictable transaction processing environments, whereas dynamic SQL will continue to dominate *ad hoc* query environments.

For instance, Sybase targets high performance applications—like transaction processing—by offering a variation of SQL built around the equivalent of database remote procedure calls. These RPC permit client applications to invoke a compiled query on a SQL server.

Other systems specialists believe that since flexibility and the ability to face a growing unpredictability are at a premium, such approaches to the rejuvenation of SQL have evident limitations. And they conveniently forget about query language transparency.

The degree of SQL transparency which we could expect among architectures is largely dependent on how well the client interface is established. To the extent that this interface is well defined and relatively permissive, software products may be made to offer significant transparency. But is "interface permissiveness" a reasonable hypothesis?

Possible difficulties may develop in the areas of system catalog access and collating sequences. No doubt more constraints will be needed as we progress toward more sophisticated environments. Hence the wisdom of supporting and maintaining open architectures the way it has so often been underlined, in which SAG's SQL efforts will provide one of the protocols.

10.7 The Open SQL Version

There is as well an *Open SQL* species in the market, seen by some people as a refinement of SQL2, OSI/TP, and RDA SQL. The so-called Open SQL Group[8] aims to function as an independent consortium open to all interested parties. As a first installment, it is committed to produce two documents:

1. An application programming interface (API) to enhance applications portability in diverse environments.
2. A formats and protocols definition to specify the message interface to different heterogeneous SQL approaches.

The output of the work on API is scheduled to be directed toward the SQL2 effort, while that of the FAP will go to the RDA and teleprocessing (TP) endeavors.

Among developments to be expected are prototypes using API, FAP, and RDA (discussed in Chapter 11). They would consist of client and server processes, the former acting as an application sending SQL queries to access data and receive data from a server. The latter are projected to empower the database server itself.

Remote database access will be provided by using Open SQL protocols and formats, with clients and servers exchanging information. The server processes are expected to understand the Open SQL syntax, formats, and protocols, converting them to their native dialect(s).

The reference to *native dialect(s)* statement is made in appreciation of the fact that though most relational database vendors give lip service in supporting SQL, there are many differences such as syntax, schemata, data types, catalog naming, data stream, data representation, functional

---

[8]Still another group with incompatible "standards" and compliance aims.

support for outer joins, as well as transaction management. Such differences make the different versions of SQL incompatible among themselves.

As it cannot be repeated too often, precisely because of the prevailing parochialism and its incompatibilities it is difficult for a user to write a single application that can access more than one vendor's relational database. The user is also faced with different interfaces, with the database vendors failing to supply software which is resident at distributed workstations, and is able to efficiently exploit the capabilities of their DBMS.

Open SQL is supposed to come as a response to such problems, attempting to solve distribution and interoperability issues. It is developed as an *ad hoc* standard to facilitate access to databases on workstations and other systems, helping to define vendor-independent:

- SQL syntax
- Data types
- Catalogs
- Transaction models
- Formats
- Protocols

This is accomplished in two parts: (a) The application programming interface, and (b) formats and protocols (we talk of both in the next chapter). The work being done for Open SQL is coded in C, with the body of code expected to form a reference model for API and FAP.

As we will soon see, API presents extensions to ANSI/ISO SQL aimed to clarify and specify details that allow an application to converse with heterogeneous distributed SQL systems. FAP provides message formats and associated communications protocols that permit heterogeneous SQL systems to interoperate exchanging queries and data.

According to its proponents, if Open SQL was adopted by most vendors, it would allow applications to access data on different systems using a standard SQL API. It would also permit users and third-party vendors to write applications that are portable from machine to machine and operating system to operating system. In this case,

- A user could employ the same front end to access several different databases
- A single database could be shared by a population of users with different workstations

All this is, however, conditioned by a big IF. Open SQL will be a success only if several major vendors cooperate in a common effort which produces universally viable API, FAP, and reference model within the perspectives consistent with RDA.

Furthermore, only solutions acceptable to the standards bodies and the population of important computers and communications users can be lasting. User organization acceptability presupposes that a standard's implementation has both functionality and performance. Sophisticated customers are demanding, and they become increasingly more so by the day.

CHAPTER 11

Application Programming Interface, Formats and Protocols, and Remote Data Access

11.1 Introduction

Approved by ANSI and ISO, the existing SQL standard is consistent with the simplest case covered by the ISO Reference Model for Data Management. According to this model's description, a user processor has a direct connection to a SQL database controller for a single environment. The ANSI/ISO standard defines SQL host language embeddings and an equivalent module for interfacing to the host language. However, it does not define the time or method of binding the application to the DBMS, thus leaving a major loophole to connectivity.

The current approach is indirect. For instance, in the client–server model, the user processor issues requests to the remote data access (RDA) SQL client, rather than directly to the SQL database controller.

The RDA SQL client employs a communication connection to an attached server, which delivers the processing request to the database controller. The implicit SQL module interface between the application program and the database is at the RDA SQL client level where local data values are encoded into standard SQL data types for transmission as parameters to a SQL statement, and the results of that SQL statement are returned, in local variables form, to the distributed networked databases.

The SQL Access Group has added several statements to support session management, while X/Open has defined extensions to support dynamic SQL (which appear in X/Open's Portability Guide Issue 4).

X/Open is a consortium of eleven international computer manufacturers with a stated commitment to bringing open systems to the marketplace. It was formed in 1984 as a loose affiliation of manufacturers; it is now incorporated as an independent, nonprofit organization. Its members include AT&T, Bull, DEC, Ericsson, Hewlett-Packard, ICL, Olivetti, Philips, Siemens/Nixdorf, and Unisys.

X/Open does not endorse products, it publishes specifications. By adopting but also adapting accepted standards it hopes to create a common applications infrastructure. The X/Open hypothesis is that this will allow the portability of software applications among different systems from various vendors.

It is important to appreciate that X/Open is *not a standard body* like the International Standards Organization (ISO), American National Standards Institute (ANSI), or the Institute of Electrical and Electronic Engineers (IEEE). It does, however, work closely with these groups to determine acceptable "standards."

Another organization with similar goals is the Open Software Foundation (OSF). OSF was formed in 1988 to develop a standard version of the Unix operating system able to compete with AT&T's Unix System V. Its sponsors have been Bull, DEC, Hewlett-Packard, Hitachi, IBM, Philips, and Siemens/Nixdorf.

As of recently, however, questions are increasingly being raised about OSF's impartiality in choosing technology and whether it plays an anticompetitive role in the market. It has been widely reported in the United States that this vendor consortium is being investigated by the Federal Trade Commission for unfair trade practices.

User organizations will be well advised to keep in mind that the so-called "OSF standards" are *not* truly standards. Practically every one of the OSF promoters has a Unix version of its own: IBM pushes AIX, DEC advances Ultrix, and the other computer manufacturers have more or less their own versions to peddle.

All of this is sad; it is all a matter of ill conceived competitive advantages and of misjudgment on behalf of the different vendors. Rather than betting on imagination and low cost to gain market leadership, they follow the red herring strategy. User organizations dislike this arm twisting and those with contractual power respond to it.

11.2 Gateways and Database Tools

Throughout business and industry many database managers are investing in gateway products. *Gateways* supersede the already popular extract and propagator tools because they do not involve the overhead of creating and maintaining a shadow relational database.

Some of the currently available gateway products map the SQL implementation of a particular relational database onto outside source files and databases. The simplest gateways which are transparent to the user provide the DBMS with only read access to the foreign source data. More sophisticated gateways assure the DBMS with write access to the source data, hand-holding across the databases.

To give the user transparent read and/or write access to a foreign data source, gateways must feature some form of translation procedures for dictionary, catalog, and schema. This way the queries built using any of the DBMS' SQL-based tools can be completed.[1]

However, gateways can and do introduce I/O performance and data integrity problems. While data accessed by gateways is much more current than data made available by extract approaches (and this process also avoids having to move data into a shadow database of info center type), there are overhead penalties associated with the solution in reference.

Another current problem with gateways is the nonstandard "standards" being employed. Figure 11.1 gives an example with the X/Open approach integrating:

- Applications programs (AP)
- Transaction managers (TM)
- Communications managers (CM)
- Resource managers (RM)

With IBM's LU6.2, TM and CM are an inflexible "one-wired model." Commit protocol usage and program-to-program communications are not easy or even possible to separate from one another. Acceptable a dozen years ago for lack of better alternatives, this monolith is the computers' equivalent of the Middle Ages.

The XA approach to protocol design, promoted by X/Open, is much more flexible and agile. But its two-way TM-DBMS linkage still offers very little by way of truly interactive transaction processing, although the new "XA Plus" gives additional primitives to dynamically bind resource managers while a given transaction is running.

The XA Plus designers should also have known that, in a long-transactions environment, the two-phase commit poses several problems. Communications to resource managers becomes complex because the protocol does not just pass a transaction but also needs to transmit other associated messages, some of which are just for housekeeping.

[1]See also in Chapter 10 how IBM is handling this problem with DRDA.

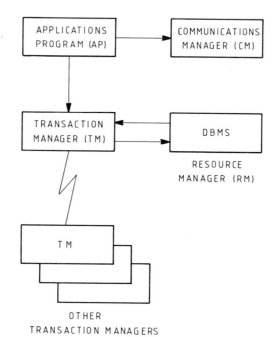

Figure 11.1 X/Open's XA protocol approach in
a transaction environment.

Besides this, XA is described rather than defined as a set of standard
interfaces. All that "X/Open compliance" means is that an X/Open
standard will be incorporated in the different vendors' solutions *if* and
when it becomes defined—and at the start it will not interoperate with
anything but CICS(!). The Transaction Processing Working Group of X/
Open is still some way from:

1. Specifying the interface between a transaction manager and
    multiple networked DBMSs in a distributed environment
2. Sorting the problems associated to a Distributed Transaction
    Processing (DTP) model
3. Going beyond two-phase commit to serve conversational
    transactions and similar functions

Yet, an able response to the critical references made in these
three points can be instrumental in serving multiple distributed XA-
compliant databases and in getting a valid networked solution in spite
of the database heterogeneity from different vendors.

As a general principle, database tools and interactive front-end products need to know the definition of the tables that comprise a database. In the past, each vendor has defined its own set of system tables to contain this information. Now the SQL Access Group and X/Open have agreed to support several of the information schema tables proposed for SQL2—the ANSI designed transaction-oriented construct. These include:

- TABLES, to allow an application to determine the names of accessible tables
- COLUMNS, to furnish information about the data types and names of the individual columns in each table
- SQL-LANGUAGES, to describe the level of SQL that the DBMS can support
- SERVER-INFO, to provide local server information, such as the collating sequence supported by the server

There will also be situations in which the target remote database management system is known in advance. An extension of the SQL comment facility should account for this fact, allowing vendor-specific SQL language extensions to be flagged in a networked sense.

Once this is achieved, the intended DBMS satisfying the aforementioned criteria can extract and process language extensions while the same statement is also sent to other SQL access servers where those extensions would be ignored. This facility is designed for situations where optional, performance-oriented features should be used.

Flexibility underpins the concept behind this statement. As in the case of dynamic and static SQL (discussed in Chapter 10), because of the polyvalence of situations currently encountered in information technology, solutions should make feasible more than one technical choice. Otherwise, they do less than half of their intended job.

The API, FAP, and RDA approaches which we discuss in the following sections should be seen in a similar manner. Today most vendors talk of API, but this does not mean that it has yet been productized. SAG standard API is still in development. There are many incompatible application program interfaces today in the market with each vendor having its own to offer, but the fact that the API-implied modularity sets in permits more flexible approaches to be found.

11.3 Working toward a Standard API

In response to the growing need for simplifying the interface between applications programs and independent, remote database management systems, the SQL Access Group has defined a specification for an application programming interface:

- The SAG API is based on the SQL ANSI X3.135-1986 and the corresponding International Standard IS 9075:1987.
- The chosen approach also features some characteristics from the current SQL2 and SQL3 drafts of new database query standards.

The scope of the SAG API is to provide transparent access from a client to SQL access compliant remote servers. But given the SQL 1, 2, 3 features, the projected SQL access specification will probably be a compromise, or at least that is the way to bet.

Industry experts foresee still another compromise between SQL 1,2,3 specifications and the current capabilities supported by the different SQL vendors, as well as their incompatible wares. While the intent is to achieve interoperability at a generally accepted core of the SQL environment, no vendor would ever accept buying someone else's standards wholesale.

On the positive side, since its inception, the SQL Access Group platform has been distributed. The underlying computer resources are assumed to be a network of intelligent servers with the SQL access standard available on all SAG-compliant servers. However, SQL Access Version 1.0 restricts a client from accessing multiple servers simultaneously, this being left for better times. While this limitation is indeed restrictive, quite important is the fact that with SQL Access an application is not required to know where the IE are located. Nor does it need to know what communications method is used to access the data or which vendor's DBMS is being accessed.

In terms of implementation, the SQL Access Technical Specification focuses on a single client–server model of database services with application programs residing in one computer environment able to access database services in another system environment. Future versions of SQL Access will quite likely permit a single request from one client to simultaneously access multiple servers.

Keeping the aforementioned limitation in mind, a SAG-compliant application can access any conforming server in the network without modification or recompilation. This is being further extended by other standards efforts—like the Multivendor Integration Architecture—to include software compatibility and portability at the operating system level. MIA's portability allows users to have a set of OS sources that can universally support applications programs. While the current SQL

Access Group Version 1.0 aims to achieve a standard level of interoperability under the stated constraints.

Version 2.0 will most likely address other technologies pertaining to interoperability including user requirements in the areas of the call level interface and TCP/IP support (including a call level interface subroutine library) and TCP/IP networking for databases and associated tools.

It is important to address the call level interface because, when developing relational database management system applications, some programmers prefer a subroutine style of programming to an embedded SQL interface. TCP/IP can be very helpful because it is the most widely used protocol at the fourth layer of the open system interconnection level of ISO.

All this should be seen within the perspectives of a more global solution involving remote database access protocols also being established by ISO/ANSI (as briefly discussed in the preceding chapter). The same reference is valid in regard to formats and protocols (FAP) necessary for a client to communicate with a server. The SQL Access Group API communicates through the network with a server process which provides access to the target database.

This user–server association runs in the context of a client account, based on information provided during the connection establishment. It employs a message-based protocol virtually transparent to the application program. This is precisely what is referred to as the formats and protocol, which fits within the RDA norms.

Another part of the work done by SAG is *prototyping* applications with commercially available relational DBMS operating in an open-systems environment. API specifications are therefore handled as an extension embedded in the SQL language that can be used by an application operating in an open system to reach any conforming remote SQL database server.

This effort centers on approaches which can be used for both local and remote DBMS access. Current and projected results are therefore of a more general applicability, permitting the source code of an application to be portable to different environments and interoperable with heterogeneous DBMS systems.

In a similar manner, the fact that the selected FAP specification fits the OSI remote data access service and protocol permits application users to select the target database server at run time. This is accomplished in a way independent of the hardware and software of the SQL database server node. The development work, however, assumes that all attached computers and the network itself observe the ISO/OSI model.

11.4 Heterogeneous Database Implementation and the API Technical Specification

As any system architect should know, a major requirement of database management is the level of independence between the application's view of the information elements and the form in which these IE are stored. The extension from a single database to a generic architecture makes this approach indispensable.

The layer of independence which should separate the applications from the distributed database services is provided by distributed *deductive* database (DDDB) facilities. These typically involve knowledge engineering but are not part of the SQL Access Group goals.

The Japanese computer vendors as well as the New Generation Computer Institute (ICOT) are very active with DDDB. American commercial DBMS vendors, particularly those offering products of a relational nature, have developed proprietary file management extensions for network environments, but only those who aim to provide gateways for heterogeneous database access are using knowledge engineering.

As it is to be expected, there are significant differences among the different projects under way today and the offers coming out of them. This greatly complicates the interoperability of databases. Without a metalayer to cover the incompatibilities, differences due to language syntax, schema definition, and semantic behavior of SQL statements tend to become visible—and the same is true of data types as well as with error handling and reporting.

Looking into this subject in an applications programming sense, due to these differences, it becomes very difficult for a user organization to write applications that can access more than one vendor's database without significant modifications. The goal, however, should be quite the opposite: namely, not only to achieve but also to continue supporting a high level of data independence, providing common syntax and semantics for access to both the application (client) interface and the database server interface.

This amounts to *any-to-any connectivity*, which offers important competitive advantages. Any application running anywhere in the network should be able to access any on-line file server or host, and it should receive very consistent results from each one of them.

In response to these requirements, the SQL Access Group is currently developing a common embedded SQL language interface for user–server interoperability in OSI environments. This specification covers most of the features in the current ANSI/OSI SQL standard, includes some new features from the proposed SQL2 normalization, and maintains upward compatibility with X/Open applications.

These developments by SQL access are closely followed by MIA and the Carnot Project[2] of MCC. They are seen as a cornerstone for a comprehensive architecture for relational database connectivity which is necessary to provide a method for application programs to access IE from multiple relational DBMS vendors.

Providing transparent access for a host client to SQL Access compliant remote file servers and databases, API integrates into the distributed heterogeneous environment in the way shown in Figure 11.2. The same chart also demonstrates the role played by the RDA emerging international standard which specifies:

- Communications disciplines and protocols to be used in distributed database environments
- A method for accessing the capabilities of database servers within distributed open systems

This API/RDA platform is positioned in the ISO/OSI context, providing a solution which helps in simplifying communications between local and remote heterogeneous relational DBMS. SQL Access tunes its communications mechanism around such norms. In terms of functionality

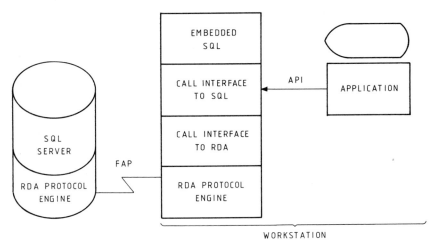

Figure 11.2   API, RDA, and FAP within the SQL Access Technical Specification.

[2]Started by the MCC consortium to promote interoperability among heterogeneous networked databases.

API interconnects the application itself to the intermediate database application environment. As an ISO specification, RDA links the application (user, client) to the local or remote file server. The formats and protocols artifact provides the logical bridge to the remote databases.

Through these services, a SQL application running on one vendor's platform will be able to access information elements residing on several other vendors' platforms.

As the preceding chapter underlined, while the original work has been done on the basis of the American National Standard document Database Language SQL ANSI X3.135-1986[3] and the corresponding International Standard IS 9075:1987, new versions now reflect the need for transactional-type implementations and the growing requirement of enrichment with triggers, graphics, and other features.

For all three versions: SQL1, SQL2, SQL3, cross-database solutions advanced by SAG more or less presuppose that the underlying computational system is a network of intelligent file servers—a sort of distributed deductive database whose software has not yet been developed.

Another important assumption, which is limiting in its nature, is that the capabilities of all features in the SQL access standard are available on all compliant servers. Only in this manner, an application conforming to SQL access norms can address diverse networked databases without program modification and/or recompilation.

11.5 Formats and Protocols (FAP)

With these basic assumptions in mind, which in a pragmatic sense it must be stated that they are not always fulfilled, an environment can be developed compliant to the SQL Access Technical Specification. Within such setting API deals with SQL syntax and semantics as well as its usage in connection to an application program.

ANSI and ISO define a syntax to access SQL data. This syntax centers on the application programming interface giving source-level portability among SQL solutions. But ISO/SQL does not provide a syntax to access remote SQL data or servers.

Formats and protocols specifies the request and response message formats between a user and a server. FAP also establishes the protocol and rules that both user and server must obey in order to *interoperate*. As the preceding discussion underlined, FAP is based on the ISO RDA specification which consists of two parts:

---

[3]Now called SQL1; both SQL2 and SQL3 are ISO/ANSI replacement standards for SQL1 (SQL89).

- The generic RDA services
- Norms for accessing different types of databases

Today, the only specialization really being worked on is SQL1. There is also some coordination with the ISO SQL2 committee to make sure that the ANSI SQL being productized is a proper subset of SQL2.

Besides this, participants in the SQL Access Group have made contributions to the ISO/RDA[4] standard in areas such as the mapping of SQL statements to RDA services, encoding of SQL data, inclusion of dynamic SQL, as well as authentication and access control.

For its part, FAP addresses message formats for open SQL requests and replies, as well as for connection to a SQL server. Data types, lengths, and representations are also defined in FAP, and the same is true of formats for data streams that flow between a client and a server.

These protocols assume the server invocation mechanism and transaction mechanism of OSI/TP, which in a way is similar to IBM's LU6.2. For its part, open SQL defines some syntactic extensions to ISO/SQL, making it feasible for the application to name and access remote data or servers. It also addresses:

- Network naming
- Catalog definitions
- Error reply structure (SQLCA)
- SQL descriptor area (SQLDA)

SQLDA is needed to receive the number of variables and their types and lengths in a prepared statement. There are some commercial DBMS products that provide multidatabase access capabilities of a similar sort, but they are not standardized.

For the time being, diversity is the rule. For instance, the language Transac SQL is an extension of SQL with multidatabase access features. To bring some common ground to these approaches, the SQL Access Group uses ISO's remote data access as a communication mechanism between database applications and servers.

RDA employs the *distributed transaction processing* (TP) standards for coordination between a user and multiple servers. Its implementation exceeds the SAG perspectives as the SQL Access Group does not

---

[4]In the United States, the X3H2 committee has a Technical Advisory Group responsible for RDA and has formed a Task Group (X3H2.1) to coordinate technical work with ISO/RDA.

address data and schema integration, being limited to the SQL language and relational DBMS.

11.6 Implementing the Remote Data Access Protocol

The remote data access protocol is based on the user–server model which was shown in Figure 11.2. RDA operations typically require either a *normal* or an *error response* and they are always invoked by the initiator (RDA user) of the connection.

As a matter of deliberate choice, RDA operations are asynchronous. This provides flexibility to distributed operating procedures:

- The user may continue to invoke further operations without awaiting a response to those already under way.
- When obtained, results of RDA operations are usually returned in the order that operations are received by the RDA file server.

RDA fits within the ISO/OSI application layer. It uses the *association control service element* (ACSE) for establishing and releasing connections between a client and a server.[5] RDA *protocol data units* (PDU) or messages are specified through *Abstract Syntax Notation One* (ASN.1). They are encoded using the *basic encoding rules* (BER).[6]

The ISO RDA specifications define services and protocols over a single association between a user and a server. At the basis of RDA is the distributed transaction processing standard still under development. Its aim is to provide the needed norms for coordination between user (client) entity and multiple database servers.

The remote data access standard defines a number of services which can be requested by a user. These include dialog management, transaction handling, resource administration, database language commands, and control activities.

Dialog management services permit an RDA client to establish a two-way communication with an RDA server. This is basically a logical connection between a client and a server with interactions occurring within the context of the RDA dialog norms.

A *unique identifier* is assigned when such interaction is first established. A "Begin Dialog" command is used for the interconnection

---

[5]ISO 8649:1988, OSI-Service Definition for the Associated Control Service Element.

[6]This BER should not be confused with the abbreviation of bit error rate. The basic encoding rules are enscribed in ISO 8825:1989 (E) (ASN.1); OSI-Specification of Basic Encoding Rules for Abstract Syntax Notation One (ASN.1).

between a client and a server. An "End Dialog" command allows the user to request the termination of an RDA link, but it cannot be executed when a transaction is active.

RDA transaction handling services support a one-phase commitment protocol. Distributed transactions, however, require a two-phase commit protocol for which RDA prescribes the use of ISO distributed transaction processing services.[7] In the one-phase commitment protocol:

- "Begin Transaction" is used to initiate an RDA transaction at the server.
- "Commit" helps to indicate that the current RDA transaction should be completed.
- "Rollback" sees to it that an ongoing RDA transaction should be rolled back.

Hence, RDA has two modes of operation with respect to transaction management. The RDA *basic application context* provides one-phase commitment protocol through the RDA transaction management services. The RDA TP application context will provide two-phase commitment for distributed transactions when available.

Resource administration helps assure that information elements available at a server can be organized into a set of interoperating databases. It controls the availability of such resources, whose contents are accessed and manipulated and therefore employed.

Data language services permit a user to send SQL commands to the file server for execution, as well as to obtain the results thereof. Prior to their invocation, the target database resource must have been opened through the "Open" service. Other commands are "Execute," "Define," and "Invoke."

The "Invoke" service can be employed by the client to request the execution of an already stored SQL statement and to inform the user of its outcome. The latter specifies the wanted command through the "Define" service and any parameters necessary for the execution of the SQL statement in database storage.

A crucial role in this whole range of operations is played by control operations. Given the asynchronous capability of RDA, several requests may be outstanding at one time. Among supported control activities are:

- Query *the status* of outstanding requests
- *Cancel* one or more of them

---

[7]TP is also an ISO/OSI application layer standard.

Successful cancellation of requests is indicated by individual responses. Control services are the only RDA commands whose results may be returned by the server before the results of previously issued requests.

SQL data and schema manipulation statements flow as part of execute commands to the server. By contrast, SQL transaction statements do not flow as part of execute requests. Instead, they are mapped to the corresponding transaction management services in RDA or TP, depending on the application context which has been chosen.

While the organization of this distributed interactive environment makes sense, much still remains to be done both in normalization and in the provision of the necessary software. As a result, organizations which need an immediate implementation develop their own projects, examples being General Motor's *Dataplex* and GTE's *Intelligent Database Assistant* (IDA).

PART III

Applications with Federated Databases

CHAPTER 12

IBM's Distributed Relational Data Architecture (DRDA)

12.1 Introduction

Introduced in 1990, IBM's Distributed Relational Data Architecture (DRDA) is a System Application Architecture (SAA) construct designed to assure communication among heterogeneous relational databases in the IBM world. The long-term aim for DRDA is, most likely, to extend beyond SAA into an open environment, but this will take years to materialize.

Like any other vendor, to position itself against the forces of the 1990s, IBM has to face significant trends not only in technology but also in the customer base. They need to respond to these trends. An able and timely response is the only way to hold control of the computer market. Among the trends in reference, we distinguish:

1. Cheaper but also increasingly more powerful workstations which must communicate with each other and with servers
2. Faster communications with LANs and WANs, including T1, T3 lines and fiber optics
3. The popularity of independent business units leading to an increasingly distributed environment of enterprises, both domestically and internationally
4. Fast-growing demand to serve customers on a global basis, driving users of computers and communications to require high performing distributed access from their database vendors

According to IBM's own account, DRDA has been developed to answer these prerequisites. More precisely, it has to be developed to satisfy the needs of application programs requiring connectivity to and among the different relational DBMS in homogeneous or heterogeneous operating environments, starting with IBM's own products.

201

DRDA supports IBM's own different versions of SQL[1] as the standard database application programming interface (API) for execution of networked processes. Within this perspective, it defines flows that program development and operations can use to bind SQL statements at a target relational DBMS.

Speaking in a fundamental system sense, rather than being looked at as a product, DRDA should be examined as a set of *rules* which enable some distributed relational databases to communicate. At the present time, the "some" means RDBMS in the IBM world with the goal of interoperability.

As a set of rules and protocols, DRDA describes prevailing information flows between participants in the selected distributed relational database environment. This includes information elements requested by processes from databases. It also addresses how to handle communication failures or interrupts.

Other supported issues regard the format of the data and what conversions take place. To establish rules, DRDA uses several already existing facilities. It might be said that this is what ISO's remote data access (RDA) also intends to do. Yes, but RDA and DRDA are not compatible at the present time, all the way from their scope to their primitives.

The net effect of such incompatibility is to cut the world of databases into two parts: IBM's and that of all the other vendors. For the time being, there is no way that DRDA and RDA communicate, though IBM has said that if RDA becomes the international standard, it will support it. Today, DRDA addresses only the different (read: incompatible) SQL versions of IBM, not IMS or Codasyl database management systems.

As we will see in Section 12.2, IMS and a number of non-IBM relational databases are being addressed by the recent Enterprise Data Access/Structured Query Language (EDA/SQL).[2] However, EDA/SQL only permits queries, not transactions. DRDA can handle transactions.

One way to look into EDA/SQL functionality is to say that it is doing what DataLens by Lotus Development does: pass-through among different heterogeneous databases for query purposes. A major difference, however, is that DataLens operates on a PC while, as part of IBM's Information Warehouse, EDA/SQL is based on a mainframe—at many times the cost.

12.2 The Philosophy of a Cross-Database Solution

Backing up the more advanced pieces of software, particularly those having to do with interoperability, are some philosophical considera-

---

[1]SQL DB2, SQL/DS, SQL OS/400, and SQL OS/2.
[2]Developed by Information Builders, the makers of Focus, and marketed by IBM.

tions. In terms of the philosophy of DRDA, much comes from the R* concepts of the late 1970s and early 1980s elaborated at the Santa Teresa Laboratories of IBM. Both centralized and distributed operating modes are at the kernel of this reference.

At the centralized side, which is operational, DRDA has implemented remote request services with each statement taken as a unit of work. This operation is executing under the Systems Applications Architecture, which DRDA serves. As we will see, DRDS is implemented at lowest level of reference with the remote unit of work able to handle multiple statements. Not implemented today is the distributed side with the distributed request connected to units of work. The distributed facility is, quite likely, a long time away.

While the nature and mechanics of the distributed request are not yet analyzed, the distributed unit of work, as such, has been conceptually worked out. However, implementation will not be available prior to 1995, and besides this it will be done one DBMS at a time. We will return to these issues.

Critics of the cross-database products IBM brings to the market tend to comment that there is, in terms of user population and implementation objectives, a certain functional overlap between DRDA and EDA/SQL (briefly talked about in the introduction to this chapter). But as we have seen already, there are also significant differences.

- DRDA is *read/write*, hence usable with transactions
- While with very few write exceptions EDA/SQL has *read only* capabilities

A technical way of looking at this is that EDA/SQL is a mapper, not a database manager. By contrast, DRDA provides unit of work support, including two-phase commit.

Neither EDA/SQL nor DRDA are standalone architectures. DRDA for instance uses the following software products as building blocks: LU 6.2, Distributed Data Management, SNA Management Services, Formatted Data Object Content, and Character Data representation. It is the task of DRDA to tie them all together into a data stream protocol that supports cooperation between the different participating resources.

In terms of coverage, DRDA addresses itself only to relational databases, using relational primitives. The mix of relational and nonrelational commands in the same request is not recommended, as one may end up with many SQL statements which are not executable.

Since DRDA is mainframe-based, its software and protocols are built into the DB2 manager; they are not a separate product. The only exception to this statement is in connection to OS/2, which uses the distributed data control system (DDCS).

For networking capabilities, DRDA is based on SNA and LU6.2. The LU6.2 services, such as those found in current releases of VTAM, are required to support DRDA on IBM computers.

Access to distributed relational databases requires connectivity to and among database managers. DRDA provides this connectivity, allowing relational information to be shared among networked multiple computer systems.

One of the functions of DRDA is to assure the formats and protocols needed for distributed processing under database management. Such functions include extensions to SQL's application programming interface (API), but not in a manner normalized by the latest versions of ANSI SQL.

Service protocols defined by DRDA extend the SAA common communications support (CCS), assuring the ability to access and use distributed relational resources. This is done in a way which provides transparency between applications and distributed relational databases, through application requester (AR), application server (AS), and database server (DS) functions.

Application request services for information elements use SQL API by means of the AR. The routing of the request through the database network is handled by the AR, AS, and DS functions as well as appropriate protocols.

The *application support* protocol provides the connection between AR and AS, serving the application end of the DRDA connection. The *database support* protocol assures the connection between AS and DS. The DRDA DDM processing model defines an application requester and an application server. It then provides a conceptual framework for constructing common interfaces between systems.

Among supported functions is the establishment of connectivity between the AR and AS, binding SQL statements to a remote database, executing SQL statements, and completing a logical unit of work or terminating the connection between the AR and AS.

Fitting within the architectural perspectives of SAA, however, DRDA provides formats and protocols which are not compatible with ANSI's and ISO's RDA, perpetuating the schism which we discussed in the introduction. The IBM cross-database environment includes:

- Logical unit type 6.2 (LU6.2)
- SNA management services architecture (MSA)[3]

---

[3]The term *architecture* is awfully misused by computers and communications vendors the world over.

- Distributed data management (DDM)
- Formatted data object content architecture (FDOCA)
- Character data representation architecture (CDRA)

LU6.2 supports general communication between programs in distributed processing. It defines communications, unit of work, and security handling requirements.

MSA addresses network management problems. It also cares about network performance, collection of accounting information, network configuration, change control, and reconfigurations.

DDM permits an application program to work on data residing on a remote system. For this purpose, it defines the management of data, connectivity language, commands, and replies. The information elements being manipulated may be in files or relational databases.

Introduced in 1988, *distributed access management* (DAM) assures transparent access to sequential, direct, and keyed files between different SAA environments. To this end, it uses programmed file I/O statements such as "Open," "Close," "Read," "Write," and is supported by distributed data management.

Correspondingly, Distributed Relational Database,[4] provides transparent access to distributed relational database tables between environments supported by SAA. It employs SQL as the SAA database interface and uses DRDA services.

For its part, FDOCA is an architectured collection of constructs employed to interchange formatted data. Through FDOCA, DRDA sends data formatting information either imbedded in or along with the exchanged information elements.

DRDA uses the set of rules of the formatted data object content architecture to describe the information elements which will flow through the system. It is doing so for both numeric and character information. If data is to be passed between systems with like representations, no conversion takes place. But if data passes through a number of heterogeneous systems, conversion takes place once only.

FDOCA permits data descriptors to be sent along with the IE, as separate objects, or to be cached for later use. It also identifies code points which are used to represent characters.

CDRA defines values needed to identify codes employed to represent characters, as well as the conversion of these codes. The chosen approach helps in preserving the characters and their meanings, which is a major housekeeping service.

---

[4]An anagram which sometimes is confused with DRDA.

12.3 A Predominantly Centralized Perspective?

Since its conception, DRDA has been applying the original goals of a centralized, single site DBMS environment to distributed perspectives. A truly distributed goal, however, can only be proven through real-life applications of a peer-to-peer nature, and for the time being the DRDA construct is rather centralized.

There are of course reasons for this design choice. The technical reason IBM advances is that even if for the time being DRDA operates only within its own relational environments and rests on DB2 support, coordinating between unlike DBMS and platforms requires substantial technical understanding. This is true if one of the issues is the perennial conversions between ASCII and EBCDIC across programming language barriers. This has to be accomplished on-line, among SAA's own heterogeneous platforms, as data moves from mainframes to workstations and vice versa.

EBCDIC to ASCII translation and vice versa is necessary for unlike platforms, and this has to be done in full observance of other requirements like network-wide two-phase commit. There is no way to take short cuts and manual intervention is clearly unfeasible.

Another issue which computer vendors chose not to discuss so much is that transactions get increasingly complex, and cross-network coordination requires many cycles. The commit protocols we have available today were originally designed for simple transactions,[5] but long transactions present much more extensive requirements.

Ironically, the extensiveness of commit requirements does not imply at all that the software for processing cross-database transactions should be centralized. If anything, long transactions are best handled in a distributed, client–server environment.

In this sense, following a predominantly centralized perspective is a matter of choice rather than of necessity.[6] It is also a way of retaining control as, quite likely, sometime in the future IBM sees the need for extending DRDA toward other vendors' relational database management systems which support one of the main SQL dialects such as SQL2 or SQL3.

Will DRDA migrate to other DBMS environments? While an easier path may be that of non-IBM relational DBMS, for evident business reasons the first candidate seems to be IMS. That job would be tough even if IMS were still MVS territory.

---

[5]For instance, of the credit/debit type.
[6]See also in this section the discussion on the global distributed catalog.

AIX too needs support from DRDA, if for no other reason than to integrate, in a transaction processing sense, two different and largely incompatible IBM worlds. In principle, IBM seems committed to providing reasonable interoperability between the SAA and AIX environments, but there are no timetables.

Industry analysts believe that once IBM has delivered an AIX DBMS, users will want to connect to SAA. Some think that users may even want the predominant Unix vendors to connect to SAA, more particularly DB2; but other analysts have a totally different opinion.

While there is some degree of speculation in these statements, in concrete implementation terms IBM has defined three levels of functionality for distributed database processing:

- Level 1: Remote unit of work (RUOW)
- Level 2: Distributed unit of work (DUOW)
- Level 3: Distributed request (DR)

DRDA support that is currently available addresses only the first level (remote unit of work), and does not yet address the distributed unit of work (where several DBMS jointly participate in executing a transaction). Most likely, there will be many more years before Level 2 is available, and even that service could be limited in what it offers. With the distributed unit of work, each SQL statement goes to only *one* location.

Greater functionality requires full support for Level 3, which means several more years after DUOW becomes available. Besides this, the distributed request has the added problems of two-phase commit and referential integrity, which also have to be solved.

In the meeting at Santa Teresa, IBM suggested that network-wide integrity constraints may exist between different tables and handling them is a very complex issue. Something similar is true about handling the challenges posed by nonrelational databases (IMS, etc.). Every vendor faces these problems.

Let's repeat the message this chapter has given so far. Currently, DRDA handles *only* relational structures. EDA/SQL, which is not from IBM, can also handle nonrelational structures but in a *read only* manner, while both DRDA and ISO's RDA are *read/write*.

Not yet supported by DRDA is the global distributed catalog. Its aim will be that of promoting a noncentralized structure, as IBM evidently understands that since database networks expand, a centralized approach has major disadvantages. Two of the more important disadvantages are:

- A high degree of contention which can develop with a myriad of workstations and servers addressing a central resource
- Low systems availability, in case the central site crashes or, for whatever reason, is temporarily off

The design idea along the line of distributed facilities is to use a three-part name: name of creator, of table, and of original location site. Some systems specialists think that there may be no reason to have a central catalog as long as these three ID prerequisites are observed, but neither is there a guarantee that they will be observed by all applications.

Since DRDA is aiming to keep site autonomy, the three-part name has in the background the wish to promote this concept. However, the maintenance of autonomous sites is not yet an acquired facility in terms of implementation perspectives. It is always wise to make the distinction between intentions and applications reality.

12.4 Operating under DRDA and EDA/SQL

Today, the way to start DRDA operations is by means of a simple remote request, making it feasible for the user to process a single SQL statement in another location. In this connection, the concept of a unit of work doesn't really apply as it is just a single request, though technically it is defined as one statement in a unit of work and one DBMS in a SQL statement.

The reason for making this distinction is that the remote unit of work may well include more than one SQL statement. This is, however, still limited to one location per unit of work and one DBMS per SQL statement.

Like RUOW, a distributed unit of work will eventually be able to have multiple SQL statements wrapped up as one unit. Also eventually, more than one location could be accessed in a unit of work. This will likely be the next step, but available evidence indicates that it will still be limited to just one DBMS per SQL statement.

Industry analysts think that IBM is already planning, for sometime in the more remote future and after DRDA's distributed requests become operational, to have more than one statement per unit of work, more than one location per unit of work, and more than one location per SQL statement.

Such solutions would lead to a network of multisite joins and unions, but it is not for tomorrow. It is also true that the solution will be quite complex, requiring robust software that is of the best quality technology makes feasible.

The wisdom of proceeding level by level is documented by the fact that many named resources, such as relational tables, must be uniquely accessible from anywhere within a set of interconnected networks. Such names must also be convertible to routings or addresses to complete connection between an application that wants to use information elements and the DBMS that manages them during transaction execution.

Besides the mechanisms of handling many heterogeneous databases and their information elements in a dependable sense, there are also security and protection considerations, as well as issues connected to continuity in the data space.

A user's identification and the privileges that have been granted to that ID should not change if the user enters the environment from different computers. The handling of the *name space* is one of the challenging issues in a heterogeneous environment.

Throughout the network, endusers must be uniquely identifiable by the participating DBMS to properly determine if the access request being made is allowed. This does not necessarily pose a problem to the database to which the user is locally attached, but when remote systems are involved there is a need to differentiate between users.

As current experiences help document, it is necessary to take into account that there may be several users accessing the remote database with the same ID, if these ID are handled in a local rather than global sense.[7] To face this challenge, the DBMS needs a globally unique name space. Typically this contains DBMS code, catalog, and all objects known to the catalog—such as the different networked DBMS.

It goes without saying that conventions, protocols, and a fair amount of sophisticated software is necessary to handle such problems in an able manner. As seen by a program, tables may really be views upon tables, or other types of views. They may also be synonyms or aliases of tables which have to be resolved by the DBMS by means of special software.

Cross-database access software, like DRDA, should also be able to define performance of any remote unit of work processing. For such purpose, limited block fetch helps in optimizing data transfer by guaranteeing the transfer of a minimum amount of information in response to each request from the applications program.

---

[7]In the early 1970s we had a similar problem with new customer numbers assigned by local branches but operational in a debit/credit sense in a global real-time banking application.

DRDA aids in the performance of retrieving data by using a single conversation to transfer blocks of information between machines each time they communicate. EDA/SQL sets for itself a similar goal, but referential integrity is not part of the problem as *read only* operations are involved.

Like DRDA, EDA/SQL operates under MVS and is part of IBM's *Information Warehouse* (IW) offer. While superficially the Information Warehouse may look like another information center—and in terms of support there are similarities—there is also a major difference between them:

- Through RDA/SQL, the Information Warehouse operates on-line.
- In the IBM world, the infocenter depends on an overnight batch extract made through DXT.

This makes a significant difference in terms of helping the enduser access the needed information elements and constitutes the good news. The bad news is that IBM carefully spells out that the Information Warehouse takes two approaches to the information problem:

1. A universal access to data in place, hence the on-line feature
2. Access to duplicate storage the infocenter way, which both operationally and culturally is unwise

On the side of the positive news to the user community, EDA/SAL helps provide a univeral data access to any language or tool able to communicate requests through ANSI/SQL. But the user organization should be careful not to fall into the number 2, negative domain.

User organizations will be well advised to appreciate the fact that both the infocenter and the Information Warehouse address themselves to management-type information. The risk is in creating duplicated databases in a way which cancels the benefits which cross- database accessibility can provide.

One of the central points of EDA/SQL is *change management*. This impacts both processes and information elements, hence requiring establishment of data definitions which in turn calls for first class data dictionary assistance.

Another pillar in change management is the provision of appropriate communication links. For this purpose, EDA/SQL supports major communication protocols: TCP/IP, NetBIOS, Named Pipes, LU6.2 (both APPC and CPI-C), LU2 (the old 3270 data stream), as well as DECnet.

The implementation of EDA/SQL also brings into perspective the issue of *response time*, dear to every user organization all the way down to the single user. IBM makes no commitment on this issue, suggesting that the level of depth a query goes into, for instance IMS, determines what the response time will be.

12.5 DRDA and the Information Warehouse

We said that DRDA is a protocol developed within the context of the System Application Architecture. Hence, by definition, it is *not* an open system. It has been designed with the intention of linking IBM's four incompatible relational database platforms which fall under SAA: SQL of DB2, SQL/DS, SQL/400, and OS/2 DBM.

Some industry analysts suggest that a way of looking at DRDA is as an indirect admission on behalf of IBM that it has cornered itself into four heterogeneous SQL versions—precisely those related to the relational references just made. "One would have expected better internal coordination by a major vendor," said a cognizant executive of a major user organization.

As evidence that the mainframer wants to make up for the different incompatible approaches presented by the relational solutions in question, industry analysts bring forward the fact that IBM's DRDA features an application requester as client interface and an application server as server interface.

They interact with each other in an overall concept as shown in Figure 12.1. The transport mechanism is based on the verb set of advanced

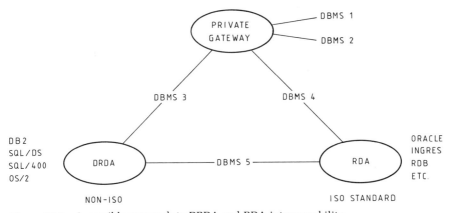

Figure 12.1 A possible approach to DRDA and RDA interoperability.

program-to-program communications (APPC),[8] which uses the SNA LU6.2 protocol. Part of an LU6.2 transport is the support for transaction management, providing the commit and rollback function.

To better understand where DRDA fits within IBM's plans and views for serving its customer base, reference must be made to the Information Warehouse, which was introduced in September 1991 with mainframe announcements. We briefly spoke of it in connection to EDA/SQL in Section 12.4.

The Information Warehouse is a structure within the auspices of SAA that allows access to different relational and nonrelational data types. But we already said that the services are read only, provided in a pass-through manner like those of DataLens by Lotus Development and DAL by Apple Computers.

To avoid criticism that it has announced yet another architecture with no products attached to it, IBM enlisted the help of two third-party developers to deliver IW-connected products:

• Information Builders elaborated the data access in the form of the Enterprise Data Access/Structured Query Language.
• Bachman Information Systems worked in supplying the warehouse modeling functions which are being developed.

The functionality provided (and to be provided) by the Information Warehouse is divided into three parts: *data*, the information elements in the user organization's DBMS; *decision support*, focusing on the data retrieval and manipulation mechanism; *data delivery*, the gear that makes it all turn around.

This approach is being promoted by IBM as an extension to the distributed relational data architecture, having the IW rather than DRDA extend its capabilities to nonrelational and non-IBM databases. But, as stated, in IW cases the emphasis is on *access*, not on update.

The fact that IBM focuses so much on *read only* in the cross-database sense is interpreted by many systems specialists to mean that there may be a dual policy conditioning this move:

1. Gathering into DB2 information from a range of different DBMS types in the IBM and non-IBM world.
2. Through protocols, presenting this information by preference to engines which are IBM's own.

[8]Former low-entry SNA.

Some securities analysts following the computer industry closely believe that, with the exception of EDA/SAL, for the time being the Information Warehouse mainly has propaganda value for IBM, which has been trying to reposition SAA as an open architecture, albeit with limited success.

Cognizant people understand well that an approach that promises to bridge the gaps between different data structures and incompatible DBMS is welcome. But not everybody realizes that *promises* are not enough. What user organizations want are *solutions* which go well beyond the much simpler pass-through supported by DataLens on PC.

The big question of course is: "Where will IW go from here and what precisely is it intended to do?" Some industry watchers think that IBM is not really planning to create an open forum for users, which explains why, at least in a first time, access is provided only to its own environment.

Critics of what might lie behind the dual DRDA/IW effort suggest that IBM's view of multivendor data management is very similar to its perception of multivendor network management. Namely, that all traffic flows *one way*:

- Making the mainframes with DB2 the focal point from which to manage disparate data resources
- Having OS/2 data manager as the best place to manipulate information at workstation level

Though some people think that OS/2 is not going to be long-lived and eventually will be replaced—at least as a workstation workhorse—by the operating system code named PINK, the change in OS does not necessarily mean a change in strategy.

What about other IBM computer products? SQL/DS and SQL/400 fall somewhere between the gaps the DB2 and OS/2 reference pillars. But while the overall strategic aspects are still unclear, and risk remaining so for some time to come, technical issues seem to be somewhat better examined.

Flowing through the LU6.2 conversion are data structures composed of the other DRDA components: DDM, FDOCA, and CDRA, which nest into one another between an upper layer of environment *protocol rules* and a lower layer of *name space* as well as directories.

- The character data representation architecture nests into FDOCA.
- The formatted data object content addresses itself to data descriptions and nests into DDM.

- The distributed data management handles commands and responses, nesting into LU6.2 whose job is transport and unit of work.

The distributed data management commands provide the basic functions of connecting to databases, binding SQL statements, fetching result rows, opening cursors, and so on. Whenever data flows exist between the AR and AS, data is described using the formatted data object content and, in the case of character data, the character data representation architecture.

DRDA provides support for a bind function, implying that *static SQL* is the normal mode of processing SQL statements.[9] Various efficiency issues have been addressed, such as sending data in its native format and converting at the receive end only when necessary.

This is of course necessary to overcome the EBCDIC–ASCII schism deep in the IBM product line and probably is not going to change.

In an effort to improve efficiency, DRDA supports single-row fetch with updatable cursors and multiple-row read-only accesses. It also presents various system management features such as generation of NetView alerts. The same is true of a collection of accounting information for networking.

In conclusion, a major reason for IBM designing and promoting DRDA is to cope with the significant heterogeneity existing among the different SAA database platforms—that is, within its own relational product line. As a result, the new offering is permissive in its tolerance of SQL syntax and datatypes. This may be exploited at a later date to tackle database heterogeneity problems concerning other vendors.

12.6 Differences between DRDA and RDA

We said that remote data access is the emerging standard by the International Organization for Standardization and the American National Standards Institute. RDA and DRDA are not compatible, but both advocate that their norms are the best possible way to distributed database processing.

Let's start with the premise that RDA and DRDA have quite similar goals, while they also try to hide the complexities of distributed database processing behind the SQL application programming interface. When

[9]While IBM's original SQL announcement of 1979 regarded what is now called "dynamic SQL," static SQL is constrained.

the technical cross-database problems are resolved, every user organization is going to profit. But from a business viewpoint, there is a fair amount of confusion among user organizations because of these conflicting norms.

Companies which pay big money for computers and communications are evidently entitled to believe that in the future there will be some sort of mechanism or gateway which will permit interoperability between clients and servers, integrating RDA and DRDA. But this is a wish or at best a hypothesis, not an assurance.

Those who make such a hypothesis based their thinking on the fact that slowly the computer industry is being driven toward common architecture. The momentum is provided by simple economics. We cannot continue forever with fully heterogeneous solutions even within the same vendor's wares, and we can no longer afford to build individual solutions case-by-case over and over again because operating systems and protocols are different.

For their part, the disbelievers of a convergence hypothesis suggest that basically RDA and DRDA address two different aspects of operability in a networked environment. While they both aim to provide solutions to issues such as portability, functionality, and distributed administration, they take different roads.

The foregoing statement is true in a number of ways which go beyond hardware and software configuration. The two approaches use different systems solutions, though they both have to cope with rather similar heterogeneity requirements.

The philosophy of DRDA is to try to handle everything the receiver can understand but also may not understand, providing in the latter case the proper support. To the contrary, RDA permits much greater interoperability but takes the low road—the common denominator.

The higher road and the lower road evidently have to do with the supports being provided. As we have seen in Section 12.3, DRDA has a centralized concept, maintaining integrity through a tightly coupled system. RDA will operate on a global/local concept of decentralization.

The challenge with RDA is that assurance of transaction execution in a multiple environment must be guaranteed in the applications programming side. This is feasible given the increasingly more sophisticated workstations which we have, and it is recommended when products from so many vendors have to interoperate.

A metaphor reflecting the difference between the two philosophies which we are discussing is that of *packet switching* and *datagram* as it developed in the late 1970s. With packet switching, it is the network that cares to bring into line for delivery out of order packets. With the datagram approach, this function falls on the receiving host or workstation.

That is why in the 1970s and 1980s, when computer cycles were expensive, packet switching carried the day. But now the economics have been reversed and datagrams are back, making feasible high performance technologies such as asynchronous transfer mode (ATM) and frame delay.

Looking at this subject both from a technical and from an organizational viewpoint, RDA seems closer to standardizing a client–server environment by specifying the duties of both parties in a two-way connection. This specification includes transfer syntax and semantics along the approach just described.

With RDA, as far as SQL operations are concerned, the client is acting on behalf of an application program or remote process. The server is

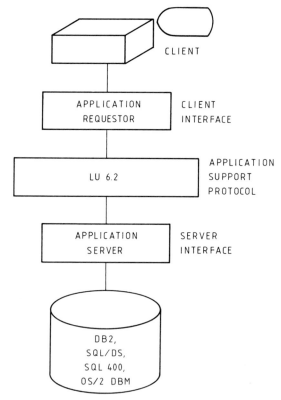

Figure 12.2 IBM's DRDA approach to client–server interoperability.

interfacing to a process that controls data transfers to and from a data-base. There is no central, mainframe-based authority in the execution of such duties.

There exists another key difference between RDA and DRDA. The former is more general in regard to the platforms it covers and the specification which it provides has two parts:

- One is *generic* for arbitrary database connection, thus making feasible greater flexibility.
- The other concerns a SQL specialization for connecting databases conforming to SQL norms.

While given their origin it is normal that differences exist in software as well as in the background concepts between RDA and DRDA, it is also true that when their usage involves systems which are still in design, it tends to perpetuate incompatibilities. Usually, heterogeneous solutions are not arrived at by accident.

During the May 1992 meeting at the Santa Teresa Laboratories, IBM suggested a possible approach to RDA–DRDA interoperability (as shown in Figure 12.2). But at the same time, IBM denied what DEC had said a day earlier at a meeting in New York: that the two companies are currently working on a RDA–DRDA gateway.[10]

Of course no statement is valid forever. In this case, the door was left open for an eventual bridge by saying that: "It might be that RDA becomes the standard. In this case IBM has made the commitment to develop the gateway." User organizations would prefer that the gateway be available today.

---

[10]In fact, as stated during the Santa Teresa meeting, IBM will eventually support Oracle and other relational DBMS but not necessarily RDB and Ingres.

CHAPTER 13

Development of the DataLens Concept and Its Productization

13.1 Introduction

The line of reasoning which led to the DataLens effort dates to around 1987.[1] Initially, Lotus Development envisioned putting together a driver which permits multiple accesses through a DBMS interface in partnership with DBMS vendors. But this did not find an echo.

The apparent rejection of cooperation by DBMS vendors had an aftermath on Lotus Development. The concept used in DataLens moved toward addressing a growing number of local database platforms while the company avoided a close association with any one DBMS vendor.

"We do not want to be linked to one single major vendor," said a cognizant executive. "Though we will work with some third-party vendors." Eventually, this provided a competitive advantage to the implementation of DataLens and its cross-database capability.

As far as the developers are concerned, an approach independent of DBMS vendors had other advantages. It led to focusing on database technology, starting with the fundamentals and proceeding with database management. Eventually, this approach can open new product perspectives in terms of:

- Visualization
- Multimedia
- Object orientation
- New forms of storing and retrieving information

[1]Out of what seems to have been research work at MIT, though Lotus does not confirm this point.

218

Whether or not Lotus Development chooses to pursue these domains is not the subject of this book. What is important is that a broader perspective permits better accommodation of the developing requirements on database usage across an expanding topology with increasingly *ad hoc* query requirements and the handling of long transactions.

Cross-database solutions have a better chance of survival when they rest on flexible structures assuring *program and data independence* and enabling their users to change the focal point of database access without affecting the applications that access the IE.

Among the basic principles underlying the DataLens design approach is that existing data should not have to be modified in order to achieve integration of files from different databases. The local IE should remain in place; only a copy would have to migrate. At the same time, existing applications should not have to be changed, unless it is desirable for processing reasons.

Another design prerequisite for the solution in reference is that users should not have to adopt a new language for communicating with the integrated system. It must be possible to access local database resources independently, and the procedure should not have to change when additional resources are integrated.

The DataLens software helps the user in envisioning the components which enter a system solution in database accessing terms, automatically defining relationships as well as interfaces. As we will see, the use of drivers provides the stability needed to address distributed databases.

Such an approach provides good advice to be kept in mind regarding the architecturing of current and future systems which need to work together. As new technology evolves, it can be incorporated without disrupting database access solutions.

13.2 Putting in Practice a Multidatabase Access Scheme

It is to the credit of Lotus designers that they started with a simple, straightforward database access concept and kept to their original idea, avoiding more ambitious approaches to connectivity of heterogeneous data resources. An example is their construction of global schemata or complex interoperable heterogeneous solutions.

As it presently stands, DataLens resolves architectural dilemmas related to data types, character sets, system catalogs, and different capability sets. But it stops short of addressing schema integration issues and inner-schema conflicts.

By contrast, once the information elements have arrived at the requesting agent (client, user), there are good facilities for transforming them within applications—in this particular case, the Lotus 1-2-3 spreadsheet. This is good enough for many implementations where the primary requirement is to be able to access IE, wherever they might be stored, for a specific job.

On the belief that most data is now stored in nonrelational systems, particularly by a VSAM file created and managed through a Cobol program, Lotus designers included VSAM in their effort. Hence, while DataLens is a good match for SQL servers, it does provide interfaces to more primitive, less intelligent back ends. This is manifested in two main areas:

1. The simple requirements placed on a DataLens *basic driver*, the simplest possible version of supporting specification
2. The choice of the call interface over a given string language

Under this approach, simple drivers do not need any sort of parsing facility which simplifies the database connectivity issues and makes them more accessible.

This sound, easy to implement technical solution helps in doing away with current *manual methods* often used in transferring data from databases (typically retyping this data by hand or changing tapes and floppies). Such manual approaches, which can be found in many installations, are not only time consuming and costly but also error prone.

It's worth noting that other developers also retained the solution used by DataLens, an example being Apple Computers for the Macintosh line. In the Macintosh case, the driver functionality is embedded in the applications software, an approach which has also characterized the first release of what became the commodity product DataLens.

Subsequent to the establishment of the initial concept, Release 3.0 of Lotus 1-2-3 incorporated some of the original ideas. Connectivity was made available for Sun and Vax computers as well as in relation to All-in-One and Windows software.

Some of the technology subsequently implemented in the DataLens has been embedded in Release 3.0 as part of an internal advanced technology project. The first specific DataLens driver was developed somewhat in parallel to Release 3.0 for dbase III/IV and was shipped three months later than the Release in reference.

To better understand the connection between DataLens and Release 3 of the 1-2-3 spreadsheet, it is necessary to differentiate between the component modules of DataLens and the database engine embedded in 1-2-3.

Differences and relationships between these two items also help explain why today Lotus 1-2-3 is the only application supported by DataLens, though future developments could include any Lotus product: Graphics, Notes, and so on, as well as a multi-applications perspective.

Quite clearly, any application can benefit from the fact that a generic data translation program exists to aid in the manipulation necessary after the access and transfer of data. This is a great improvement over current approaches where IE transfer itself is cumbersome, but the *ad hoc* development of routines for data translation is very time consuming. Typically, today, if the IE happen to reside on a mainframe and are needed on a WS, the turnaround time for a request is often measured in days. If a custom-made extraction program has to be written, the wait can be measured in months or years.

Clear-eyed companies have come to realize that the only elegant approach is to assure an on-line real-time connection to the distributed heterogeneous databases. The solution must preserve local type information and save the user from having to learn different one-to-one interfacing routines.

Lotus Development perceives DataLens as a critical component of *a new generation* of cross database software. This artifact is designed to provide multivendor data access across hardware and operating system platforms.

The Lotus solution assures good connectivity that helps capitalize on the existing computers and communications architectures, allowing users to transparently access information elements throughout diverse and incompatible database structure.

13.3 The 1-2-3 Database Engine: A Partner of DataLens

Figure 13.1 presents in a block diagram the two main components of a spreadsheet, the *presentation facility* and the *database engine*, as well as how they interface by means of DataLens to different DBMS. This is achieved through *virtual tables* handled by DataLens which may come from relational or nonrelational DBMS.

Within this context, DataLens is a specification that describes how Lotus 1-2-3 communicates with a range of databases. As we will see in subsequent sections, a DataLens driver is created for each data source by using appropriate function calls and data structures defined in the DataLens specification.

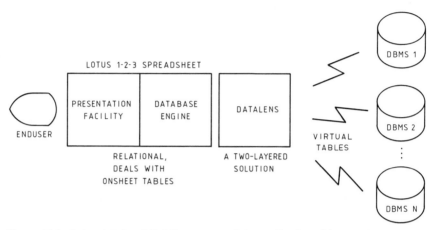

Figure 13.1   Lotus 1-2-3 and DataLens connectivity to distributed heterogeneous databases.

Correspondingly, the DataLens driver and the DBMS communicate using the DBMS's standard interface. The driver receives requests for information from the 1-2-3 spreadsheet and translates them into DBMS commands which are submitted to the DBMS for which they have been made. Then, the driver receives the results from the DBMS, translates them into a standard format, and forwards them to 1-2-3.

As this brief description helps document,[2] the database access capability mechanism allows considerable flexibility with respect to the location and extent of a distributed environment. A particular function, such as sorting, might be implemented in the DBMS server kernel or in the DataLens driver above it. This distinction is transparent to the application, except for possible performance implications. Alternatively, the application itself may either provide the function or prevent the user from invoking it.

It is precisely this last choice which leads to the two major modes of DataLens usage which we saw in Section 13.2: *basic* and *value added*. The application allows the user to invoke only those operations that are supported by the respective driver. This provides for flexibility in a user interface, restricting the complexity of queries that can be constructed in a function of the DBMS being accessed without losing consistency in the handling and presentation of the human–machine interface itself.

The 1-2-3 presentation facility and its associated database engine deal with on-sheet tables. These are presented by DataLens, which accesses

[2]We will examine in detail the functions of the driver in Sections 13.6 and 13.7.

the heterogeneous DBMS. This happens in a point-to-point fashion but can be executed in parallel through several point-to-point accesses to an equal number of databases.

The 1-2-3 database engine processes tables unaware of where they come from. Such a function is made feasible by the fact that DataLens takes care of virtual table construction besides the data access proper. It also uses standard platform-independent data types such as integer, packed decimal, and floating point to transfer IE between the application and the driver. Nonstandard data can be converted to one of the standard data types, or the driver can define extended types as needed.

This brings in the value added perspective, or high road, which we discussed in Section 13.2. For instance:

- With Sybase, a two-records join is supported because the DBMS has a richer repertoire.
- With Dbase III there is no join. DataLens describes the situation and the database engine of 1-2-3 compensates.
- With IMS, the translation into ASCII is within the driver supported by the Lotus multibyte character set (LMBCS or Lambecs).

Lambecs is part of the DataLens driver and at the same time it is the standard of 1-2-3.

13.4 Application Programming Interface

A different way of explaining this reference is that DataLens drivers and Lotus 1-2-3 communicate across the DataLens applications programming interface (API) through LMBCS, which is a portable and expandable character set similar to DEC's multilingual character set. As such, it can represent every character in any character set, regardless of language and computing platform.[3]

By means of such facilities, files created in different languages can be read and written without being corrupted. This is true even if there are conflicting definitions among characters in the respective languages. Furthermore, a capability definition mechanism permits description of the different treatments of isolation—that is, level of interference with

---

[3]Lotus Development is a member of the SQL Access Group and closely monitors its work. Semantically, DataLens is a superset of the API functionality, but the API offered by Lotus is not compatible with the SQL API since the latter has not yet been officially released.

other server users—to be found across servers. This makes feasible read repeatability as contrasted to read-only connections.

- Some servers have a transaction ability so that the application can commit and abort transactions; others do not.
- The facility to break out of a currently executing query is often tied to the server's transaction model, hence part of the high road.

The DataLens driver uses a capability bit mask to tell applications which *optional* features, if any, it supports. Value added features include updating, querying and subquerying, nonsequential fetching, long data handling, record selection, breaking out from an executing query, and transactional and concurrency control.

Other value added features include operators and functions relating to the following list of items:

- Logical
- Arithmetic
- Financial
- String
- Date
- Aggregation
- Set

The same is valid regarding functions such as prepared statement handling, privilege handling, system catalog querying, and data definition.

The DataLens driver supports optional capabilities through standardized function calls. It is also possible to define *extended* features corresponding to server-specific functions not covered by basic or optional functionality bits, but there is no standard protocol for manipulating extended facilities. Through this approach DataLens supports types including character data, number data, and time stamps.

If records are time stamped, the time stamps will be handled as part of the record. DataLens also respects different levels of passwords provided by the DBMS. The driver(s) take advantage of security mechanisms such as user IDs and access privileges, assuring that existing security and integrity levels are maintained.

For security purposes, the user can manipulate what is available in the distributed DBMS database, taking advantage of available value added features. Hence, security is at two levels: the DataLens driver and the DBMS.

13.5 The Layered Architecture of DataLens

We said that DataLens software defines how 1-2-3 talks to a given database and suggested that this is done through a layered structure which permits endusers to extract their own IE and create their own reports using 1-2-3 commands which they already know. This is a major improvement over different uncoordinated practices which result from multiple database sources and end in heterogeneous human interfaces.

The ability to provide more efficient database access accommodating new applications strengthens ties between computer professionals and endusers. Familiar query commands are being employed to extract selected IE, with the user performing any number of extracts or updates without reconnecting or creating new ranges.

The existence of templates eliminates the need to set up input, output, and criteria ranges. Macros can be created to establish the connection to the data source with a single command. This is helped through the chosen two-layered structure shown in Figure 13.2:

- *Layer 1* interfaces to the database engine of Lotus 1-2-3 and is the first to receive the request for database access by the spreadsheet.
- *Layer 2* is composed of family drivers, one created for each database management system. The drivers do the communicating.

The application programming interface which is employed has become a standard in the relational query and DBMS worlds, therefore the

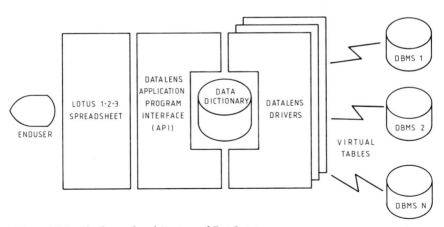

Figure 13.2 The layered architecture of DataLens.

choice is properly done. It is the job of the drivers to send requests from 1-2-3 and the applications layer to the data source and return IE to the worksheet. Such information elements can be almost anywhere: on mainframe, maxis, minis, a LAN server, another workstation, or a CD-ROM. They can also be in any format.

This layered approach to the access of diverse databases with incompatible DBMS has two advantages. First, it lets 1-2-3 users get the data they need without complicated procedures. Since DataLens integrates with the recent versions of 1-2-3, users do not have to learn a separate interface for data access; they work with familiar 1-2-3 commands. Second, the layered approach avoids the cumbersome process of rewriting the entire software for every new and incompatible DBMS being supported.

The applications layer is common to all database accesses and the same is true of the supported data dictionary. What needs to be written to include a new heterogeneous database is the driver, and even in this case some modules are reusable software.

DataLens defines about 100 standard error conditions as well as a mechanism for drivers to deliver detailed event-specific and back end-specific error descriptions to an application. This permits DataLens applications to manipulate a range of error conditions.

Precisely because it incorporates multiple drivers, DataLens enhances the ability of work groups to share information elements. User organizations can choose different hardware, but 1-2-3 provides a common data access tool on all supported platforms.

Furthermore, data access criteria can be customized for a given work group and shared between members the same way 1-2-3 macros, templates, and models are customized and shared. This assures a greater flexibility in terms of end usage.

Embedded functionality permits us to filter and dynamically screen, the latter not always being necessary as lots of screening is done at the level of the DBMS. DataLens services are augmented through AI constructs; two which are currently supported are:

- The *solver*, which is also a component of other Lotus products and is shipped in some installations and beta tested in others.
- *Improve*, the new generation spreadsheet for the next computer, which includes both data and rules (of which we spoke in the preceding chapter).

Knowledge-engineering routines left aside, current DataLens technology is implemented by means of code built into the application software that communicates with the data source through the appropriate Data-Lens driver. A focal point of the architecture is therefore the drivers connecting the application to the distributed databases.

Drivers receive requests for information from the API, translate them into DBMS commands, and send the results back to the application. The study of the way driver functions are implemented reveals the vital role they place on the whole interconnection process.

13.6 Services Rendered by the DataLens Drivers

The applications interface layer of DataLens does not directly define a distributed database support. But it allows an application to simultaneously connect to multiple drivers, which correspond to servers and databases in heterogeneous systems.

Lotus 1-2-3 uses this functionality to support queries across distributed resources. For instance, a table residing in one database may be joined with one or more tables under a different DBMS. API distributes the parts of the query to be handled independently at each site and assembles the answer. For cross-database support, it depends on servers which address the distributed databases.

Drivers translate *metadata* queries and updates, which are expressed as DataLens functions, down to the basics of the underlying system. The mask mechanism mentioned in the preceding sections is used to specify whether the server supports views, user authorization, synonyms, row IDs usable for update, and the like.

As a minimum, all drivers feature a set of simple catalog browser functions that allow applications to obtain fundamental information about tables and columns in the database. An optional capability makes feasible direct queries against system catalog tables, such as finding all columns in a table.

Given a whole family of drivers, endusers can take full advantage of the features of each specific DBMS being supported rather than settling for a small but standard set of features. This assures significant flexibility when working with distributed databases running on diverse platforms.

Given that drivers can be written to use data types most suitable to each DBMS, endusers are able to extract IE from these sources with standard and nonstandard data types. Furthermore, a DataLens *Developer Toolkit* makes it easy for DBMS vendors, with proprietary data sources, and systems programmers to develop new drivers.

Provided by Lotus, this toolkit contains the DataLens specification plus tools and documentation to write a driver. Its usage helps extend the access to external databases for new or existing applications which must reach additional DBMS. This is also an efficient approach to developing connectivity from multiple applications to multiple data sources.

The Developer Toolkit permits a driver to be written only once for a particular data source, supporting all DataLens applications. In a similar manner, once an application understands DataLens, it needs to do no other work to gain access to different databases.

As the number of applications and drivers grows, the connectivity perspectives increase significantly while the development cycle is reduced, given that software developers no longer need to constantly modify database extract routines and programs. Drivers can be ported rather easily, with the driver developer providing access to different DBMS from applications on different platforms, shielding the user from the actual data access process. The application program interface handles function calls whose arguments include data structures. The enduser does not see these calls directly, greatly simplifying the use of the database access software.

Unlike many other database APIs, DataLens has no string sublanguage that is passed into the server. There is an execute string trap door for passing arbitrary strings to the server, but this is transparent to the user. Queries are formulated by building what amounts to a parse tree, passing that form over the interface. This removes most of the frequent syntactic particularities of different dialects of query languages. Such functionality also helps in resolving the interpretation of nested algebraic expressions, allowing drivers for simple DBMS or file managers to avoid implementing the equivalent of an SQL parser.

From enduser query to database access, the sequence of events is shown in Figure 13.3, which also explains the interplay between Data-

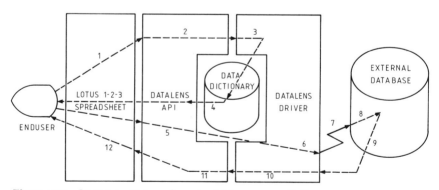

Figure 13.3   Steps 1 to 12 in enduser to database connectivity.

Lens API and driver. Through a command or interface of the application, the enduser makes a request calling for access to database(s). This is step 1. In step 2, the application programming:

• Loads the appropriate DataLens driver
• Establishes connections
• Allocates control blocks
• Passes the control block pointers to the driver

In step 3, assisted through a data dictionary, the driver obtains database connection information. It supplies such references by filling in the control blocks and passes a function vector of entry points to the application (step 4).

By means of the commands or user interface of the application, the enduser makes a request to access data. This is step 5. In step 6 the application uses the function vector to call specific DataLens functions within the driver.

The driver translates the request into the DBMS-specific API and the associated language used by the database. During step 7, it transmits the request for information elements to the DBMS.

In the course of step 8, the DBMS processes the request for information elements, retrieving the appropriate IE. These are returned as results to the driver during step 9.

Subsequently, in step 10, the driver converts the results to DataLens standard format and passes them to the API layer. In step 11, API communicates the IE to the spreadsheet. The latter's application facility displays the data and returns control to the enduser in step 12.

There are only a few system services needed to support run-time driver connection by applications. These are catalog and dynamic loading routines provided on most platforms by a small piece of code, called GAB, which assures a rudimentary naming service for browsing DataLens drivers.

The latter can be a stand-alone implementation or assured through a real naming service, if the operating environment provides one. GAB also manages the loading and sharing of multiple DataLens drivers.

By centralizing such activity on a file server or host, rather than the workstation, multiple applications can share drivers simultaneously. Similarly, they can be updated independently of API and drivers when the underlying services evolve toward a more sophisticated implementation.

Leveraging of DBMS functionality is assured by the fact that DataLens drivers use the existing DBMS interface to communicate with the database management system. This solution is nonintrusive to the host server while exploiting the power the server makes available.

13.7 Mechanics of the Driver's Interconnection

The DataLens drivers are specific to the characteristics of the back-end engine, that is, special to the DBMS they address and its primitives. This helps explain the architecture and functionality of DataLens. We can distinguish the following steps:

- Open the driver connection
- Connect through it to the DBMS
- Understand its schema and capabilities
- Execute simple fetch back to the driver
- Close down the driver connection

Management schemes concerning each member of the family of drivers, one per supported DBMS or file, explain how server differences are overcome in terms of data types, character sets, and system catalogs (*metadata* access).

This approach is well suited for exception handling. It permits us to uphold an isolation model in regard to distributed database capabilities. It also provides an efficient manner of interconnection to heterogeneous servers and databases. Such an operation takes place in two parts:

1. The driver itself translates between virtual machine and the programmatic interfaces of the database.
2. On-line connectivity integrates into the network's transport primitives and supports open-system principles.

As far as the access to the data dictionary is concerned (shown in Figure 13.3), this retrieves, among other issues, the specs and table formats of known (supported) databases. There is no global schema, with the data dictionary acting mainly as *directory* and *format reference*.

The DataLens driver depends on the underlying servers for replication, fragmentation, and query optimization. Connectivity to the DBMS is assured by means of network-based remote procedure calls (RPC).

Problems relating to global consistency control are eased by the fact that distributed database connectivity is mainly done for analytical query purposes—hence read only. If update is necessary, then the system uses raw ID by DBMS.

Hence, in terms of mechanics the precise solution depends on the underlying servers for doing some of the fancier things which may be needed. Some relational DBMS, for instance Ingres, have themselves the capability to coordinate among multiple servers.

It is precisely in regard to this reference, in terms of coping with server differences, that in the opening section we have spoken of alternatives such as:

- The *low-road* approach using only the most basic common functionality
- The *middle-road* approach defining basic capabilities and treating the others as value added
- The *high-road* approach looking out to find the same advanced functionality everywhere among the networked databases

As it has been appropriately explained, the basics are connect, browse, fetch, and the native string pass-through. Add-ons include select joins, updates, break of queries, handling of subqueries, and the use of a queriable catalog.

Generally, the more the approach becomes value added the more the solution is going toward the high road and away from the *passive* implementation, which is staying at the basic level. Just the same, the more the solution is value added the better it permits leveraging of the interconnected databases and the implementation of escape mechanisms. But it becomes less and less applicable in real-life database environments where file management and hierarchical DBMS dominate.

The low road is important because a crucial aspect of DataLens mechanics is the underlying conceptual *universality*, thus providing a cross-platform access for interconnected workstations.

This is a good example of principles which should characterize system design: carefully avoiding the often followed path of doing strange and difficult things instead of using a simple approach with the goal to:

- Ease enduser chores
- Make the mechanics transparent to the enduser
- Permit operation in real time
- Provide a solution which is ready for use within a short time frame

One lesson worth learning from the DataLens experience is the wisdom of editing out of the system complex approaches such as those implied by a global schema. Another lesson is the need to assure a good match to

SQL as well as nonrelational servers while at the same time supporting a range of applications products.

To recapitulate, in terms of the mechanics of implementation, it is the driver which handles both the network link and the interface to the DBMS while, at the DBMS level, the anchor point is the aforementioned remote procedure call executed in a networking sense. An alternative to this solution is to split the DataLens driver into three sets, leaving the first part at the WS as network surrogate and bringing the other two parts as resident at the database server. This approach has been chosen by Lotus Development in connection to a Unix environment.

13.8 Implementation Opportunities with DataLens Software

If raw connectivity has been the first and foremost requirement in using on-line database resources, polyvalence in accessing heterogeneous databases is the second. This has taken place by stages, starting with a short-term solution which permits the usage of commodity software able to address the immediate connectivity needs for managerial purposes.

Such functionality is precisely what the DataLens solution offers. No doubt, for the medium to longer term, more generic alternative will need to be developed including both multimedia gateway architectures and federated approaches to heterogeneous distributed databases.

While these are solutions which have first to be studied in depth and then supported through well-focused projects, it is wise to lose neither time nor money in waiting for "perfection." Currently available productized software can save lots of trouble as well as errors and delays.

Provided benchmarking is done with adoption as a goal, DataLens has much to offer, starting with the fact that platform-specific DataLens Developer Toolkits are currently available for MS-DOS, OS/2, Sun Unix, and VAX/VMS.[4] They include:

- An example driver
- Code libraries
- A LMBCS character-handling routine
- Diagnostic tools
- A test application
- Documentation

[4]The CL/1 connectivity language for the Macintosh also needs no intermediary between application and driver, but it lacks the concept of server capabilities.

Table 13.1 Heterogeneous Databases Supported and
to Be Supported by DataLens

* DB2	* Oracle
* SQL/DS	* Vanguard and RBASE
* Adabas	* CCA Model 204
* IMS	* Paradox
* VSAM	* dbase III
* Teradata	* Netware SQL
* Sybase SQL Server	* SQL Server
* RDB	* SQL Base
* RMS	* OS/2 Extended Edition
* Ingres	Data Manager
	* DB Accelerator

On the application side, DataLens technology has now been incorporated into the 1-2-3/3.0 for MS-DOS and OS/2, 1-2-3/M for IBM mainframe environments, and 1-2-3/G for DEC VMS and All-in-1. Thus, 1-2-3/M users can now access DB/2 directly; 1-2-3/G and 1-2-3/3.0 users can access the Sybase S1L Server, and so on. In the future, DataLens technology will be used for Lotus database tools.

Users invoke external data access by choosing the Lotus 1-2-3 menu commands "/Data External" to connect to the database and "/Data Query Extract" to bring data into the spreadsheet. In addition, users can create and update data using other familiar data commands. DataLens leverages users' knowledge of Lotus 1-2-3, providing a known environment for accessing distributed heterogeneous databases.

As demonstrated in the preceding sections, incorporating the DataLens interface into applications creates a consistent and transparent means for Lotus users. Through commodity software they can move data into their applications for analysis, manipulation, and storage.

Table 13.1 outlines the maximum possibilities. Lotus Development suggests that through the IBM PC the following systems can be reached via DataLens: dBase, Paradox, Novell Netware SQL, Sybase/Microsoft SQL Server (running on an OS/2 server, under Unix or VMS), DEC RDB, and IBM AS/400.

In addition, the following systems will be supported by the end of 1991: IBM EEDM, Informix (on PC, under Unix or VMS), Oracle (on PC, under Unix, VMS, or IBM mainframe), Ingres (on PC, Unix, or VMS), Focus (PC, Unix, VMS, or IBM mainframe). Also IXF, SQL/DS, DB2, Adabas, IMS, IDMS, Teradata, and VSAM files are supported through the Focus DataLens Driver.

A different way of making this statement is that DataLens is implemented and supported on DOS, OS/2, several versions of Unix, VMS, some versions of MVS, and different versions of VM/CMS. Furthermore, with the Lotus Macintosh Spreadsheet available DataLens can run under the Macintosh operating system.

All this seems impressive and it is so. However, a negative aspect has also to be retained: Not every DBMS is supported under every OS mentioned in the preceding paragraphs. Lotus Development developed a road map which helps identify available drivers by hardware and OS platform.

To recapitulate, some 20 heterogeneous databases are being supported presently as shown in Table 13.1. There is also a driver to manipulate simple ASCII files and a plan to support DMS II of Unisys.

Lotus also gave a special software example concerning the building of DataLens drivers with add-ons to its spreadsheet for *security* purposes. It has been done on Sun workstations for a financial institution in New York.

To the query regarding examples of past collaborations on the development of focused constructs, Lotus mentioned a joint project with Xerox on a *budgeting application* which involved planning, reporting, and outlooking.

This *plan/actual* implementation involved heterogeneous databases as well as an enhanced dbase-spreadsheet (Spreadbase) coordination. The value of these examples is to document that once a *properly designed* solution becomes operable, it can be amenable to *customization*, fitting in a better way the user organization's requirements.

CHAPTER 14

The California Intelligent Database Assistant (CALIDA)

14.1 Introduction

The California Intelligent Database Assistant (CALIDA) has been designed and implemented by the GTE Laboratories, Weltham, Massachusetts. It is the first practical usage of the IDA[1] shell made by the same laboratories whose object has been to provide global, integrated retrieval from multiple heterogeneous databases. CALIDA features include:

- Easy communication with the enduser via a high-level query specification language, adjustable to the enduser's computer literacy level
- Menu guided interfaces enriched with user-defined macros
- Sizing up and estimation of the query results for resource utilization and associated planning reasons
- Warning given to the user about expensive queries as the complexity of queries increases
- Automatic generation of subqueries and heterogeneous database targeting
- The generation of multiple database access and query integration programs as necessary
- Automatic join generation and other utility functions
- Transparent network utilization in reaching the appropriate databases
- Automatic generation of target database queries as necessary
- Automatic join generation and other utility functions
- Data protection from unauthorized use, for security purposes

[1]Intelligent Database Assistant. For a description of IDA, see D.N. Chorafas *Risk Management in Financial Institutions*, Butterworths, London and Boston, 1990.

Since December 1988 CALIDA has been put into practical implementation accessing corporate data from relational and hierarchical databases, variable record type files, and flat files. Apart from offering interoperability, its usage permits the reduction of average query turnaround time.

CALIDA has been optimized for an applications environment characterized by a relatively small number of very large, complex queries addressed to heterogeneous databases. The latter are largely independent from one another in the sense that there is no global schema to be observed and local databases have data definition autonomy. With this solution, each database is represented in the federation through its local characteristics. Semantic rules are used to improve upon integration, as we will see shortly.

The first release of CALIDA has been implemented on the Xerox AI workstation using Interlisp-D. Since this first release, the artifact has been endowed with network links to remote databases.

14.2 Employing the Concept of the Expert Schema

The overriding architectural concept of IDA and CALIDA is that of a federated database solution which contrasts to that of a global schema. As Dr. Gabriel Jakobson suggested,[2] "The global schema seems to be more elegant since it is able to shield the user from multiplicity of different heterogeneous schemata. But it is not feasible." If the global schema were feasible, it would have been nice to have an interface between the user and the distributed databases presenting all information elements *as if* they were in one homogeneous database. But, as we have already seen on several occasions, experience shows that this does not work.

One of the hypotheses studied by the GTE Laboratories, among others, concerned the feasibility of constructing a virtual database layer liberating the user from the diversity of the logical schemata of the underlying databases. This, however, posed several other problems such as:

• Preserving data consistency and integrity
• Resolving the challenge of the global naming problem
• Overcoming low efficiency in manipulating large databases

Effective solutions to these problems are still forthcoming. By contrast, the chosen solution of *federated databases* leaves the local databases

---

[2]As stated during the meeting which took place in the course of the research at the GTE Laboratories.

logically independent. With, in each heterogeneous database in the federation a subschema is defined: the *export schema*, which determines the possible connections with the other databases.

The export schemata does not preserve the data integrity and uniqueness of the IE names in a cross-database sense, as the global schema might do. But it has the advantage that it provides a practical cross-database environment, making it easy to deal in an able manner with a large number of heterogeneous database structures. Figure 14.1 helps one appreciate the CALIDA contribution along this line of reasoning. The graph is based on the components of the IDA engine.

- The shell's user interface provides the basis for an agile interactivity.
- The expert module of the database acts like a knowledgeable dictionary facility.
- The database communications module reaches incompatible databases through the network.

As can be appreciated, the chosen architecture is applications independent. There is, however, a specific applications knowledgebank steadily being enriched as the implementations horizon expands. Another key component is the knowledgebank's data dictionary edit facility.

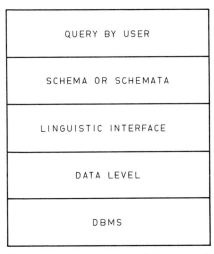

Figure 14.1 Constraints and functions of the layered CALIDA structure.

Given the autonomy of local databases in the network, logical attributes may vary, but overall design goals address themselves to the necessity of gaining the inherent efficiency advantages of distribution while providing a fairly integrated environment. In an engineering design sense, when we exploit distributed resources, the *price* we pay for our solutions lies in the provision of structure and functionality. The *benefits* we derive come from fusing, coordinating, and assuring the consistency of information elements across geographically and logically dispersed databases.

We also try to capitalize on the fact that linguistic specifications and semantic elements enrich the knowledge domain. The rules which the knowledge domain contains make it feasible to explore new logical combinations capable of facilitating real-time search of what are certain to become enormous knowledge-based semantic networks.

With the CALIDA implementation example, the integration is achieved on the logical level by defining global join fields between the networked databases. Their descriptions are stored in the IDA data dictionary. Knowledge modules help in automatic generation of joins between the distributed files which satisfy a given query, thus helping to integrate the response.

14.3 Targeting CALIDA-88

As has been explained on several occasions, one of the major goals of systems development during the 1990s is that of presenting the enduser with an integrated interface to heterogeneous databases. To do so in an able manner, we need to reconcile many differences, some of which can be resolved by a uniform user language—though not all of diversity prevailing in the networked databases can be handled through interfaces.

In this perspective, in the CALIDA solution the necessary services are provided by means of four major functional components: user interfaces, a database expert system, network communications, and the knowledgebank—all of which have been mentioned in the preceding section. The user interface is interactive and menu driven.

Constructs needed for query formulation, such as logical and arithmetic operations, different comparisons, output conditions and sorting specifications, are entered through menus. Menus are also used for selecting databases, as well as the files and fields they contain at the level of the desired information elements. Through a macro facility the user can customize the interface by defining new metaphors.

A linguistic construct has been designed for *ad hoc* interactive queries. Known as CALIDA-88, it is similar in nature to SQL, but it also assures more enriched database operations such as aggregates on secondary records as well as grouping and summaries within the same query which are not found in SQL.[3] Requests that integrate IE from multiple databases can be specified within a single query. This permits the user language to serve as a basis for database integration at the highest level of reference.

CALIDA-88 has a core set of features needed to express most of the frequently required database operations but does not have every feature of every target language. Queries expressed in this query facility are first transformed into DELPHI, an intermediate database language. They are then translated into different relational and low-level languages to access heterogeneous files.

This approach resembles the one taken in the early days of higher level languages (mid-1950s) with FORTRAN, where the internal translator (IT) played the intermediate-layer role. In fact, FORTRAN's first name was FORTRANSIT, with the double meaning formula translation into IT and a construct written for transit purposes.

Always with reference to Figure 14.1, the database expert system module performs the following added tasks: It plans and optimizes query execution for integrating the networked databases, transforms the query execution plan into the target database image, and estimates the number of records to be returned before actually accessing the databases.

However, since CALIDA does not have a global data manager, not all of its features are applicable for all databases. To help itself in its mission, CALIDA extensively uses constraints and semantic correctness rules. These assist in dynamically disabling features inapplicable to a specific database. The chosen process employs the facilities of IDA's knowledgebank, which contains the data dictionary of each heterogeneous database in the network. It uses explicitly designed software modules for generating the target database program.

The data dictionary edit/browser allows users to modify the data dictionary itself as well as file, record, and field specifications. A security package has knowledge of all the authorized CALIDA users and their passwords, which can be modified only by the database administrator.

The GTE Laboratories underlined that five levels of reference are important in dealing with heterogeneous databases, each presenting its own capabilities and constraints. As is shown in Figure 14.2, these start at the user level and end at the DBMS:

---

[3]Which speaks volumes about the obsolescence of SQL.

- Query by user
- Schema or schemata
- Linguistic reference
- Multimedia data level
- Database management systems

The GTE approach has been that of achieving integration at the query language level by using CALIDA-88 in a uniform way to access all databases supported by the system. Access to heterogeneous databases is helped by the macro facility, enabling users to define and employ domain-specific concepts as macros.

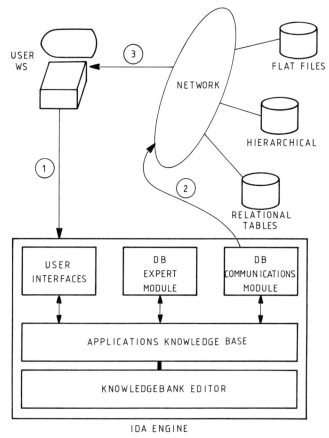

Figure 14.2 Component modules of the IDA engine.

There is another aspect of CALIDA-88 which is fairly interesting because it supports the integration of networked databases. During schema definition time, it generates a full database join tree. To do so, it uses heuristic guesses about inter- and intradatabase join fields—the way it has been explained in the preceding section.

14.4 Query, Schema, and Language Performance

CALIDA-88 is targeted for three types of databases: relational, hierarchical, and flat files. It supports relational language features such as multilevel grouping, sorting, and aggregate summary and also generates the joins, both at intra- and cross-database levels.

Nonrelational structures are handled by permitting the user to define complex conditional compute statements which are evaluated during query execution. This makes it feasible to get aggregated information elements from secondary records with multiple occurrence. Queries expressed using CALIDA-88 may have several sections, which range from simple to complex, and can be independently specified, greatly increasing system flexibility.

The *compute* section, for example, defines new variables that can later be used in the condition, output, sort, or summary sections or reused in other computations. The *destination* section indicates the destination of the query output—be it a file, terminal, hardcopy, or softcopy (visualization).

Endusers can specify the condition for accepting or rejecting databases entities. The sort section defines the sorting and grouping order of the output; the output section addresses the tabular output of fields and/or computed variables and column headings. A summary section focuses on the aggregate computations for each group and for the report summary.

To test the user friendliness of this approach CALIDA was benchmarked through users with five different levels of qualification and experience. All of them found it easy to comprehend and employ. It takes one week to learn to use CALIDA with sufficient proficiency, and three to four weeks of utilization to become an expert who can solve complex data requests.

In terms of results, in 85% of the test queries, CALIDA was more efficient than the then prevailing mode of operation. In the remaining 15%, results were at par with the prevailing mode. Most significantly, substantial savings were found for complex requests and in some cases the time taken to formulate a query using CALIDA was very much shorter than with the classical approach.

To make the whole approach agile and user friendly, syntactic constraints based on the CALIDA-88 query language grammar have been embedded into the user interface so that any query—even from naive users—is syntactically correct. In addition, a special module checks the field data type to prevent comparison of incompatible data types. Some of the database specific constraints are also addressed at query level.

The GTE Laboratories underlined the wisdom that particular attention is paid to constraints associated with the *schema*. It is rather common that a database has many physical generations of the same logical file. If these are precisely the same, there is no problem in using the same schema for them. A problem arises when a change has been introduced into the logical schema. In this case, the schema for such files is handled as a union of the different schemata.

For this reason, CALIDA checks that the appropriate generations, automatically determined from the prevailing conditions, do contain the requested fields. If this is not the case, then it informs the user through an error message.

Since there is no global schema, CALIDA uses the join fields in its data dictionary which specify how IE from the different databases are to be combined. The local and global joins are being determined at run time from the query.

There are also aspects of the adopted systems solution which should be brought into perspective. For instance, given their size, the already existing distributed databases are kept unchanged even when there is a need to change the schema. For ease of use CALIDA maintains a single logical schema for all physical generations. It is the employment of semantic rules to assure that requested fields are valid for all the required generations of IE.

The linguistic level of reference is multifunctional and this includes query reformulation. The GTE researchers have found through practice that naive users frequently misformulate the query. Such a query may be syntactically correct and even produce the right answer, but it is not what the user really wants. To deal with this issue, GTE knowledge engineers developed and implemented a set of intelligent *query improvement* rules. These rules use heuristics to guess what the user wants to do. They assist the user by presenting a knowledge-enriched query version.

In other terms, the approach which was chosen is that of making intelligent guesses about maximum likelihood of user profiles, which lead to a query improvement rule. This is supported in an able manner through knowledge-engineering artifacts which help in creating an intelligent interface.

14.5 Data Level Solutions through CALIDA

References on the support provided at the human interface level have a counterpart in data-level solutions. On the data level, CALIDA generates and executes an optimized plan for evaluating a multidatabase user query. A file-transfer join method is employed in which separate requests are sent to different networked databases and intermediate files are moved across databases, as necessary. Database requests are translated to specific target languages. One of the databases is used to compute and integrate the final results, hence avoiding the need for a global data manager.

Semantic rules, at the data level, help in checking database-specific constraints, such as the maximum number of sort fields or the length of a field header. The designers chose to use near-maximum functionality, checking constraints as the target query is generated. When a constraint is violated, CALIDA gives users the choice of either continuing with the query automatically adjusted to satisfy the constraint or modifying the query.

Most important are the constraints applied at DBMS level. Every database management system has limits on the maximum size of many of its parameters. These might restrict the number of lines in a query title, maximum number of sort fields, or size of a field header. As every specialist knows, however, restricting the user language to the minimum common functionality is not a good solution for many of the problems faced by distributed databases. Hence the wisdom of establishing a more flexible but also secure solution.

Another of the goals in terms of optimization is to obtain the maximum potential out of each networked DBMS. In this case, two strategies are possible. In heterogeneous database systems with a global data manager, the manager can compensate for some of the operational deficiencies.

But since with CALIDA the choice was made not to proceed with a global database manager, because of the stated global schema inoperability reasons, the designers adopted a different approach. The system sets the user interface parameters to the near maximum value across all DBMS. These parameters are checked in the module that generates the target language.

When a parameter is exceeded, the user is warned of DBMS specific constraints. These cannot be easily checked at the query specification time since multidatabase queries call for global optimization as well as query separation steps. The latter are needed to establish which subquery will be sent to which database in the distributed environment.

As seen in Figure 14.3, there are delays in obtaining on-line responses from CALIDA, sometimes reaching several minutes. This multiminute delay, however, is *not* CALIDA's; the expert system works in subsecond speed. The delay is caused by getting the query through the networked databases and accessing the information elements through multiple incompatible DBMS.

Benchmarks by GTE have established that without CALIDA it would have been virtually impossible to respond to most *ad hoc* queries. When this was feasible, under the previous conditions, the searches necessary to respond to unstructured dynamic queries have been found to take *two days*. These are the delays associated with classical approaches. All of this has a significant impact on business competitiveness. It should properly be recalled that, in a dynamic business environment, *ad hoc* queries are increasing in frequency as they have come to constitute one of the pillars of market leadership. Hence, long delays can be deadly.

The more we bring the computer to the level of supporting the interactivity of the manager and the professional, the more we gain in competitive edge. Let's always keep this business principle in our mind.

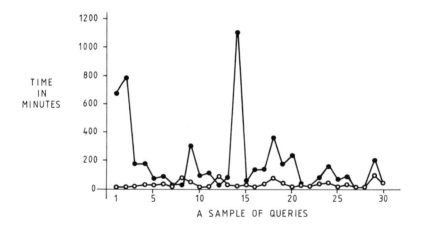

● PRESENT MODE OF OPERATION

○ CALIDA

Figure 14.3 Response time for complex queries to heterogeneous databases; CALIDA field results.

To recapitulate, database integration at the language level of CALIDA is achieved by implementation of a universal query language. This is an interactive, syntax-driven, menu-type artifact which has given good results.

The chosen solution sees to it that each database is represented by its own schema. Using a relational representation of each database and global join fields permits employment of a simple pruning algorithm, for instance, for determining missing joins. This approach calls for an intelligent linguistic interface impacting the functions CALIDA performs at the data level.

- Decomposing the user's query into the database queries accessed by the system
- Using a file transfer algorithm to support interoperability functions between databases
- Generating the target database queries and compiling the response to the user

A file transfer algorithm implemented in CALIDA helps in determining which specific database to access first. An extract file command is sent with the immediate results from the server's database transfered to the workstation's database to perform a cross-file join.

Query optimization and cross-database integration as performed by CALIDA affects the business operating environment. This contains database and semantic constraints, query editing facilities, user derived macros, and mechanisms for policing correct data types. Functions such as data dictionary editing and security are, as stated, basic ingredients of the chosen approach.

14.6 Estimator and Optimizer Functions

In its original release CALIDA was primarily constructed for database analysts. Subsequent improvements addressed endusers who know the basics of query specification procedures and understand the contents of networked databases. Among the functions provided for this user population has been that of merging horizontally partitioned files, automatically generating local joins as well as global joins across the databases.

As the early results of the research project got productized, the system's knowledgebank was divided into three parts, depending on the knowledge which it contains:

- Database specific
- DBMS specific
- Communications specific

Part of the *database specific* knowledge is the data dictionary as well as the field and join statistics needed for estimating the query result size. *DBMS specific* knowledge focuses on the rules for generating the target database query languages. *Communication specific* knowledge includes network communication protocols and database access procedures.

The network communication module links CALIDA workstations to remote databases over the network with the database expert module generating the query execution plan for integrating the distributed resources. A key role is played by the estimator, whose rules are able to warn the user about costly queries.

Capitalizing on these facilities, CALIDA integrated customer service information from the decision support system (DSS) and management information system (MIS) databases at GTE West. This implementation demonstrated that query response time in connection to complex integrative programs can be reduced significantly, often from hours to minutes. At GTE, such reductions were achieved through:

- The elimination of manual procedures needed to integrate multiple databases
- The ability of IDA (the shell) to generate and send only correct queries to databases
- The use of an intelligent user interface which facilitates human–machine communication

Among the resources CALIDA addresses are two large IBM mainframe databases, CUSTOMER and REVENUE. The former is an on-line Dataquery database with about half a million records. The latter is a historical batch file system, containing horizontally partitioned data for several months. It is accessed using the Datareporter.

In both cases, the ability to estimate the size of the query result before execution has proved to be quite instrumental. Such estimator action is a prerequisite to optimization, as it can prevent runaway queries that produce too much output—a good deal of it irrelevant.

If an estimator is accurate enough, it may even be used instead of running a request. The GTE Laboratories commented that estimating becomes particularly important:

- With on-line access to an expanding network of heterogeneous databases
- When a poorly formulated request becomes very expensive in executing

The CALIDA estimator produces *low* and *high* estimates. It uses algorithms to evaluate the number of distinct field values in the file *population* based on the number of distinct field values in a *sample*.

The approach which has been chosen applies join selectivity statistics to estimate the size of joins. Sampling has been preferred because a single estimate is frequently misleading, since the user does not know the range of possible error. The estimator therefore computes low and high estimates.

Using quartiles, the module derives formulas for single file queries so that query results will be within the low and high bracket at least 95% of the time. These formulas were extended to multifile queries under the assumption of independence between joins and the query conditions. When this assumption is not true, the low and high estimates lose their accuracy; they become a heuristic evaluation—and a very useful one for that matter.

Subsequently, the CALIDA optimizer selects the query execution plan with the smallest expected cost. It then provides the user with an estimate of the cost of a query, letting the user decide whether running the query is still warranted. Generalizing from the CALIDA application, we can project a layered conceptual structure for estimating and optimizing purposes.

This functionality is important in all cross-database applications, particularly when addressing multiple heterogeneous resources. Its implementation includes a procedural part and an application-specfic knowledgebank. The latter is composed of:

- Database references
- Specifications of the networked DBMS
- The module's own rule base
- Interfaces for efficient communications

Concepts and tools from knowledge engineering enabled the developers to easily adapt the system to changes in database structures, type of DBMS, specific rules, and network primitives. Knowledge engineering artifacts see to it that CALIDA provides a unified environment for query specification, database integration, and communications.

14.7 Lessons to Be Learned from the CALIDA Experience

What can we learn from GTE's CALIDA? The first lesson is to appreciate that heteroegeneity in database structures has many origins, and a solution should address all of them rather than just those due to DBMS design. Other leading companies who undertook similar efforts have come to the same conclusion.

Database incompatibility is due to many factors. For instance, one DBMS handled by CALIDA has aggregate operations while another does not support aggregates. This difference increases the housekeeping time. Also, it is to be expected that database semantics not only vary among nonhomogeneous DBMS but also are interpreted in incompatible ways, thus complicating the search for solutions.

Such a complication has not only technical aftermaths but also business fallouts. In an interactive environment, the slowest response sets the pace in which a system works. Furthermore, as Dr. Gabriel Jakobson noted in the course of our discussion, some of the *ad hoc* query requests made by endusers are in themselves very complex.

The point of course is that, like long transactions, complex user queries are increasing in frequency and classical data processing cannot handle them. An integral part of this reference is the fact that dynamic, *ad hoc*, analytical queries have come to constitute one of the pillars of business competitiveness. If this is true for a telephone company, it is even more so for a major financial institution, a transnational manufacturing firm, and a merchandizing organization.

The ability to answer customer demands on-line in real time may not close a deal, but lack of it will spoil the business. This is the conclusion at which a significant number of the companies which participated in this research have arrived.

Therefore, one of the major effects of using CALIDA is the boost in business service. The GTE Labs credit a good deal of this betterment of service to the substitution of the manual process of coding in a low-level language with automatic code generation.

The adopted strategy also affects the logic design phase in that the enduser can now manipulate the logic for more compact, simpler, and higher level queries. This is a field where an intelligent database system offers a significant breakthrough in terms of boosting the functions of management.

Dr. Jakobson remarked that: "Using IDA, it does not really matter how complex the query is. We can be sure that the solution will be found—and this in spite of organizational delays due to database incompatibilities, non–on-line archives, still existing batch procedures, and errors in files and process bugs.

Essential to the GTE solution is the fact that CALIDA is able to handle urgent customer requests, which are now given priority in an attempt to shorten the overall response time.

Another lesson learned from this experience is that optimization is feasible in a distributed database sense because in addition to the core programs of IDA, its practical implementation:

- Contains information describing the data dictionaries and database management systems of accessed resources
- Maps into itself the different network communication protocols which serve the interconnection purpose
- Incorporates specific notions and expressions frequently used by database analysts to formulate complex queries

The chosen structure enables CALIDA to generate access queries by automatically translating the high-level request specifications of a user into a program for accessing relational databases or, alternatively, into a query program for accessing hierarchical databases including JCL[4] code generation.

Mort importantly, IDA and therefore CALIDA approach their task by distinguishing three levels of reference. Shown in Figure 14.4, these levels permit a modular approach to:

- The enduser's query, without implying the use of a global schema
- The analysis and subsequent integration of different DBMS schemata
- Efficient handling of specific schemata at the distributed heterogeneous DBMS level

Still another lesson is derived from the wisdom of making the data dictionary transparent to the user from the fact that it is not really necessary to reflect the actual formats and protocols of the databases the system interfaces with. At the same time, a uniform data dictionary maintenance policy makes CALIDA's usage easier.

During run time, a loader allows the user to select which of the databases to update. The loader then loads the changes, alters the central data dictionary if necessary, and remakes the appropriate files.

As a precaution, the loader saves the previous version of the central data dictionary. Also, it has a simple mechanism which assures that

---

[4]IBM's Job Control Language is a paleolithic tool, but still widely used in data processing.

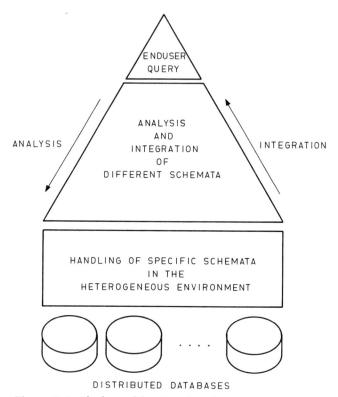

ANALYSIS

ENDUSER
QUERY

ANALYSIS
AND
INTEGRATION
OF
DIFFERENT SCHEMATA

INTEGRATION

HANDLING OF SPECIFIC SCHEMATA
IN THE
HETEROGENEOUS ENVIRONMENT

· · · ·

DISTRIBUTED DATABASES

Figure 14.4 The layered functionality of a user query.

only files that will not generate circular lists during join generation are loaded.

14.8 Using Federated Database Principles

The federated database principles adopted by GTE and mapped into CALIDA have been a refreshing new departure, even with all the risks this represents during a pioneering implementation. So far these risks have been contained and the results have been good.

The fact that the loosely coupled databases in this chosen federated approach maintained their locality (and local independence) waived the requirement other companies had concerning needed changes in their applications programs. This simplified the implementation perspectives, enhanced software reusability, and made feasible other improvements, such as greater security.

One of the important lessons learned with CALIDA relates to the ability to design an integrated transparent *data security* environment. The system centrally maintains and assures the correct user identification and password for each distributed database to be accessed. A security package had to be written for CALIDA to protect user identifications and passwords, fix workstation security loopholes, and prevent unauthorized access to corporate databases. Security awareness today is a crucial issue with most organizations. This reference is particularly pronounced with financial institutions as well as with the treasury operations of industrial firms.

The basic principle of the CALIDA security package is to maintain and store database user identifications, passwords, and any other pertinent user information in an *encrypted* form. Such information can be accessed by the database administrator but not by the user. Users may be added and deleted to accurately reflect the current CALIDA community.

The GTE Laboratories also emphasized that if database integration and access transparency are to be maintained, the CALIDA user database must accurately reflect the user identifications and passwords for all databases the system accesses. As this information changes, methods are provided to update the user and database populations, and checks are done to assure that information elements are being correctly identified and protected.

Furthermore, the knowledgebank sees to it that the validity of online, interactive references can be checked, with provisions made to dynamically change user identifications and passwords. Checks assure that the user identifications and passwords have been correctly entered and meet requirements. A number of functions are also provided to permit the DBA to maintain the CALIDA user database. Other functions see to it that a user trying to log into the system can in fact be admitted into the CALIDA environment.

Functionality tests are made to assure that the system performs according to established tolerances. While many databases organizations are adequate for the utilities which run on them, they lack the sophistication and flexibility increasingly desired by endusers today. This is especially true in large companies where tens or hundreds of thousands of files need to be kept track of, and the number of users requiring access is large and steadily increasing.

In conclusion, the problems of today's distributed database management are compounded by the fact that there is a significant number of networked workstations addressing files in very large databases. Such files need to be moved around. This environment is flexible and efficient, but structurally it contrasts to centralized mainframe solutions with users logging into the same machine and accessing files from a fixed location in the centralized system.

While a distributed environment presents major organizational and functional advantages, it also poses prerequisites to be answered in an able manner. CALIDA takes care of these prerequisites and is particularly valuable to those users that have or will be acquiring multiple discipline applications. The needs of many professionals and managers increasingly fit into this class.

CHAPTER 15

The Data Access Integrated Services (DAIS) as a Solution to Heterogeneous Distributed Databases

15.1 Introduction

As the case study on CALIDA demonstrated, the technology challenge faced today by most corporations is to enable efficient and transparent data sharing among networked databases, some using incompatible DBMS facilities and others with simple file management schemes. To better handle the necessary integrative effort, companies focus on semantic data models and languages which are tailored to a specific industry sector.

The ease of usage of a data access mechanism which addresses itself to heterogeneous databases arises not from any single feature all by itself but from a collection of features that cover both databasing and enduser services. Such features are underpinned by a set of specifications that can satisfy different commercial DBMS. Typically, the latter would involve both existing products, such as relational, Codasyl, hierarchical, inverted files, and new ones, such as object-oriented DBMS implemented in a distributed sense.

This is the goal that the American Electric Power Research Institute (EPRI) set for itself. The solution being elaborated addresses both open networking standards, through the adoption of ISO/OSI, and the development of generally valid Data Access Integrated Services (DAIS). DAIS is a sponsored effort which aims to promote a job-oriented, common data declaration language and access mechanism. This *federated databases approach* contrasts to the global schema which, as often stated, has been tried on different occasions without particularly successful results.

As a project, DAIS facilitates communication with diverse and heterogeneous databases in electric utility networks. It aims to provide linkage
to distributed systems that include relational and nonrelational DBMS,
file management structures, business applications, and real-time control
programs. Among the objectives is the assurance of a common method
of describing different data structures, providing common data access
operations, and guaranteeing essential support functions.

The latter two are served through DAIS facilities which include a data
dictionary, directory, and distributed data access management capabilities.

Like Japan's Multivendor Integration Architecture (MIA),[1] the DAIS
project develops *specifications* intended for vendor and third-party
implementation. But it only writes such software as is necessary to
implement a demonstration of integrated data access. Richer software
endowment is expected to be provided by vendors.

Figure 15.1 shows how the DAIS approach can be employed in a
distributed database involving, for example, three heterogeneous
DBMS. Since there is *no common schema*, the information elements in
each of the local databases cannot be accessed by the other two systems

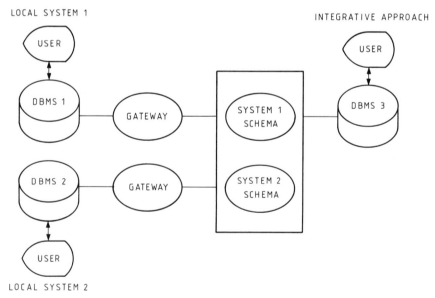

Figure 15.1   An integrative system concept with DAIS.

[1]Which is covered in the subsequent two chapters.

unassisted. By contrast, each of the three systems can access the other two through DAIS, by means of an integrative approach implemented at the schema level.

Due to the observance of security restrictions, each site must first be granted access to the other sites' IE. This being done, database-to-database communication is assured since the remote local system's schemata exist in the DAIS inventory.

15.2 The Development of a DAIS Architecture

The architecture adopted through this solution is policy neutral regarding issues such as local or central data administration or standardization of information model contents. Notice, however, that all by itself DAIS does not provide for:

- Administration of data storage facilities
- Tightly coupled schema integration
- Distributed transaction management
- Cooperative processing between applications

Rather, the developers look at DAIS as a project complementary to these functions which can be used in connection with other programming products. DAIS itself is keyed to:

1. The implementation of an architecture
2. Independence of operating platforms
3. Uniform access to heterogeneous databases
4. Remote update capabilities
5. Coexistence with local data systems which retain their autonomy
6. Extensibility, while observing OSI compatibility
7. Security and access restriction enforcement

The overriding architectural concept is one of a database federation to which many banks and industrial companies subscribed during the April 28 to May 8, 1991, research. Said one of the financial institutions in regard to the concept of *federated databases:* "While we work towards integration, we seek to keep existing systems and think this is a valid argument. It has *huge payoffs."*

American utility companies think in precisely the same way. For this reason, the first phase of the DAIS project focuses on the access technology to be adopted by surveying relevant products to determine to what extent those existing meet DAIS requirements for standards and evaluating present standards to establish which could be incorporated into the DAIS specifications under development.

Such specifications are being developed for an information architecture defining various levels of description, as required to make the information elements globally available. This ports emphasis on universal access procedures by which widely scattered information elements can be retrieved and updated.

One of the components shown in Figure 15.1 is a utility database access *gateway* with software modules able to support necessary communications channels for database access integration. A *DAIS instance* comprises access to several types of database systems on a variety of platforms.

A vital component of the project is that common data sharing does not imply loss of control over local data. The local databases are not physically or even logically merged into a single system. Local control is retained even if each local system donates part of its IE, as appropriate, to local access procedures. This is a very important point which distinguishes federated databases from other solutions.

- The local database administrators can define who has access to what IE and the security level of that access.
- Local database users continue to work with local access procedures and security mechanisms.
- The global database administrator does not affect the functioning of local databases, which remain identical to what they were before and after making their information elements globally visible.

Such definition work is done interactively with EPRI, which affects the specifications based on industry feedback.

Computers and communications vendors are expected to implement a *DAIS compliant system*. The latter will address, in a manner transparent to the enduser, a variety of computers supporting *functional sweeps* across many areas.

15.3 Approaches to Effective Data Sharing and Modeling

An access method is a technique for moving information elements between central memory, secondary storage, and input/output devices—or among the different networked databases themselves. The access mode helps in obtaining a specific logical record from a storage place, or inversely sending it for storage to a local or remote data system. Both access methods and access modes need efficient tools.

Data independence is the property of a database management system that enables data to be processed in a manner independent of the access mode, storage method, or arrangement of data. The tools DAIS provides for data sharing, in an applications independent manner, can be summed up in the following three classes:

1. A federated data model able to describe any IE in the variety of databases supported in the environment, by means of a single formalism.
2. Common access procedures for manipulating distributed IE through a common interface.
3. Means which enable restriction of access to local databases, particularly for security purposes.

As the preceding sections underlined, local computers contribute part or all of their IE to the global data access mechanism; they do so by writing a description of them. This is done through the DAIS data declaration services.

The conceptually unified but physically distributed data dictionary facility is an integral part of the DAIS system architecture. It helps in managing the schemata as well as in implementing access restrictions specified for each of the local systems. This is a procedure instrumental in preventing breaches of security.

The interactions between endusers, applications software, and DAIS typically follow a sequence of steps:

• Creating the schema needed to share local data
• Connecting local computer resources to the DAIS module[2]
• Generating an application to access databases (through the module)
• Interacting between DAIS and the running application

For instance, the software developer may create an application that contains calls to DAIS data access procedures. These include the necessary schema name and information element identification.

Typically, the application program makes a database access request using the universal access procedures supported by DAIS. Then, the access setup module establishes connection with the local database,

---

[2]Which we saw in Figure 15.1.

passing the request to the global command mapper. The latter translates the application request into the canonical format.

The result of modeling a local data resource is a schema. DAIS accepts a schema for each data system making it globally visible.

- Application programs use data from all local databases through a common data manipulation language (DML).
- The common data model (CDM) and data manipulation language are powerful enough to express the semantics of IE in the local databases.
- Data dictionary and directory facilities are also provided through this solution.

A common data model is a set of concepts and abstractions that provides a way of describing information elements. In the case of DAIS, the CDM uses a modeling approach to describe all available IE through the static properties of their information content and the operations that may be applied to such data.

The DAIS common data model has been studied in a way to support *concurrent operation*—that is, a mode of processing allowing the performance of two or more operations within a given interval of time. Provisions have also been made for *concurrency control*—the correct sequencing of concurrent operations—so that each one of them is accurately processed.

15.4 Preserving the Consistency of Networked Databases

Consistency is preserved, assuring agreement among IE that are replicated at various locations within the supported distributed database management. Typically, consistency is assisted through CDM, as the data declaration services of DAIS assure the means to describe IE in a local database in a commonly valid manner, while defining the mapping from CDM to the local data and vice versa.

After retrieval, the canonical format is transmitted over the network via the appropriate protocols.[3] It is translated into the local database format and this is done at the *local site* by the *local command* mapper. The request is executed at the local data system, and the result is retrieved in the local database format.

---

[3]Of which we will talk when we discuss the *Utility Communications Architecture* (UCA).

Subsequently, the information element(s) is (are) translated by the local data mapper into the canonical data format. The IE is (are) sent over the network, via communications protocols, to the node originating the request. The global data mapper translates the IE received in the canonical format into the universal data format. The latter is presented to the application program which has formulated the request.

Uniform representations of the globally visible portions of the local conceptual schema or schemata are written in DAIS's common data declaration language. Such an approach does *not* propose to integrate the local conceptual schemata, but *local schemata* will be represented in the form specified by the common data model. This provides the nearest solution to one *common data schema* associating heterogeneous local conceptual schemata.

In the solution shown in Figure 15.2, the *external views* are subsets of this common data model. They present a group of DAIS users with only the portion of the information that is relevant to their needs—doing so, most importantly, in a way which is understandable by these users.

Such external views can be employed for security and access control. Multiple views may be associated with a common data model, and a view may be defined over multiple common data models without integrating such local schemata.

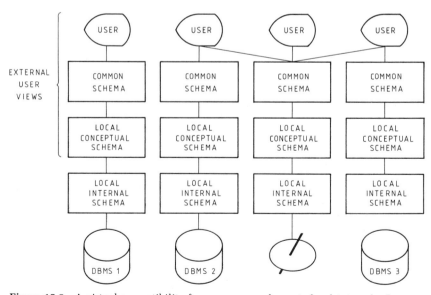

Figure 15.2 A virtual compatibility from common schema to local internal schema.

In contrast to the common schemata, a *local conceptual schema* will reflect conceptual (logical) descriptions of the information content of different databases, files, and real-time feeds. The mapping between the local conceptual schemata and the schema of a common data model *addresses the heterogeneity* of databases in the system.

Typically, there is a local conceptual schema associated with each local database. It is expressed in data model form and supported by DAIS. However, depending on the DBMS, in some cases the conceptual and internal schemata may be combined. In others, these are not separate entities but viewed as such by operations on the processor. In still other cases, one conceptual schema can represent data from multiple processors.

Among the concepts shown in Figure 15.2, those better known relate to the *local internal schemata*. As a number of past implementations have established, internal schemata provide descriptions of low-level storage structures and different access paths.

The latter are associated with different DBMS file management systems, operating systems, and teleprocessing routines. Each database, and DBMS under which it runs, is considered as having its own local internal schema whose format is particular to it.

This distinction of a common schema, local conceptual schemata, and local internal schemata simplifies both the implementation and use of DAIS. Like any valid distributed architecture, it supports evolutionary data access integration without mandating changes to existing database management schemes. This allows local users and distributed applications to continue using local schemata while integrating into the global one.

15.5 Accessing and Using Distributed Information Elements

We said that DAIS is a federated database solution. Its *concept of data sharing* does not mean schema integration but access to the same IE by several applications and sites through *a uniform interface*. The latter is supported by a common data model encompassing all computer systems and database structures being supported.

An information element resides on one database, with the primitives of the DBMS defining its semantics. Applications using that IE assume precisely the semantics of the originating database. In some cases, however, different computers and databases may appear to contain instances of the same IE. Such instances may be endowed with somewhat different semantics, and hence the need for a homogeneity algorithm.

Applications using that IE choose one instance from one local database and accept the semantics defined by it. This sets the nature of data modeling parameters.

Along this line of reasoning, the development of DAIS specification has been done by first working on an architecture that contains the information levels needed to provide uniform database access. Then, the universal database access procedures are established.

This approach has led to the design of a utility data access gateway, with the specifications developed for the DAIS covering three key issues. These are presented in Figure 15.3 in a layered form:

1. The database access *gateway*, which is the software system able to implement the procedures of the next higher layer.
2. The *universal database access*, which is a set of uniform procedures and conventions for accessing diverse on-line databases.
3. An overall, loosely coupled *information architecture* constituting the higher layer.

Such an architecture describes the levels through which the user's view is translated to the local schemas of individual databases.

This research has documented that a layered structure such as this is fundamental in providing data independence, as well as in assuring the separation of logical from physical representations of IE. It also identified how tools and application programs can employ only a high-level logical schema (data description) to define user queries.

```
┌─────────────────────────────────┐
│        LOOSELY COUPLED          │
│    UNIVERSAL INFORMATION        │
│        ARCHITECTURE             │
├─────────────────────────────────┤
│                                 │
│      UNIVERSAL DATABASE         │
│      ACCESS PROCEDURES          │
│                                 │
├─────────────────────────────────┤
│                                 │
│       NETWORK GATES             │
│     FOR DATABASE ACCESS         │
│                                 │
└─────────────────────────────────┘
```

Figure 15.3 Three levels of sophistication of a utility data access gateway presented in a layered form.

According to the EPRI project, access procedures within a heterogeneous distributed database environment must effectively cover operations for all supported types of implementation. Since such operations will be communications intense, DAIS has been designed around the ISO/OSI network model.

Data access primitives integrate with the ISO/OSI architecture and they are expected to evolve into a standard for the American utility industry. The ISO/OSI layers assure a standard network architecture with its communication protocols. The functionality being provided by these layers is necessary to handle the traffic initiated by DAIS and by other applications running on the corporate network. DAIS proper is looking after data access, declaration, and manipulation services.

In this sense, the DAIS concept depends on the communication system provided by ISO/OSI as all sites involved in database sharing are connected by means of it. As we will see in the following section, DAIS uses the communication service routines of the OSI lower layers.

With this well-architectured approach, common access allows databases that were previously accessible at only one site to be shared by the entire network. The issue of heterogeneity is bypassed, providing the ability to make *globally available information elements* through common interfaces.

Basic to the DAIS system concept is the provision of a set of tools and software able to assure that the direct users of DAIS (whether applications or humans) will not be handicapped by database incompatibilities. Typically, human use will be made indirectly through software which uses the DAIS standards.

Another basic premise is that this approach does not require all local databases to be globally accessible since data sharing is, by agreement or policy, under security clauses. Local database administrators control how much, if any, of a local system's information elements can be shared by which users.

In other terms, what DAIS assures is common database access, provided security criteria are satisfied. This is guaranteed through:

- A *common data model*[4] powerful enough to capture all of the IE contained in the interconnected heterogeneous databases.
- A set of *common access procedures* that permit a variety of computers to communicate through a single programmatic interface.
- *Security and protection* clauses which can be set to limit access to globally available information elements.

[4]But no universal schema.

This approach makes it feasible to support a means for global transparency and at the same time uphold local independence. DAIS sees to it that a local database can reveal some of its IE, while the remaining elements are available only through special permission—including authentication and authorization.

Hence, DAIS supports more than a single set of globally available procedures that allow read and write access to the databases. Such a policy is in conformance with the fact that most companies require a richer solution than that provided by a single interface able to assure a common access facility for distributed IE.

The evolving distributed applications environment (with its analytical queries) requires a good deal more than the act of learning the details of each access procedure pertaining to a local database. This is the opinion of cognizant systems architects based on what is suggested by current and projected implementations.

The EPRI project is also after the establishment of a standards policy which can be of longer term interest to its members. Its plan is to see that software developers adopt the common access procedures, and computer vendors are motivated to produce interfaces to their systems that meet that standard.

The grand design asks for access procedures to translate operations, expressed in the language of the common data model, into local database operations. The local system performs the actual data manipulations while maintaining local integrity and security constraints. The global solution supports the functionality that exists within the local systems, plus seamless access to heterogeneous databases.

In terms of applications design, programming products using DAIS can reside on any processor on the network. This promotes the evolution of integrated solutions while the network's fully distributed nature is upheld.

15.6 Mapping DAIS into the ISO/OSI Infrastructure

DAIS fits within the ISO/OSI applications layer and therefore uses the facilities provided by the lower six layers of ISO's Open System Interconnection model, as shown in Figure 15.4. This choice enhances the implementation capability of the data access solution under consideration.

In the DAIS version of ISO/OSI's seventh layer (applications level), we distinguish four sublayers:

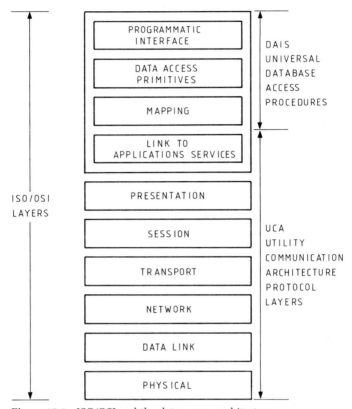

Figure 15.4 ISO/OSI and the data access architecture.

1. *Programmatic interfaces* are enduser oriented and aimed to facilitate communications with the distributed heterogeneous databases.

In the EPRI project, the primitives of this sublayer are job-specific, oriented to the needs of the power production industry. However, nothing excludes another sublayer being written to support financial applications—or even better, a family of sublayers, with a member written by each specific applications sector.

2. *Data access primitives,* addressing themselves to the distributed database network.

These primitives exhibit the characteristics which we have been discussing in the preceding sections in terms of universality, modeling, and the actuation of the access mechanism.

3. *Mapping,* which is the layer of the universal database access procedures.

We will see in the following paragraphs what the mapping level contains and therefore supports. But prior to this, the functionality of the fourth sublayer must be brought into perspective:

4. *Link to applications services,* interfacing to the presentation layer of ISO/OSI.

As is clearly demonstrated in Figure 15.4, the link to applications services is not part of DAIS but of the Utility Communications Architecture.[5] The latter is oriented toward networking, also incorporating the other (lower) six levels of ISO/OSI.

Hence DAIS occupies the upper three sublayers of the ISO/OSI applications level, of which the top one, programmatic interfaces, is enduser specific. While, as stated, the current project addresses itself to the needs of EPRI and the power production industry, layering has the advantage of permitting adaptation of DAIS to other domains (for instance, banking) just by changing the specs of the topmost sublayer.

Another way of looking at the architecture under consideration is that underlying the DAIS sublayers is gateway and networking software. The appropriate routines reside in each local data system. They handle requests that come through DAIS by mapping between DAIS common access procedures to the local system's access procedures and passing data and error messages from the local system back to the DAIS sublayers.

The services which are supported by the *mapping* sublayer can be defined in the following sense:

1. *Data mapping* algorithms for each supported schema
2. *Command and data mappers* that affect the translations required between the common data model and local data models
3. *Mapping rules* able to sustain the chosen information architecture

---

[5]The specification for UCA is being developed for EPRI by Andersen Consulting under contract RP2949-1. The specifications for DAIS are worked out by Honeywell under contract RP2949-5.

4. *Mapping algorithms* needed to implement the mapping rules

Three sorts of mappers are maintained within this layer: *command,* *data,* and *schema.* Each has specific and well-defined functions to perform.

Command mappers translate commands in the common command format to different command formats for individual networked databases. Two sets of common command formats are needed: one suitable for user and application program interaction and another for efficient network transmission.

Command Mapper I maps the universal command format to the *canonical format.*[6] Command Mapper II maps the canonical command format to the different heterogeneous command formats for accessing IE from the individual distributed databases.

15.7 Data Mappers and Schema Mappers

According to this approach, access requests from programs are translated in two steps: from the universal command format to the canonical, and from the canonical command format to that of the different databases. This job should not be confused with that of the *data mappers.*

Data mappers, supported by the sublayer in reference, translate the common data format to the data formats for the individual heterogeneous databases and vice versa. Two sets of common data formats are needed: one suitable for the programmatic interface to DAIS and another for efficient network transmission.

Here again there are two data mappers: Data Mapper I, which maps the universal data format to the canonical data format and vice versa; and Data Mapper II, whose job is to map the canonical data format to the data formats of the distributed individual databases and from the latter to the former.

The third class is *schema mappers.* They translate local conceptual schemata to the form specified by the common data model. This approach does not attempt to integrate the local conceptual schemata into a single global schema. Each local conceptual schema will be represented in the form specified by the common data model representation. Hence, there is one common data schema associated with each distrib-

---

[6]A canonical format is a standard or common internal format for efficient access and transmission through the network.

uted heterogeneous database. But at the same time, each database retains its own local schema as a federated environment obliges.

Quite significantly, the schema mapper for a given database contains *knowledge of the structure and representation* of the local databases, as well as of the common data model. The translation algorithm may be written in firmware and embedded in the mapper or retrieved from the directory.

Another important contribution of this approach to universal access design is done by the *view manager*, which provides functions able to define, delete, and modify views. Such views regard the common data model representation of the database. The view manager also supports functions needed to validate and implement queries expressed on different views and assure that updates to views are consistent with view definitions.

The view manager interacts with the dictionary/directory service to retrieve such view definitions. However, the functionality provided by the view manager may be different for different databases in the system, depending on the primitives of the latter.

Still another important software module is the *access scheduler*. It provides the functions needed for handling response time issues; for instance, prioritizing exchanges and serving specific response time requests.

Along this frame of reference to the supported features of DAIS, the *performance monitor* is an aid to the work of database administrators. Its mission is to gather performance statistics about universal database access procedures such as number and type of data exchanges taking place, priorities of the exchanges, communications times, response times, and profiles of time spent in different procedures. Still another module helps in doing performance optimization.

15.8 EPRI and the Implementation of DAIS

The *American Electrical Power Research Institute* (EPRI) has initiated a broad research program in integrated communications for the U.S. power production and distribution industry. The DAIS project is an integral part of this program.

EPRI's objective is to lay the foundation for interconnection of processors and database engines within an electric utility using the ISO's OSI reference model. This closely parallels the goals of NTT's Multivendor Integration Architecture as well as Project Carnot of the Microelectronics and Computer Development Corporation (MCC).

Within the scope of EPRI are the two projects of which we spoke in the preceding sections: The Utility Communications Architecture and the Database Access Integration Services. The best way to look at these two projects is in terms of interoperability and joint-implementation perspectives.

This can be done through the appreciation of the facilities which they support in conjunction with one another. Each layer of UCA, for instance, is providing a particular type of service to support communications between computer systems.

While DAIS makes use of the UCA services, its specific goal is to help in *the definition of functional requirements* for the access of heterogeneous databases. Most particularly, its goal is to assist in identifying and documenting what is necessary for an integrated database access within the operations environment of an electric utility.

In order to follow this aim in an able manner, it has been necessary to start with *organizational prerequisites*. Typically, the functions in a utility industry are divided into areas of responsibility, such as power generation, transmission, distribution, and corporate support.

Developed quasi-independently from one another in terms of systems approaches, each one of these functional areas uses different types of computers as well as incompatible software for its processing needs. This is no different than what has happened in many other industries. In an electric utility power plants have millisecond requirements for process monitoring and control.[7]

There is a whole family of real-time data systems with subsecond response requirements. Such applications typically include plant monitoring, efficient energy management, network analysis, reliability studies, cost optimization, emissions monitoring, and so on. By contrast, customer accounting primarily employs business systems which have classically worked as batch systems.

At the top of the list of priorities in the power production industry is the support of very fast response time, as Figure 15.5 demonstrates. But there also exist other time-relevant systems, addressing such fields as chemistry, physics, engineering, and environmental studies, and quality databases for trouble reporting and analysis and for customer service.

Typically, all these databases are distributed and are heterogeneous. However, they contain a variety of data types which have common themes:

• The IE which are contained in these data types present historically important, time-relevant information.

[7]As we will see in the next chapter, a telephone utility has similar millisecond response needs.

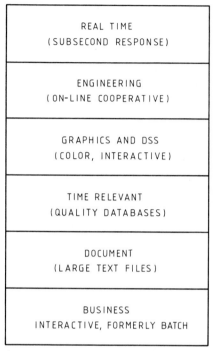

Figure 15.5 Functional requirements for
the implementation of computers,
communication and software from lower
to higher complexity.

- The system as a whole typically records many instances of values
  about entities along a time dimension.
- Operations on historical quality data most often refer to the time
  line of their origination.

Retrieval functions in connection to quality databases are not necessarily real time but must be *agile, on-line,* and executed *cross-database* in a way transparent to the enduser. A similar requirement exists in other industries such as banking—for instance, for global risk management.

15.9 Integrative Corporate Solutions

Corporate utility solutions also include many more business chores such as scheduling and optimization. This is often done off-line from control centers which manage power generation and transmission as well as simulation models for system regulation, preventive maintenance, and reliability studies.

It is often said that the main information processing activities within a power production plant, whether nuclear, thermal, or hydroelectric, are *engineering, operations,* and *maintenance.* This argument, however, often forgets the synergy of other areas, such as security, performance measurement, and administration, which are just as important.

Another failure of years past is that in the power industry[8] automation took place piecemeal. Yet, transmission and distribution automation involves not only technical issues but also operational and decision systems for dispatching, monitoring, control, protection, and investment studies.

Over and above these references, during the mid-to-late 1980s an increasingly important role was being played by customer interfaces. These include interfaces with industrial, commercial, and residential users of power at the customer's own site, as well as customer service which requires increasingly on-line interface functions, with rich database access and expert systems support.

Another example on the need to convert to on-line procedures is company-wide inventory management. Each power plant, for example, keeps on site a large spare parts inventory to assure quick maintenance. However, major high-cost components can fail for which no spares are kept on site; they have to be searched for long-distance through human-to-human communication.

If the local spare parts inventory computer could communicate with dissimilar machines at other plants, and possibly at other companies (asking about the availability of such components), critical spare parts would be acquired faster. This can lead to *lower costs* and *better uptime* by reducing the mean time to repair (MTTR).

In addition, each factory's local system should be able to communicate with corporate purchasing, leading to *just-in-time inventory* (JIT). Such a requirement can be met by:

• Attaching all the participating databases to a standard communication system
• Providing for properly planned database integration services
• Enriching this network with JIT algorithms and knowledge engineering constructs

A similar reference can be made regarding *concurrent engineering.* Design engineering studies must be accomplished in a cooperative manner

---

[8]As well as in practically all other industries.

with cross-database interaction. Typically, such studies are concerned with experimentation, circuit breaker stress studies, nuclear core analysis, vibration monitoring, system-wide fault diagnosis, and a variety of estimating missions.

Within this perspective, the creation of virtual database homogeneity while necessary is not enough. Text and data are another frame of reference, and Figure 15.5 makes reference to document handling. Graphics and other multimedia requirements include:

- Engineering drawings management
- Computer-aided design
- Mapping of power distribution facilities
- Topological type studies

There is a growing range of multimedia implementations both for engineering and for management. A good deal of these have to do with document handling.

Document databases are typically connected to the new wave of office automation. Procedures associated with them have to do with controlled document handling as well as browsing and the automation of executive libraries. Document handling has to be on-line and increasingly uses optical disks.

Active business databases of a multimedia nature involve many categories from plant mechanical and electrical maintenance records to plant equipment files, materials management, work-in-process tracking, employee information, budgeting, plan/actual control, and a fast expanding customer information system.

The point often missed in terms of systems design is that all these databases typically contain business-oriented data, such as names, addresses, machines, costs, parts lists, and schedules. For these, the information elements must always be current and accessible no matter where they are stored.

On-line access to heterogeneous databases becomes a "must" as a growing range of applications comes on-line. DAIS aims to provide a valid response to this requirement.

CHAPTER 16

Multivendor Integration Architecture and the Communications Environment of the 1990s

16.1 Introduction

Computer-based solutions must be able to provide a broad range of business services. Hence, they should be *flexible* enough to include different computer makes and models, each covering the area of business in which the vendor's approach is the most profitable or the most advanced.

The trend toward multivendor environments is not only due to the corporations' needs to answer their software requirements in an able way but also to the active competition that has developed during the last 10 years. This permits corporations to *swamp costs* through a well managed computer procurement policy.

Companies which know how to put into effect a *multivendor* approach to procurement have been able to reap considerable benefits. However, they also found that *multisourcing* is not a simple process as it involves many issues:

- Avoidance of duplicating the development and maintenance of application programs (AP)
- Overcoming allocation and scheduling difficulties in resource sharing in a network-wide sense
- Efficient operation in spite of differences in operating systems and methods
- Network-wide access to heterogeneous databases classically designed along local reference terms

Every one of these tasks requires significant investments in *human capital*, as well as in *time* and *money*. As every company knows, the development of application programs takes vast amounts of time and skill. For obvious reasons, porting the AP among different computer platforms saves time, labor, and finances—but this process is handicapped by the *diversity* which exists in basic computer software.

In a multivendor environment, computer connectivity is often difficult because different computer equipment typically uses incompatible communications interfaces. This limits machine capabilities in resource sharing. The usual result is duplication in resources such as databases and workstations, programming products developed for incompatible operating systems, and work such as data input and clearance addressed to a variety of computers.

Furthermore, the special hardware and software to be developed for interfacing reasons raises the overall cost of system development, installation, and operation. At the same time, it decreases on-the-job efficiency.

By contrast, the ability of defining a common application program interface (API) makes porting possible, thereby reducing development time and cost. Another advantage is that systems personnel can be uniformly trained, thus improving the overall productivity of the whole group.

Making it feasible for computers from different vendors to talk to each other at a common platform level enables users to share resources such as databases and networked workstations. When a sound system interconnection interface (SII) is established as a common communications protocol, it is possible to:

- Bring together into one system a variety of platforms
- Eliminate wasteful duplications which currently exist in applications programs and skills
- Reduce operating expenses for system design and implementation

Another prerequisite for sound systems design is that users should have virtually the same display and visualization standards on whichever workstation they work and wherever they go. This can be achieved through a common human user interface (HUI).

A common HUI will also permit integration of the training of users, helping to reduce overall expenses and improve job performance. These are *goals* all clear-eyed companies set for themselves. The challenge is to reach them.

16.2 Pillars of Multivendor Integration Architecture (MIA) by Nippon Telegraph and Telephone (NTT)

API, SII, and HUI are the pillars on which rests the strategy of NTT's Multivendor Integration Architecture. It came about through the appreciation of the fact that when user organizations upgrade their systems based on common interfaces, they are able to choose the most efficient products from the appropriate vendors. Changes in procurement become feasible without making existing resources such as APs obsolete, incompatible, or unusable. Over the longer run, software portability between the computers a company employs is assured.

This issue of *reusable software* is particularly acute in industries where the information systems infrastructure and product line offerings tend to merge—as presently happens in the banking industry. In a similar manner, the foremost telecommunications companies face the challenge that there should be compatibility between the two fields of switching and information processing.

These integrative issues are increasingly significant as the wall between the two fields (switching and computing) is being torn down. As a result databases, communications protocols, and workstations need to be fully incorporated into networks in order to keep providing competitive solutions. Efficient approaches require the standardization of *software platforms* and *interfaces.*

Based on these premises, the Multivendor Integration Architecture elaborated by Nippon Telegraph and Telephone leads to *the establishment of an open-vendor policy through standardization.* The specific goals are:

- Easy portability of applications software
- Emphasis on user-friendly human–machine communication
- Simpler networking interfaces
- Seamless integration of heterogeneous databases
- Continued growth of programmer productivity
- Protection of investments in applications software

NTT bets on the size of its procurement of computers and software to obtain *vendor adherence* to the MIA standard.[1] Hitachi, Fujitsu, NEC, DEC, and IBM Japan have not only accepted this principle but also

---

[1]NTT is today the largest carrier in the world with 1990 revenue of about 6 trillion yen ($45 billion).

participate in MIA's development, that is, the definition and implementation of the three common vendor interfaces we spoke about:

- The application program interface between system software and APs
- The systems interconnection interface affecting communications protocols
- The human user interface for visualization and workstation operations

These three standard references have been worked out for all general purpose computers to be procured by NTT and NTT DATA—from large scale hosts to 32-bit workstations. Figure 16.1 displays the overall relationship among the three standard interfaces of MIA.

The goal is to *define, apply,* and *maintain* a common vendor application platform that allows use of the wealth of functions already implemented in existing proprietary operating systems (OS) as well as those to be developed in the future. Once established, the common software platform constitutes the *specification* for computer procurement. This should be valid all the way from business applications to office automation.

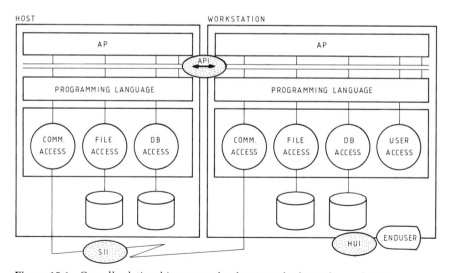

Figure 16.1   Overall relationship among the three standard interfaces of MIA.

As NTT's Dr. Fukuya Ishino[2] suggested during our meeting, the roots to this development can be found in the Telecommunications Intelligent Network Architecture (TINA), elaborated by one of the two leading telecommunications companies of the developed nations of the world. Its basis is the adoption of the ISO/OSI model for system integration.

Dr. Ishino further underlined that the successful design of an intelligent network depends above all on the *internode protocol* and the *software architecture* being adopted. Homogeneous solutions for all future developments are even more necessary given that the functions needed by the carriers are largely performed by means of software, while most communications carriers lack manufacturing facilities to make their own hardware equipment. This shows the wisdom of adopting a universal software architecture to avoid needless duplication in the development of programming products needed in a multivendor hardware environment.

One of the key decisions underlying MIA is the switch from hardware compatibility in procurement, which has characterized telecommunications companies worldwide, to *software compatibility*. Given the deep-rooted processes associated with hardware compatibility policies, which have been followed over a long time period, this amounts to a *cultural change*.

16.3 Version 1 and the Implementation Timetable

At the origin of the switch from hardware compatibility standards to the definition and implementation of a *common software platform* has been the realization that technology today provides plenty of room for improvement. Any such improvement will increasingly be software based as well as AI enriched.

As computer hardware becomes cheaper, it makes sense to exchange machine cycles for the savings realized in software development—and for a rapid deployment timetables. These are the concepts which underlined MIA's Version 1. In its essentials, the Version 1 implementation timetable has followed a reasonably fast track:

• January 1988, NTT called for partners to participate in the MIA concepts.

[2]Director of NTT's Communications and Information Processing Laboratory at Yokohama, Dr. Ishino has been both the designer and the project manager of MIA.

- September 1988, the partners have been selected (the five aforementioned computer companies) and the MIA study started.
- June 1989, the MIA concepts have been detailed and approved by all partners.
- February 1991, 13 books have been published, defining in detail (not just describing) all MIA *protocols, interfaces,* and *gateways* appropriate to Version 1.

These 13 publications defined the common software standard which permits program portability at the computer level as well as *real-time network interconnection.* The 13 books also describe *the process of certification* to be done by NTT. *Conformance tests* include those using the test suite presented by NTT and authorized organizations, which outline inspections for products and their manuals. The actual *test method* is also defined. As it depends on the type of the test suite, some further details are specified when MIA products are procured. All MIA version specifications of a given class must be implemented for a vendor's product to satisfy conformance requirements. If a vendor-specific interface is implemented in addition to the MIA interface, it must be clearly specified in the product manual.

MIA Version 1 specifications cover *processing types from on-line transactions to batch, and computers from mainframes to workstations.* Implementation is flexible in the sense that individual application areas do not always need all interfaces which have been established in advance.

The nine conformance classes in column 4 of Table 16.1, are based on the difficulty of function implementation, suitable processing type, and system configuration as a whole. Interfaces are viewed as function items of each conformance class and they include selectable options.

In SII specifications, OSI protocols and Internet protocols are selectable options. Both of these include LAN options, such as token ring and CSMA/CD. At least one selectable option shall be implemented to satisfy the *conformance condition.* Examples of selectable options in connection to MIA Version 1 are given in Table 16.2.

Above the lower levels of the LAN reference will be transaction processing (TP) specs. However, these SII specifications are not required until OSI TP becomes an international standard.[3] Other multivendor protocols providing the same API and distributed transaction processing capabilities can be selected during this interim period.

---

[3]OSI TP is important to the SII specification since an estimated 80% of MIA utilization is being targeted for transaction processing.

Table 16.1 Conformance Classes and Options

	Computer		Conformance	
Processing type	Configuration	Capability[a]	Class[b]	Remarks
Transaction-oriented	Workstation	Low	TW-1	
		Medium	TW-2	
		High	TW-3	
	Departmental computer/ host	Medium	TH-3	
		High	TH-4	
		—	TH-0	Stand-alone (for black-box model only)
Interactive	Workstation	Low	I-1	Personal computer class (including MS-DOS–based workstations)
		High	I-2	
Batch	Mainframe	—	B	

[a] High, medium, and low indicate relative capabilities within each processing type.
[b] The exact specifications of each conformance class are given in the 13 volumes published by NTT.

Table 16.2 Selectable Items within the MIA Standard

Scope	Selectable Options
SII, LAN level	OSI and Internet protocols; CSMA/CD, token ring
HUI	OSF/MOTIF Style Guide; Open Look, AT&T's graphical user interface; CUI, from IBM's SAA[a]

[a] See also in Section 16.8 the problems this interface may present.

16.4 Specifications for Technical Interconnection

As these examples help document, MIA can be seen as a family of *technical interconnection* and *pass-through* specifications. Each vendor will be able to implement them in a practical manner in order to operate within a standards environment. The distributed systems architecture will use 32-bit workstations and their successors. The telecommunications side will use ISDN, digital leased lines, and related developments.

As we will see in subsequent sections, particular attention has been paid to the provision of standards for *operating system compatibility* for engineering and business data processing applications, as well as in the office systems environment. Key industry organizations with a strong history in proprietary OS—like DEC and IBM—are now committed to the NTT-developed *cross-OS standard*.

The best documentation on this reference is that DEC has asked Project Carnot, by the Microelectronics and Computer Development Corporation (MCC),[4] to bring the MIA standards into its definitions. This is a dramatic reversal in the way major vendors start operating and can be characterized as a very important development for the 1990s.

The common software standard to which five different operating systems will abide (by IBM, DEC, Hitachi, Fujitsu, and NEC) can be seen as both a complement and an alternative to Unix (which has had to face significant problems, many of which are yet unresolved). Stemming from a research laboratory environment, Unix has been developed by too many competitive organizations and as such has significant inconsistencies. Unix is not designed for data processing applications nor for communications, resulting in random additions to the basic operating system which have created even further inconsistencies.

While hopes for a manufacturer-independent standard were undergoing disruption by add-ons, extensive AT&T-inspired marketing thrust has hyped expectations for Unix. In the meantime, cooperative efforts such as Posix and X/Open are influencing not just Unix but many other developments.

Competing developers OSF and Unix International are showing signs of some settlement of their disagreements and promise to bring other semistandard versions, such as Berkeley Unix and Xenix, along with them. MIA has chosen the Unix OSF standard which, some people believe, could have a unifying influence.

All this should be seen as part of a global effort aimed at promoting truly internationaL standards for the office of the future. As a cooperative project, MIA is committed to creating international standards which could be a major boost to computer-based productivity.

16.5 A New Concept in Establishing Computers and Communications Standards

Today, the general purpose computer market features a large variety of hardware and operating systems of vendor-specific design. Heterogene-

[4]MCC is the largest cooperative effort in America among computer vendors, acting as a national laboratory supported by the Department of Defense. Project Carnot roughly follows the same cross-vendor goals as MIA.

ity starts there and then. Therefore, MIA specifications have been projected as a feasible extension of, and able to coexist with, vendor-specific OS architectures.

Both the shorter term and the longer term must be considered. In the longer term, *flexibility* is counterbalanced by *stability*. The MIA definitions have to remain stable, because among themselves they establish the basic requirements for general-purpose computer implementation.

MIA's Version 1 provides the following three levels of standards definition for multivendor integration purposes with a reasonable stability perspective.

- *Level 1 (L1)* defines hardware and software *interface* specifications.[5] Interface standards are a long-standing issue in the computers and communications business worldwide. MIA attempts to rationalize them in an implementations-oriented sense.
- *Level 2 (L2)* addresses minimum functions and management requirements which hardware and system software must meet. At L2, for example, functions are defined for specifying priorities in AP execution and other parameters required for transaction processing. But L2 does not yet define syntax and related semantics.
- *Level 3 (L3)* covers the users' guides that supplement L1 and L2 to assure AP portability and interoperability.

We have seen three sets of L1 specifications: API, SII, and HUI; they form the nucleus of MIA Version 1. Added requirements for system definition are meant to complement API and SII specifications to assure AP portability and interoperability.

This methodological approach by NTT's Multivendor Integration Architecture underlines the significant policy change by telecommunications companies of which we have spoken: The change from *hardware certification* for interconnection to the network to *software certification* for the same reasons.

This is a major conceptual change, and therefore an issue which should greatly interest all telecommunications companies. The fundamental reasons behind the new policy are *efficiency, technology,* and *cost.*

Standards, NTT underlined, are the key to reaping the benefits of the office of the future. If everybody does not store, access, and handle

---

[5]This should not be confused with IBM's L1 to L6.2 which address a totally different domain.

information elements in a compatible format, communication between computers breaks down. But which one should be that format? NTT and its partners have answered this query through MIA specifications based on:

1. International standards established by public organizations and implemented into products by vendors.
2. International near-standards, whose specifications were expanded by vendors and put into practical use by many users.
3. *De facto* standards implemented in many products by key vendors and actually employed by many users.

Figure 16.2 helps one visualize the connection between these issues, underlining that different *ad hoc* but not-so-popular standards need not be considered. While at the same time, within the population of

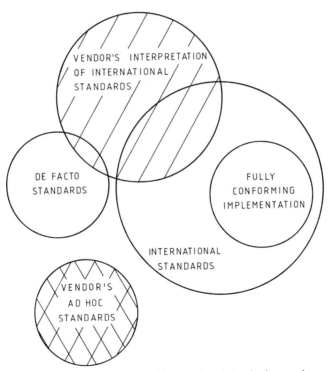

Figure 16.2 The integration of international standards, usual deviations, and *de facto* or *ad hoc* solutions.

international standards, the fully conforming implementations are the exception rather than the rule.

The MIA designers decided correctly that the best approach was to refer to existing implementation standards, making the MIA specifications consistent with these rather than developing a separate body of *ad hoc* specifications.[6] As a first option, international standards were chosen while *de facto* specs were also considered.

Seen in this perspective, the MIA standards and the process of software certification are of significant importance to all computer users, not only in home base operations but also internationally given that:

- IBM, DEC, and the three major Japanese vendors have adopted MIA.
- NTT is currently engaged in *Pathfinder*, the cooperative effort with British Telekom and Deutsche Bundespost Telekom which is expected to bring a certain degree of harmonization.

NTT's participation in this supercarrier consortium signals the intention of the world's largest telecommunications companies to become major players in the global services market. To date, some of these players have been largely restricted to their home market by regulators.

Pathfinder would offer managed links, managed private network service, and the administration of network operations. It would support multimedia—voice, data, video, text, graphics, and image-based applications—and address itself to users that seek to out-source their international private networks.

One of the considerations currently being made is that Pathfinder will be structured as two separate companies referred to as the factory and the wholesaler. The factory would handle transmission; the wholesaler would manage a specialist sales force. Both could have ample opportunity to use implementation standards regarding computers and software along the MIA normalization lines.

Standards are needed to assure that Pathfinder is able to manage different and incompatible networks coherently with a single software platform as reference. In this sense, MIA can be instrumental in seeing that value-added services are consistent from one supplier to the next and that software portability is assured.

---

[6]This decision underlines the role of the SQL Access Group and its API, RDA, FAP, SQL2, and SQL3 projects of which we speak in the following chapter.

16.6 Reconsidering Our Applications and Their Database Needs

We will be focusing attention on the development of software-oriented specifications (and the way MIA approached this problem) in the next chapter, but prior to doing so we have to take a look at the impact which our applications have on database needs. More particularly, we must discuss the *resizing of our applications* environment.

Application resizing and downsizing is being fueled by the explosion in workstations, database servers, and client–server software. The forecast is that within the next few years distributed application development will be simplified significantly by three enabling technologies:

- Message-based systems
- Distributed deductive databases (DDDB)
- Remote procedure calls (RPC)

MIA accounts for this evolution and sees to it that the developing applications architecture is fundamentally network based. Hence, its designers have focused their plans on client–server computing for an increasingly distributed application development.

With a client–server architecture, client applications and database servers can be on different platforms. The interaction between them is transparent to their user, being supported through:

- Protocols which assure steady flow of data structures between interfaces
- Agile user interfaces linking the client to the protocol and from there to the database
- File server interfaces connecting the networked databases to the protocol

MIA is an open architecture using (as much as possible) protocols and interfaces which are not specific to a type of database server. Studies by NTT have demonstrated that in the longer run this is the most efficient approach to database connectivity.

In other terms, when several largely heterogeneous types of DBMS products are utilized an open interface is in order. This is the scope of standards promoted by ISO and ANSI and productized by cooperative organizations like the SQL Access Group, as we have seen in Part II.

We have spoken of open architectures in Part I, underlining their importance as well as their future perspective. Choices made by NTT in the original design of MIA reflect the fact that companies, operating divisions, and other organizational entities that manage different databases are often autonomous. This means that their applications and databases are under separate and independent control—a trend expected to grow during the 1990s.

Another basic consideration in setting architectural perspectives is that people and companies who can control a database are often unwilling to let others specify how to design their resources. In other cases, they are willing to share their information elements only if they retain control over them. Therefore, it is important to understand the aspects of component autonomy for applications and databases, how it can be addressed in a meaningful sense, and when network-wide access is important.

A component database participating in a federation may exhibit several types of autonomy. This may concern the information elements being managed, as well as the data model, query language, and naming of the IE in the context of networked databases.

The conceptualization or semantic interpretation of the data may also be subject to local autonomy. This contributes significantly to the problem of semantic heterogeneity, which will both persist and need to be overcome in selected cases.

There is also an operational autonomy which relates to the ability of a component organizational unit[7] to exercise control over its databases. A requirement of future networked databases may easily be *design and execution autonomy.*

Correspondingly, service autonomy needs to relate to the right of each organizational unit (independent business unit in an entrepreneurial approach) to make decisions regarding the services it provides to other organizational units. Part of this reference concerns requirements related to association and communication autonomy.

Performance within an evolving environment of applications and databases is another critical reference. As a basic principle, at the end of the day few people buy technology. *They buy solutions.* Hence, the criteria to look for in an architectured approach are:

1. The way an efficient solution is being structured
2. High technology quotient for competitive edge

---

[7]For instance, independent business units, multinational division, or even business partner—client or supplier organization.

3. Results in terms of high quality *and* low cost in networked databases
4. An open, flexible, and evolving approach in global design
5. Integrative capability within the user environment
6. Implementation timetable for agreed upon applications perspectives

Solutions will never be linear. In the general case, the need to maintain local autonomy and the need to share data present conflicting requirements. Though many technical problems may impede interconnectivity, the most difficult ones to solve are those of a political and organizational nature.

CHAPTER 17

The Development of Software-Oriented Specifications

17.1 Introduction

The success of any solution depends on its acceptance by those who are responsible for its implementation and usage. In matters concerning high technology, the best strategy for gaining acceptance is to *support the enduser* all the way from the concept behind the system to real-life applications.

This has not been a widely followed policy by data processing operations. Rather than producing a valid solution to better professional quality by means of enduser computing, data processors were insensitive to enduser needs, and they also mismanaged technology.

The mismanagement of technology comes from its haphazard exploitation, and nowhere is such a statement more true than in matters concerning software. Evidence has also been provided throughout this book that another major reason for failures with technology is the limited imagination in addressing the heterogeneity of databases.

Lack of integrative solutions sees to it that today many workstations in corporate sites can make no contribution to business efficiency. Over the years, approaches to database heterogeneity were deficient in terms of both supportive software and access protocols. As a result, endusers found it difficult to take seriously the work of data processing (DP) professionals, which, over and above this reference, have not been truly competent in terms of on-line, interactive solutions.

Both the diversity and the inadequacy of interactive approaches became apparent as the computers and communications industry progressed through successive commodity programming products at the WS level, providing, for example, visualization services. Graphics are becoming increasingly important among both financial institutions and industrial organizations.

Only the foremost companies have been concerned by the fact that connectivity has remained rooted in the dark ages, as exemplified by the 3270 protocol. This protocol and similar ones can hardly be considered suitable for today's enduser requirements. This is because millions of workstations are connected to expansive local area networks (LAN) sharing common file servers, and users depend on the increasingly rich central and distributed corporate databases for doing their day-to-day work in an able manner.

The real requirement of endusers—particularly of managers and professionals—is to share the distributed database system, not just the LAN's file server. The problem starts at the level of inadequate remote data access disciplines which are hampering more imaginative cross-database solutions.

In many cases, PC-to-mainframe interconnection is still largely limited to terminal emulation and simple file transfer. This denies users a full interactive service. At the same time, a horde of incompatible software add-ons have emerged that attempt to solve the problem case-by-case by manipulation of "this" or "that" application rather than alteration at the system level.

The cost of support for such nonelegant approaches is growing fast, while the services obtained out of them is substandard. It is therefore no wonder that leading user organizations have taken the initiative in terms of providing an efficient system-oriented solution.

Since software drives hardware, a focal domain in the search for better system solutions is the use of software specifications. MIA took the right approach through the concept of a *standard software wire* cross-OS, to which all applications can be attached and therefore ported from one machine to another.

17.2 Normalizing the Application Software for Portability

The concepts underlining MIA are sound: each vendor's computer hardware and OS are taken as a unit and compared to the MIA standard. What each vendor misses in meeting this common software platform has to be provided by the individual vendor—hence the process of *certification* regarding conformance to MIA protocols, interfaces, and gateways.

The able setting of specifications is only then possible when the necessary software environment for the provision of telecommunications services is properly studied and understood. The software required by carriers largely falls into three categories:

- Communications services
- Network operations
- Administrative chores

A very significant amount of software is necessary to support communications products, control the networks, and provide customers with a growing pallet of services. Such software must meet severe real-time and performance requirements as well as guarantee nonstop operation.

Another big chunk of software which is necessary in a telecommunications setting has the role of efficient hardware operation and maintenance. Administrative programs are used in billing and accounts receivable, inventory control, statistics of all types, general accounting, cost accounting, personnel management, and countless other tasks in office work.

As technology advances, the need for more sophisticated software increases dramatically. At NTT, this has resulted in the production of some 30 million lines of code, leading to a radical revision of policy. The new guidelines are one purpose, one program, and to never duplicate a programming effort for the same purpose.

Once a piece of software has been written, it must be used on a variety of platforms to spread the benefits from the investments made in applications. Such *applications must fit multiple architectures*, including the requirements posed by distributed databases and networks.

At the same time, a multivendor procurement policy is necessary for a company without its own computer manufacturing arm to assure a stable supply of quality products at low cost. Software portability is an issue which promotes competitiveness. That's why it has become an increasingly essential goal as the volume of required programming support grows.

This is practically what led to the NTT concept of the *standard software wire*, to which a variety of hardware and basic software platforms will be attached as shown in Figure 17.1. Interfacing to this standard software wire are the operating systems of the different computers, each with its own functionality and incompatible with the next one. These need to be extended to assure homogeneity as to the standard which essentially is a universal applications programming interface.

While some applications may be competitive within a given mainframe environment, no two OS currently offered in the market have the same functionality. Hence, the missing link to be provided by the

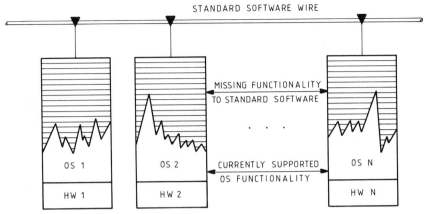

Figure 17.1   The making of a universal application programming interface.

vendor(s)—and those American and Japanese computer manufacturers who participate as partners in the MIA project are doing just that.

This helps break the very common past policy by computer manufacturers—who are competing for the same markets—of designing distinctive features into their products. The common software wire strategy capitalizes on the fact that if vendor equipments differ and OS are incompatible, then the gaps must be closed by the vendors themselves. This means ironing out differences in the interfaces between the operating system and other basic software supplied with that equipment, with reference to the common software wire norm.

In the case of NTT, the first guideline of procuring systems from multiple vendors has been that of interfaces aiming to assure software reuse, including portability from one computer to another. This policy helps integrate multivendor approaches, allowing software to be ported across hardware and operating systems procured from different suppliers.

System designers at NTT can choose an architecture according to the purpose to be reached as far as that vendor gives them software portability. As new systems are designed or existing AP revamped, emphasis is expected to shift away from the approach of hardware interface standardization toward the software interface standardization and associated methods.

Another important issue faced by the NTT project is the ability to access and use heterogeneous database resources in providing telecommunications services.

Database normalization is dependent on the operating system, database management system, and data structures. Specifications need to be defined that help in global data access. Also, solutions must be provided to avoid the need to reenter IE when the OS or DBMS is replaced, which happens in the present day for reasons of prevailing heterogeneity.

17.3 Upper and Lower Level Protocols

MIA conforms to the ISO/OSI concept, and its protocols can be largely divided into two groups: upper (ISO/OSI layers 5,6,7) and lower (ISO/OSI layers 1 to 4).

- Lower-layer protocols provide reliable information transfer between computers, independent of data type and contents.
- Upper-layer protocols enable resources such as databases to be shared among computers for each data format and attribute.[1]

Once the system interconnection interface (SII) has been established as a computer-to-computer common protocol, its functions permit seamless database-to-database exchanges over local and remote networks.

MIA Version 1 defines the media types, physical and electromagnetic characteristics of media, the number of tracks, data recording methods, codes, labels, and file structures based on specifications of the Japanese Industrial Standards (JIS) Institute. These are compatible with ISO 1001, 1864, and 3788 and aim to enable AP porting. The MIA file transfer protocol has been developed for this type of usage, and file structures are defined for AP portability over communication lines.

According to MIA specifications, upper-layer protocols corresponding to OSI layers 5 to 7 enable resources such as DBMS and file management systems to be shared between application processes. MIA Version 1 protocol implementation specifications are defined for message, mail, and file transfer as shown in Figure 17.2. The protocol for open message transfer between application processes is based on ISO/OSI specifications adopted by INTAP and DARPA.[2] This protocol defines the establishment and release of communications paths, including message transfers, between application processes. Message constants can be defined as needed by cooperating application processes. The protocol for

---

[1]See also the discussion on DAIS in Chapter 15.

[2]INTAP stands for Interoperability Technology Association for Information Processing of Japan; DARPA is the Defense Advance Research Project Agency of the United States Department of Defense.

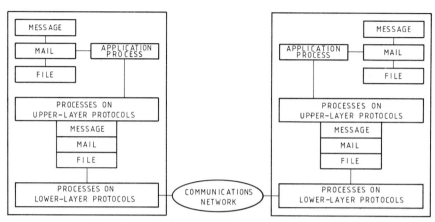

Figure 17.2 Goals reached by ISO/OSI upper-layer protocols.

transferring mail (envelope and text) between application processes is also based on the OSI implementation specifications of INTAP and DARPA.[3] This protocol defines the establishment and release of communications paths and the transfer via relay systems of mail consisting of character data, *with no document structure between application processes.* The application process is, however, the final sender/receiver in a communication.

The protocol for transferring files between application processes is defined on the basis of the OSI normalization specifications and DARPA RFC specifications. Typically files are classified as: *unstructured*, meaning that no record structure is defined, or *structured*, in which case they may be sequential with a record structure being defined.

File transfer is classified into whole file transfer and partial file transfer. MIA Version 1 covers the whole file transfer of unstructured files, for which standard implementation specifications have been elaborated. MIA Version 2 will focus on the other alternatives.

Attention has also been paid to the *network management protocol,* which defines operations between *managing* and *managed* systems, as well as the data format used for these operations. MIA Version 1 covers:

- *Fault administration,* which detects system or communication line faults and supports recovery procedures
- *Configuration management* used for network reconfiguration during recovery from a fault

[3]RFC specifications.

Standardization of the network management protocol is being promoted by OSI. However, only the common management protocol has been completed. MIA Version 1, therefore, defines the network management protocol, taking into consideration normalization activities as well as vendor products and user requirements.

As it currently stands, MIA Version 1 defines methods for interconnecting networks in an able manner, though Version 2 will cover a much more extensive domain. Version 1 also addresses other issues such as OS interfaces, programming languages, and enduser computing.

The MIA protocol specifications established so far will be enhanced stage by stage, taking into consideration the progress in international standardization. If MIA protocol specifications at a certain stage of enhancement cannot satisfy interconnection requirements of some users, these users may have to construct their networks based on vendor-proprietary protocols.

17.4 Placing Emphasis on Enduser Computing

In any company and in any conference, enduser computing is a key topic. Not only have the endusers themselves become more sophisticated as well as computer-literate, but senior management also sees enduser computing as the only means to break the huge backlog of applications programming. Results along this line of reasoning are rather positive.

The new policy starts with the premise that a significant number of people can do enduser programming, though this is not true of everybody. The prerequisite for enduser programming is not only agile high-level languages and computer literacy but also deductive distributed databases with virtual homogeneity, though such databases can be locally heterogeneous.

For these reasons, MIA has paid significant attention to system interfaces for user access. Agile user access requires:

- Windows and characters to be displayed in a specific location on a screen together with defined functions for input
- Functions to be handled through a calling interface enriched through knowledge engineering

Since no international standard has been established for user access, MIA Version 1 defines needed specifications for interactive processing on workstations, taking into account vendor products and user requirements.[4]

Furthermore, given that the success of any implementation environment is closely related to the able use of database resources and processing types, MIA has addressed the database environment. Attention has been paid to the normalization of database access through ISO's remote data access (RDA) mechanism:

- Dynamic database access requires an able definition of query and retrieval, including analytical queries.
- Database-oriented processing types include addition, deletion, and updating as well as functions to assure database consistency.
- In MIA, these are defined as extensions of programming language specifications.

The database access norms for MIA Version 1 are based on the latest JIS SQL specification, which is compatible with ISO 9075. This has been done after taking into consideration vendor products and user requirements.

Attention has been paid to file access, with reading, writing, and further functions used for sequential, direct, and other types of manipulation. Files are defined as part of individual programming language normalization. The file access specification for MIA Version 1 is based on standards for the supported programming languages.

The same reference is valid in connection to communications access, regarding the initiation and termination of remote APs as well as the sending and receiving of messages between APs. However, work is still in process in this domain and it is anticipated that normalization will include a calling interface such as the one provided by the CALL statement.

Since no international standard has yet been established for communications access, the latter are defined by MIA Version 1 *de facto*. This is particularly true for interactive applications and transaction processing.

In the general case, international standards already available for programming languages and database access were edited by adding or deleting functions to develop appropriate MIA specifications. Table 17.1 outlines the API organization for MIA Version 1. Of these APIs, programming language and database access interfaces are common to

---

[4]For a comparable effort in America, see Chapter 15 on DAIS as well as the second half of Chapter 18, which covers the activities of the SQL Access Group.

Table 17.1 API Organization for MIA Version 1

Interface	Transaction	Interactive	Batch	Base standard
		Processing type		
Programming language	C	Cobol	Cobol	C, ANSI X3, 159–1989; Cobol, ISO 1989–1985
		FORTRAN	FORTRAN	FORTRAN, ISO 1539–1980
DB access	SQL	SQL	SQL	SQL, ISO 9075
System interface[a]	Structured task definition language (STDL)	Interactive processing extensions		None

[a] User access and communications access.

all types of processing. By contrast, communications access and user access interfaces are specific to the processing type.

All user access and communications access interfaces are coded as part of a task definition. User access is executed by invoking a presentation procedure (Send, Receive, Transceive) for human interface control. Communications access is executed by invoking remote tasks (Call, Submit) from the processing steps in the task definition.

17.5 System Software for Presentation Procedures

System software for presentation procedures, such as forms packages, are basically supplied by vendors. A presentation procedure is invoked by a task to execute human interface control, including forms control. Users can prepare their own presentation procedures as needed. AP developers have to code Send/Receive/Transceive, specifying I/O in the task definition. But they need not worry about output data screen displays or how workstation users submit input information elements.

The invoked presentation procedure maps IE to display and input operations at the workstation. If vendor-supplied presentation procedures are used, the screen designer must specify mapping using:

- CASE tools integrated in the development environment (first phase)
- Vendor-specific screen (forms) definition language in the execution environment (second phase)

A pseudo-conversational mode is supported whereby data is sent from and a response is returned to a user more than once by chaining multiple sessions of basic mode interaction. This essentially means by the use of multiple transactions.

Since resources are freed at the end of each transaction, this mode offers a *higher degree of concurrency* than a fully conversational one. Still, transaction handling requirements will be restructured after the ISO norms become available.

Functions requiring support are prioritized in terms of task scheduling and database concurrency control. Necessary control information includes various time-out values as well as destination lists used by the broadcast function. The MIA transaction processing architecture has the following features:

1. APs are separated into task definitions and processing or nested procedures.

All transaction control, including enduser and communications access, is concentrated in task definitions.

For transaction processing reasons, the AP's productivity, portability, and ability to keep pace with international standards can be improved by understanding the transaction control flow. Improvement can also be made by assuring that future changes or additions to the API require only modification of the affected task definition, not the processing of nested procedures in which applications are often coded.

2. Applications with a high level of abstraction improve the productivity and portability of transaction processing routines.

The use of remote task invocation hides complex communications control chores from the communications access interface. It thereby enables users to develop distributed transaction processing applications in a more elegant way.

3. Display and operation control for the workstation are separated and hidden from the user access interface; users can easily develop transaction processing APs that execute workstation I/O.

MIA has introduced the concept of classes commonly defined for the required recovery action. This enables users to develop portable exception handlers.

MIA Version 2 will provide users with workbenches for software development and decision-support applications. MIA Version 1 defines the interactively processing API for workstations only.

This interactive processing approach taken by API includes interfaces which are required when an on-line workstation accesses a TP system, such as a departmental computer or host which acts as server. Networked solutions have dominated system design both in Version 1 and in Version 2 (which is under development).

17.6 Support for Agile Human Interfaces

MIA supports two types of human interfaces (HUI): the *display interface* and the *workstation operation interface*. These are provided through system software and appropriate applications programs.

HUI specifies the common interface as well as *a style guide with rules* which permits application programmers to sustain a consistent interfacing effort.

- The display interface defines items such as layout and format for windows on an enduser workstation.

Users can then understand displays without having to limit themselves to what is supported by a given WS vendor or model. However, to give directions to WS interactivity, users must display a menu in a window and select items from it using a mouse or keypad.

- The WS operation interface defines the broader terms of the interaction between the user and the workstation.

Users can employ their workstations in a virtually homogeneous manner, following the same procedures outlined for other computer equipment, without having to consider the WS vendor or model.

A style guide is provided by MIA to account for the fact that human interfaces greatly depend on the application, making it difficult to establish *a priori* uniform specifications. This style guide promotes design rules for application programmers in terms of window use and visualization. NTT has found that this approach helps the programmers in implementing consistent HUI structures, thus normalizing the presentation issues.

Window manipulation includes such functions as Move (change the window location); Resize (change the window size); Activate (a window for input from the keyboard); and Scroll (moving display contents in a window vertically or horizontally). MIA Version 1 defines the selection features indicated in Table 17.2.

HUI specifications in MIA Version 1 also support enduser-directed interface capabilities providing do, undo, and immediate feedback. This is achieved through a conceptual model with the following features:

1. *The ability to use metaphors:* Through windows and icons, workstation users manipulate an environment which approximates quite closely their everyday experience.
2. *Tools for direct manipulation:* Processing is performed through operations similar to those in the real world, using a mouse or typing commands from a keyboard.
3. *Keeping interfaces consistent:* The same operation always produces the same results, and similar components operate in the same manner on similar applications.
4. *Providing for user-friendly windows:* Specifications provide for basic window structure, including title and action bars, window moving and sizing, and the representation of basic components like menus and prompts.
5. *Assuring efficient dialogs:* MIA's HUI definition includes the representation and manipulation of dialog boxes, help windows,

Table 17.2 Selection Features Supported by MIA Version 1

Selection feature	Function
Radio button	Selects one of several items (single selection) A previously selected item is released when a new item is selected
Check box	Selects any number of items from several (multiple selection) If an item is selected, other items are not affected
Push button	Executes the selected function immediately Functions are indicated by icons or character strings
Text input field	Inputs and edits character strings Manipulates title and a rectangular field for text entry
List box	Selects one or more items from the displayed list The list box has a scroll bar to make item selection easier through scrolling

prompts, and message boxes. Emphasis is placed on the design of efficient dialog components.

6. *Protecting against unexpected destruction:* If an operation causes a critical result that cannot be recovered, the user is prompted into explicit action. The use of modes requiring key definitions has been minimized; the same is true of operations based on status.

7. *Making the interface transparent:* The user is released from explicit recognition of the internal processing sequence of the system. This has become transparent, greatly simplifying both WS programming and human–machine dialog.

17.7 A System Design Guide

A *system design guide* is also provided for designers and for people responsible for purchasing new software and hardware products. It specifies system design and product procurement based on the individual user environment.

A system users guide has been written for workstation users and AP developers, providing instructions and restrictions on the employment of the computers and communications network. It also indicates how to set parameter values and use tools when the system is employed.

The MIA Version 1 HUI Style Guide adopts the following standards in association with each of the outlined HUI specifications:

• *Motif*—OSF/Motif Style Guide Revision 1.0, which is Unix-based

Motif is defined in publications describing the window management facility and toolkit (Motif Toolkit) of OSF/Motif.

• *Open Look*—AT&T Open Look Graphical User Interface Style Guide; Interface Style Guide Release 1.0

We have come a long way from 3270 terminals and their variants. Graphical interfaces are the rule of the day and there is a variety of techniques for exploiting WS in conjunction with visualization standards.

• *The Common User Access (CUA)*—from IBM's systems application architecture described in the Advanced Design Guide, SC26-4582-0

CUA is also outlined in publications describing the OS/2 Presentation Manager and Japanese Language MS OS/2 (Version 1.1).

However, notice that with AIX, IBM has also produced its own Unix line of products. AIX is seen as an alternative to SAA in order to create for IBM a share of this market.

These three specifications are not completely consistent for all supported items, but differences can be smoothed by following the MIA HUI Style Guide. The Japanese-language environment is defined as an additional specification. The MIA HUI Style Guide contains additional information for users wanting to employ a combination of selectable window specifications. Within the scope of a common human interface design, it focuses on means of interaction, such as help support and messages, in a way which can be widely used in many applications.

Design guidelines are provided to identify common procedures for human–machine communications. Just as important is the proposed use of common window component features. These are used in menus and associated selection operations as well as in visualization, which is becoming increasingly important in interactive computing.

In conclusion, while there are as yet no international standards for human interfaces, the MIA developers believe that platforms such as Unix can serve as system software that runs on 32-bit workstations. Human interface specifications close to industry standards have also been chosen to work with these platforms, as long as they meet chosen functional requirements.

This solution permits multiple vendors to produce their own product implementations. MIA, however, specifies that if implementation of the specification requires execution of a licensing agreement, such licensing shall be nonexclusive and applicable worldwide. Every effort should be made to preserve homogeneity in a global sense.

CHAPTER 18

Common Goals to Be Reached by MIA and the SQL Access Group

18.1 Introduction

The Pentagon is the world's biggest consumer, spending $80 billion a year on new equipment. Any change in its buying habits can shake up not just defense contractors but a variety of other industries as well—computers and communications being a valid example.

In the same manner, NTT is Japan's largest spender on computers. Therefore, its normalization effort finds echo among computer manufacturers and, as we saw in the preceding chapter, five of them responded favorably to the normalization effort regarding the common software platform.

Such examples help demonstrate that it is important to take notice when pace-setting customers of computers, communications, and software start playing a role in establishing the technical standards on which offices around the world may one day be based. The way to bet is that these *de facto* standards will take hold; even more so when they are based on ISO and ANSI norms.

For instance, the Pentagon's entry into office automation standards has resulted in the computer-aided acquisition and logistics support (CALS), largely inspired by a project known as *the integrated weapons systems database*.[1] The idea is to store in a compatible form all information about weapons—from design premises and manufacturing plans to maintenance diagrams. Such storage takes place in vast on-line databases linking the Defense Ministry's computers with those of thousands of suppliers.

This is another example of the fact that throughout the developed nations of the world the business community is rapidly adopting the

[1]This has been adopted by France and Sweden, as well as the American military.

concept of *cooperative databases* in which multimedia resources are distributed among a wide range of computers of different types.

Typically, organizations taking the initiative on standards setting, like the Pentagon and NTT, have the muscle necessary to twist the vendor's arms. But they see normalization as a longer term process which must be properly planned from the start.

The Pentagon has already begun creating the constituent parts of that distributed database. Between now and 1995 the plan is to:

- Beef up the military computer-communications network
- Work out redesign procedures for acquiring weapons and other equipment
- Stay flexible in order to take advantage of the new technology

Like most multinational companies, the U.S. Department of Defense believes that within a decade nearly all business will be done electronically. To encourage suppliers to operate in this manner, DoD procurement policies are tuned to give preference to companies with which business can be done on-line.

As a client of the computer industry, the Pentagon has much more leverage than NTT. It is therefore a positive sign that Project Carnot of MCC is moving along the same integrative direction. This reference concerns standard protocols, like those developed by the SQL Access Group, as well as other components like OSF Unix.

The present chapter completes the discussion on NTT's multivendor integration architecture. It then highlights key issues characterizing the work done by the SQL Access Group, paying attention to standard protocols as well as to the next generation of human–machine communications.

18.2 Choosing Operating Systems and Establishing Their Interfaces

To enhance software portability, NTT has focused on the standardization of operating system interfaces and associated programming languages. This has been achieved by adopting the software wire reference for operating systems, standardizing functional primitive interfaces for business data processing. Much of this has been discussed in the preceding chapter.

Interfacing to MVS (of IBM), VMS (of DEC), ACOS (of NEC), and the operating systems of Fujitsu and Hitachi mainframes (which are MVS derivatives) was found to be the best strategy for interactive, transactional, and batch applications. By contrast, the CTRON operating system has been the one chosen for real-time switching because of its ability to support subsecond response speeds.[2]

In other terms, a two-tier approach has been adopted. For applications which are less response time critical, NTT chose operating systems that have come into wide use. This helps in promoting their acceptance as *de facto* standards.

At the workstation level, the three OS references are, Unix, MS-DOS, and OS/2. Unix and MS-DOS make it possible for multiple vendors to supply application programs that are widely portable. However, in the case of Unix there are now two separate sets of standards in existence. Both are multivendor products, including interface capabilities, but it was felt to be unwise to adopt more than one.

Consequently, the OSF Unix was adopted as the MIA standard with applications development focusing around microprocessor-based machines, starting with the currently available workstations and moving on to RISC processors. The latter are able to deliver mainframe power at far lower cost.

The Unix and MS-DOS operating systems have the advantage of commodity software availability, but are not renowned for fast real-time implementation. Therefore, as the preceding paragraphs suggested, in fields with highly demanding requirements for real-time processing and nonstop operation, CTRON has been the chosen OS.

There is currently a lack of a well-designed *de facto* or standard OS that can compete with dedicated operating systems specifically projected for millisecond response. CTRON has been developed in Japan with a set of nonproprietary, open interfaces and its features include:

- Real-time processing on the order of *milliseconds*
- *Multitasking* on the order of thousands of simultaneous tasks
- *Fault tolerant* type operations
- Localization of hardware dependency, for the sake of *vendor-independent* interfaces

CTRON design was undertaken by a committee made up of nine Japanese firms. Interface research has been done jointly, while implementa-

---

[2]The CTRON operating system was developed in Japan in the 1988–1989 time frame. See *Original CTRON Specification Series* (Ohm-Sha), by TRON Association, Tokyo, 1989.

tions are made separately by each firm. The firms developing the interface specifications do so without making any claim to proprietary rights.[3]

18.3 A Time for Critical Decisions

These are crucial references for organizations that are users of large process control, data processing, and office systems. The time has come for them to assess the strategic impact of operating systems on corporate solutions. They must examine the realistic opportunities which exist and identify the software products to be exploited in large corporate sites.

Able approaches can only be based on the analysis of key developments taking place in communications and computers, as well as standards and applications within the corporate world. A pragmatic approach suggests that traditional mainframe and minicomputer users can no longer afford to ignore the common software wire of NTT or to throw out their existing applications code.

Thus a path must be devised to take advantage of MIA within the world of commercial and scientific data processing. Communications and portable software tools are key factors in achieving this end, and the normalization done by MIA provides the needed guidelines.

NTT's approach to the virtual homogeneity of distributed operating systems supplies important examples of the current state of the art and indicates what the future may hold. The whole effort represents a milestone on a long path of experimentation and discovery.

Each one of the five computer vendors[4] has undertaken support of MIA with specific products or families of products. Each one of them carries encumbrances from the past and faces obstacles to achieving MIA's realization. The effort, however, makes sense because the MIA standards produce a complete functional statement of all elements of distributed computing. The announced object is to relate various distributed operating system features into a conceptual unity.

Eventually, all leading organizations (finance, manufacturing, and merchandizing) will be endeavoring to achieve a consistent and complete model of distributed processing, databasing, and networking. While one can argue the completeness, coherence, aggregation, and

---

[3]The results of CTRON research are made available without charge even to nonmembers of the association.

[4]IBM, DEC, Hitachi, Fujitsu, and NEC.

other aspects of MIA, the underlying message is still quite clear: We are moving toward an environment in which all the functions of computing are distributable across wide geographic distances and, so far, incompatible systems.

The virtual compatibility to be developed through *de facto* standards will help increase in a significant way the return on investment made in computers and communications. It will also provide considerable ease for program developers, systems administrators, and endusers.

18.4 Programming Languages and Industry Practices Regarding Subsetting

While international standards are followed in the MIA development wherever possible, an all-important *conformance testing* is offered to assure that implemented products (and their manuals) actually abide by the established interface specifications. The latter are steadily evaluated as to the extent to which portability is achieved.

This evaluation process benefits from the fact that conformance testing has been defined—not just described—in the 13 manuals of MIA Version 1. Real-life testing is also done through a process whereby implemented program modules are actually ported to different hardware architecture equipped with the MIA interfaces.

During the testing phase, program modules being ported are written in ANSI C language for a whole range of on-line operating procedures. Rather than trying to define a single interface for all application programs, a single definition is assigned to each functional primitive and subsetting rules are determined for groups of functional primitives.

This policy is being followed all the way to the subsecond real-time applications. More than 30 systems which implement CTRON subsets have been developed thus far. NTT mentioned that an evaluation of these preliminary results suggests the need for improvements in a number of areas, such as overhead reduction and greater efficiency in program modules across different hardware platforms. A number of obstacles to portability have also been discovered. Some are the result of violations of programming language conventions or differences in compiler operation, while others come from deficiencies in interface definitions inherent in current solutions.

Cognizant researchers suggest that there is also a need for hiding differences in memory protection mechanisms, as well as in regard to specifications covering initialization and termination procedures.

Solutions need also to be provided to assure upward compatibility in spite of inconsistencies in subsetting rules for functional primitives.

NTT researchers have further established that while the standardization of programming languages is a basic requirement for software portability at the source code level, there are constraints to software portability which are based only on the standardization of programming languages. Specifically, such portability is limited to those application programs which have very little interaction with the operating system.

An example is the Knowledge Base Management System (KBMS-2) developed by NTT.[5] This is a software tool used in compiling expert systems in the Japanese language. Applications currently employing KBMS-2 include:

- Emergency fault handling for switching system
- Fault diagnosis of crossbar switches
- The design of private networks
- Computer-aided training of network operators
- Trouble analysis of computer software
- Sales support for customer terminals

KBMS-2 is written in LISP and is designed to run on various operating systems supplied by vendors. It is being used in connection with nine different architectures, including IBM 30XX, VAX-8000, MicroVAX, SUN-3, Apollo Domain, and NEC PC-9800.

One of the problems found in these implementations is that while LISP language specifications are supposedly standardized, the actual LISP products available from vendors contain special features. Hence programs must be written within the range of common functions that are supported by the LISP executors of each machine—otherwise they are not portable.

Another issue has been that the I/O processing in human–machine interfaces depends on the specific operating systems of each vendor, so this part has to be rewritten for program porting purposes. This vendor-dependent part amounts to around 10 to 30% of KBMS-2 code, which is a major burden.

The need for normalization in language subsets and programming language/OS interaction could not be documented in a better manner. The same is valid of the COBOL ANSI[6] and FORTRAN languages neces-

---

[5]Not to be confused with the KBMS product developed and marketed in America by the AI Corporation.

[6]There exist today some 500 incompatible COBOL dialects, eight of which parade themselves as COBOL ANSI.

sarily supported by MIA, in order to provide some portability for the tens of millions of lines of code available in application libraries.

NTT's Dr. Ishino also underlined the need for higher level languages and shells which can be employed by endusers to permit self-service in the development of needed programs. The same reference is valid in regard to another set of more sophisticated high level tools to promote greater efficiency in professionally developed applications.

Both are goals of MIA Version 2. The same is true of compilers and debuggers which automatic program assembly and testing feasible—from shell to object code. For object code level, the current choice is C, with future implementation most likely centering on C++ for parallel and object-oriented computing.

18.5 Networking Computer Resources and Application Programs

The MIA project has emphasized since the start a communications-based solution running on both local area networks (LANs) and wide area networks (WANs). The LAN communications links typically cover relatively restricted areas, such as a building or campus, and they support low to medium speed, of up to several tens of megabits per second (MBPS), and high-speed LAN, a hundred or more MBPS to gigabits per second (GBPS).

The CSMA/CD bus, token ring, and FDDI ring come within the MIA Version 1 scope. The token bus is not included because there are few products available.

Two wide area network (WAN) types are supported: digital and analog.

- *Digital* includes digital leased lines, packet switching (X.25), circuit switching (X.21), ISDN, and asynchronous transfer mode (ATM).
- *Analog* incorporates current telephone and analog leased lines.

MIA Version 1 scope covers digital lines, packet switching, and ISDN. All other aspects will be the object of MIA Version 2.

Distributed processing dominates the Version 1 solution which satisfies most present-day user requirements in multivendor environments. It specifies the protocol for distributed processing where messages,

Table 18.1 Networking Goals of MIA Versions 1 and 2

	Resource to be transferred	Data structure
Version 1	Message	Arbitrary
	File	Record storage sequence
	Mail	Letter (envelope and text)
Version 2	Database	Meaning relationships among data items (semantics)
	Document	Pages, chapters, and sections. Also, figures, tables, etc.

files, and mail are transferred as shown in Table 18.1. More advanced database-to-database communications and document exchange are aims of Version 2.

To appreciate what is under the title of "File and Mail networking services" supported by Version 1, it is proper to recall that the chosen network system configuration is a three-layer structure of enduser workstations, departmental computers, and hosts, including a network control center. This three-layered structure is interconnected by means of telecommunications lines and SII interfaces, as shown in Figure 18.1.

The system is operable when all computers in the network implement interfaces which are defined in MIA Version 1. A network system model consisting only of computers with *compliance* to MIA standards is known as a *normal model*.

While several computers may operate as both departmental computers and hosts, only workstations are equipped with human interface control functions. But there exist three *operational modes*, as strategic alternatives.

Under operational *Mode 1*, the WS has complete control of user interactivity and only the application on the WS can directly employ the enduser access interface. When a host AP wants to access windows, it must ask the WS AP to perform the needed routines.

Under *Mode 2*, the WS and host share control. Host APs can also access windows directly. Under *Mode 3*, the host has complete control. The relationship corresponds to that between the host and terminals of a star-type system. All APs that access windows reside in the host.

Since the now obsolete star-type mode does not permit improvement of system performance or betterment of enduser facilities, in future

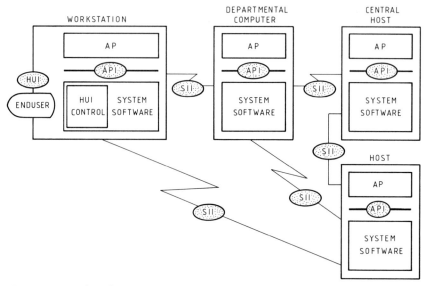

Figure 18.1   A three-layered network configuration.

installations Mode 3 will rarely if ever be used. Mode 2 has been adopted for the X Windows System under Unix and still remains to be evaluated. MIA Version 1 thus covers only Mode 1.

Other important provisions have also been done. For instance actual environments might require interconnection with existing computers having no MIA compliance. As a basic framework for dealing with this case, MIA Version 1 provides the so-called *black-box model*.

The MIA designers have also paid attention to the specific networking and processing types encountered in distributed environments, as well as to their requirements. These have been classified into four categories:

- Real time
- Transactional
- Interactive
- Batch

The specific implementation domains corresponding to each networking and processing category are shown in Figure 18.2. Notice that corresponding to each class are the specific time-dependent characteristics of the implementation domain, from subsecond switching to the long delay back office type applications.

NETWORKING/ PROCESSING	IMPLEMENTATION DOMAIN
REAL TIME*	SWITCHING
	PLANT PROCESSES
TRANSACTIONAL	COMMUNICATIONS
	ADMINISTRATIVE JOBS
	OFFICE AUTOMATION
INTERACTIVE	CAD/CAM
	SOFTWARE DEVELOPMENT
BATCH	OLD APPLICATIONS TO BE WEEDED OUT

* SUBSECOND RESPONSE

Figure 18.2 Networking and processing types and implementation domains requiring them.

Of the four processing types described in Figure 18.2, MIA Version 1 covers specifications for three of them:

- *Transaction processing* is suited for major applications for which high traffic and reliable information handling are required.
- *Interactive processing* is particularly applicable to office automation, engineering design applications (CAD), computer-aided software engineering (CASE), decision support, and expert systems.[7]
- *Batch processing* is still widely used in such areas as wage computation and structural calculation, in which large amounts of data are handled in batches.

The able execution of all these applications depends on databases; therefore, MIA Version 1 covers relational databases. Version 2 will be focusing on other types of DBMS as well as software development

[7]This is also the field where object-oriented solutions are most fruitful.

support tools (CASE) and their platforms. The study of enhanced tool functions and standardization of the interfaces between tools and platforms has also started.

18.6 A Timetable for the Implementation of Integrative Solutions

The conceptual approach to MIA specifications has been one of allowing users to *readily adapt* application programs to equipment procured from different suppliers. At the same time, from the standpoint of vendors selling equipment to a number of different users, the same arguments apply to improving the rate of reusing AP and basic software.

From a rationalization viewpoint, issues involved in arriving at a standard software wire include the:

• Classification of application fields requiring interface standards
• Definition of reference models of the software architecture for each implementation domain
• Identification of programming languages and the software written to be ported
• Logical representation of IE, allowing databases to be automatically exchanged

In order to respond to these prerequisites, the supporting documentation of the multivendor integration architecture is organized into three divisions. *Division 1* gives a general overview of MIA Version 1 rules and bylaws describing the objectives, organization, and specification environment. From vendors to users, this helps the readers to understand the sense of the standards described by Division 1.

Divisions 2 to 6 define the obligations for vendors (for example, as L1 specifications and L2 requirements).[8] These are organized into five groups of interface normalization, one per division:

• API, SII, and HUI
• Development work interfaces
• Interfaces for cross-database information exchange

Division 7 provides the users' guides, known as L3 guidelines. In MIA terminology, *users* are considered to be the application designers and system developers, as well as endusers at workstations.

[8]See also Chapter 17.

Application program interface specifications include a general description of supported programming languages, C, COBOL, and FORTRAN, as well as MIA's own structured transaction definition language (STDL) and interactive processing extensions.

MIA supports the remote database access (RDA) protocol normalized by ISO and promoted by the SQL Access Group, as well as the SQL1, SQL2, and SQL3 versions by the same outfit. As we will see in the subsequent sections, SQL2 is transaction oriented, but it has not yet been standardized. In a similar manner, ISO's RDA specification has not yet completed the definition of the distributed transaction processing (TP) standard. Hence the need for STDL.

A bird's eye view of the MIA Version 1 specification environment is given in Figure 18.3. Based on this overall development picture, the NTT timetable calls for fairly fast moves.

- In *May 1991* a request for offers was made regarding the procurement of computer systems, with delivery at the end of the year.
- *One whole year*, 1992, was devoted to implementation tests to be done in a network-wide sense.

While the testing goes on for Version 1 standards, the development effort focuses on the concept and specifications for MIA Version 2. These are written with the objective of covering fields beyond computers and networking, such as:

- Databases
- Supercomputers
- Human windows
- Advanced programming languages
- Knowledge engineering

Version 2 is tuned to ways and means for meeting these objectives. Capitalizing on the portability of several elements of the work already done, the MIA Version 2 timetable included:

- *June 1991*, call for partners
- *September 1991*, start of the concept study
- *December 1992*, definition of protocols, formats, and interfaces
- *March 1993*, publication of the standards volumes and call for offers

NETWORK	LAN	LOW TO MEDIUM SPEED LAN (UP TO SEVERAL TENS OF MBPS)		HIGH-SPEED LAN
		CSMA/CD BUS	TOKEN RING	FDDI RING
	WAN	DIGITAL		
		DIGITAL LEASED LINE NETWORK	PACKET SWITCHED NETWORK	ISDN
	NETWORK MANAGEMENT	FAULT MANAGEMENT		CONFIGURATION MANAGEMENT
	DISTRIBUTED PROCESSING	TYPE OF DATA TRANSFER - MESSAGE TRANSFER - FILE TRANSFER - MAIL TRANSFER		
	FUNCTION SHARING BY THE WS AND HOST	HOST-TO-WORKSTATION WORKSTATION-TO-HOST		
COMPUTER	SIZE	SMALL SCALE (INCLUDING 32-BIT WS)	MEDIUM SCALE	LARGE SCALE
	PROCESSING TYPE	TRANSACTION PROCESSING -BATCH -PSEUDO- CONVERSATIONAL	INTERACTIVE PROCESSING	BATCH PROCESSING
	DATABASE	RELATIONAL DATABASE		
	PROGRAMMING LANGUAGE	COBOL	FORTRAN	C
	WS TYPE	MULTIWINDOW		CHARACTER

Figure 18.3   MIA Version 1 specification environment.

At NTT, Dr. Ishino underlined that Version 2 places particular emphasis on *enduser computing*, with the standards to be developed as well as the languages designed to apply to many fields: office automation, management support, telecommunications networks, equipment sales, as well as tellers and professional advisors at banking branch offices.

Over the longer run, MIA specifications will be revised depending on progress in standardization and the expansion of application areas. Specifications will also be modified to keep pace with international standards and *de facto* norms, as well as to eliminate unclear descriptions and errors.

Modifications are expected during vendor development of products conforming to MIA, as well as in the initial stage of product introduction. Multivendor systems consisting of computers conforming to MIA Version 1 specifications would provide:

- Standardized AP development work flow
- Applications portability
- Interoperability among computers
- Common displays for workstations

However, NTT is also conscious of the fact that vendor-specific methods may have to be used to move developed programming products to and from the execution environment. System definitions and operator commands will also have to be generated and submitted in vendor-specific ways, though these are issues to be addressed by MIA Version 2.

INDEX